YOURS SINCERELY

YOURS SINCERELY

Ron Greenwood
with Bryon Butler

WILLOW BOOKS
Collins
8 Grafton Street, London W1
1984

Willow Books
William Collins Sons & Co Ltd
London · Glasgow · Sydney · Auckland
Toronto · Johannesburg

Greenwood, Ron
Yours sincerely. 1. Greenwood, Ron.
2. Soccer – England – Managers – Biography
I. Title
338.7'6179633463'0924   GV942.7.G/

ISBN 0 00 218074 X

Filmset in Ehrhardt
by Ace Filmsetting Ltd, Frome, Somerset
Printed and bound in Great Britain by
Wm Collins Sons & Co Ltd, Glasgow

CONTENTS

FOREWORD

Sir Walter Winterbottom, CBE
England team manager and FA Director of Coaching 1946–62

Ron Greenwood has always believed that attacking football and good sportsmanship are not obstacles to success. He has been a strong, positive influence on the game – and only a small and distinguished number of men can truly have that said of them.

There are managers who are really just pickers of teams but if football is to flourish both as an art and a science it needs men who are properly qualified as coaches. The game must have men who believe in it and understand it, who study to equip themselves and who have learned the best ways to pass on their knowledge and motivate players. They must have minds that are open to change and improvement and be willing to draw on the best ideas and methods from all over the world of football.

I am very aware of the problems of managing England although the game has changed in many ways since I first met Ron when guesting for Chelsea in war-time friendly football. I have followed his career closely. His interest in skill and combining players' movement drew him into the Football Association's coaching scheme where he quickly established a reputation for his deep understanding of the game. He coached the England Youth and Under-23 teams and was one of a small number of men considered for the full England post towards the end of my tenancy. As history knows Alf Ramsey was eventually appointed in 1963.

It also fell upon me to play a part in Ron's appointment as manager-coach at West Ham. My opinion was sought and Ron, as one of a new type of manager coming through, seemed admirably equipped for the post. He found full opportunity to apply his ideas about positive football at Upton Park. There were many occasions when opponents did their best to knock West Ham off their game but Ron persisted and his team won the FA Cup in fine style and then captured the European Cup Winners' Cup with a brilliant performance against Munich 1860. For that display they became the first football team to win the World Fair Play Trophy in Sport.

Ron is always angry when he sees ruthless and brutal aggression getting the better of skill, or so-called 'professional' fouls preventing goals. He deplores the spread of negative football and he is disenchanted by the modern obsession with money – an obsession which is effecting attitudes and integrity inside the game. Yet his enthusiasm for the best in football has never waned. When we were together on FIFA work in the World Youth Championship in Tunisia in 1977 he was thrilled and encouraged by the stimulating play of several sides, especially from small countries like Honduras.

Ron's coaching ability and his extensive knowledge of international football were then acknowledged by the Football Association when he was invited to become England's team manager. He was well aware of all the problems he would face and he also knew that sometimes only a hair's-breadth can be the difference between success and failure in European and world competition. Field Marshall Montgomery, a keen follower of football, once told me that a general at war and a football manager were rather alike. As well as possessing qualities of leadership they also needed a little luck on their side. In the World Cup in Spain England were weakened by injury and the lack of form of one or two key players. Their attack lost the sharp edge so evident in their opening game against the clever French and although England were unbeaten – with three wins and two draws – they failed to reach the semi-finals.

Ron accepted this philosophically, however, and I am pleased that he is now recounting and frankly appraising his fascinating career in football.

INTRODUCTION

Mine has been a good, full life and in more than forty years in football as a player, coach or manager I am proud to say I was never out of a job. I am also obliged to admit I was very lucky.

I am not talking about the sort of luck that wins the Treble Chance or sends the ball into the net off a post in the last minute. I had something better than that: luck with people. I was allowed to do things my way and to hold on with both hands to a conviction that football is a game to be enjoyed. People had faith in me and I was able to have faith in others. It is a pity my kind of luck cannot be picked off trees or bought across a counter.

There is one short but important chapter missing in this book. It was written – and then rewritten a few times – by my wife, Lucy, before she decided against its inclusion; and her single and honest reason was that we have always kept our home life private. I am sorry the chapter is not in, however, because it made me see our marriage, and my career as a manager, in a new light. The chapter emphasized how much of my time and myself I gave the game and her advice to the girls of Britain was think carefully before marrying anyone likely to become a football manager. We married during the war right at the start of my career, and she says she took on a game and a way of life as well as a man. I do plead guilty to professional selfishness – but I could not have managed without the love of Lucy and my family. They were at the heart of everything that mattered to me.

Reg Pratt and his directors at West Ham gave me my first League platform as a manager and I only wish every manager could be employed by men of such trust and integrity. They refused only two requests by me in nearly seventeen years at Upton Park. The first time was when I wanted to take on Malcolm Allison as a youth coach, and the second was when I wanted to sack Bobby Moore and Jimmy Greaves. At all other times they backed my judgement – even when I told them I was going to turn down a chance to buy Gordon Banks soon after the 1966 World Cup. They backed me, too, when Brian Clough made a big, arrogant offer for Moore and Trevor Brooking.

The rare stability of West Ham is emphasized by the fact that since the club was formed in 1900 it has had only five managers: Syd King, Charlie Paynter, Ted Fenton, myself and now John Lyall. I was the fourth and, by coincidence, I left them to become the fourth full-time manager of England. Walter Winterbottom, Alf Ramsey and Don Revie preceded me and now it is the turn of Bobby Robson to handle what he himself calls 'a roller-coaster of a hot seat'.

I took over the England job for just three games in the first place but, after beating Italy in a World Cup game at Wembley, I joined the England staff for a meal and said to them: 'Perhaps this isn't the Last Supper after all.' I stayed for five years, during which we reached the finals of the European Championship and the World Cup. I am enormously grateful, once again, for the stout and loyal support I received from the late Professor Harold Thompson, Bert Millichip, Dick Wragg and everyone at Lancaster Gate. This didn't stop me making a decision to retire a year before the 1982 World Cup finals, after an awful defeat in Switzerland, but the England players themselves talked me into changing my mind somewhere over Europe. It was a privilege to work with these players.

Twenty-two years is a long time to spend in just two jobs, but there were other offers along the way. Clubs who wanted me as a manager or as a coach include Fulham, Brentford, Portsmouth, Leeds, Workington, Sheffield Wednesday, Queen's Park Rangers and Juventus. The offer from Rangers, made after West Ham had won the European Cup Winners' Cup in 1965, was a generous one – a £10,000 signing-on fee and 'name your own salary'. Juventus approached me through the late Gigi Peronace, a good friend, but I refused this one because I couldn't even have ordered a cup of tea in Italian, and my job depended on communication. I could only have taken their money and that wasn't enough for me.

Three men above all were instrumental in shaping my ideas on the game. Billy Birrell, the manager of Chelsea during and just after the war, a quiet thinker who made an immediate impact on me; Malcolm McDonald at Brentford, who gave me belief in myself, and Walter Winterbottom, who opened my eyes to a brave new world of coaching and changed the whole direction of my life.

Walter was a wing-commander and I was an aircraftman when we met during the war but it was some years later, after he had become England's manager and director of coaching, that he got through to me. Walter was an inspired teacher. He spoke with wonderful conviction and enthusiasm and everybody listened to him – even Bill Shankly. A lecture by Walter was an event.

Many people in the game now have no idea how much English football owes to Walter Winterbottom. He launched our coaching system and gave it impetus and status; and his influence has reached on down through the years. It certainly touched many of the clubs from which England called on players to win the World Cup in 1966, and many of our best coaches, including Don Howe, Dave Sexton and Malcolm Allison, readily acknowledge their debt to Walter. He and Stanley Rous – who were both to be knighted – are major figures in the post-war history of English football.

But those early, exciting days at Lilleshall seem a long time ago. Now I am a director of Brighton and Hove Albion. 'I've become one of those people who are a blank page in Shack's book' I tell people. (Len Shackleton included a chapter in his autobiography on 'the average director's knowledge of football'. He left a complete page blank, and I suspect it is now one of the most-quoted observations in football literature.)

The idea was amusing; but untrue. I remember how grateful I was for the way in which West Ham's admirable directors let me get on with my job at Upton Park. I enjoyed the same freedom, too, when I became manager of England. No manager can ask for more.

1

More than a Game

Pelé got it exactly right when he called football 'the beautiful game'. At its best, the game is a joy: a battle of wit and muscle and character: it involves and inspires. It is always different and endlessly fascinating.

That is the way football should be but, sadly, shamefully, our professional game is slowly being ruined. It is being mutilated as a spectacle by impatient directors, accountants with acid in their pens, frightened managers, poor coaches and dull theorists. The spirit is wrong and it hurts me. Football comes from the people and it is for the people; and when they begin to reject it then something is dreadfully wrong.

I spent my whole career as a manager trying to stop this devaluation of the game. I cared more about the purity and finer values of football than I did about winning for winning's sake – and if that is a sin then I am a sinner. Football should be a game of risks. When I was manager of West Ham I sent out teams that were prepared to gamble, whatever the dangers, because I believed strongly that this was the secret of the game's appeal. We gambled with intelligence and skill, otherwise we would have been committing suicide, but I wanted to see pleasure on the pitch and pleasure on the terraces. I took on a different, heavier responsibility when I became manager of England but my philosophy did not change – even when time and circumstance clipped our wings.

There are people who will write me off as an idealist. That is fine with me. I simply see a game that is deteriorating in quality in front of half-empty terraces. I see television sucking at the game's life-blood. I see clubs who cannot or will not get their sums right. I hear a great deal of noise but not enough common sense.

I do not pretend to have a bagful of answers for football's problems. These problems did not materialise overnight and they will not be solved overnight. Too many instant solutions are offered when what the game needs before anything else are open minds, clear vision and an honest and deep concern for its future. The product is a good one; if the quality and presentation are right it is very marketable. There *is* a place for professional football in the modern world despite all the counter-attractions.

13

My all-consuming concern is for the game itself, because it has been my love and my profession. Over the years I have admired many players and teams, among them the modern Liverpool, a side of high quality and character, a side to place with the best. But in saying that I see little else to delight me now in English football, I am not claiming that football isn't what it used to be. It never was. The present always fights a losing battle with the past because the past improves with age.

Football is, inevitably, a reflection of its own time. The game used to be slower, talent had more time to indulge itself. But now the world has quickened up: communications, food and travel are all instant or through the sound barrier. Football, too, is more concerned with speed and hostility. Players are fitter today than ever before – the tragedy, though, is that this new edge is not used creatively and excitingly but to close the game down. I do not think many spectators will have noticed this because the misuse of pace has been a gradual development over a number of years. It is like the wrinkles of age: they never show in the bathroom mirror.

The English fan revels in the combat he watches every Saturday and I have always been first to champion those qualities which hallmark the British game. Courage and aggression are cornerstones of our football, but its sheer pace can mean that it is short on other qualities. Players' minds are often a couple of paces behind their whirling bodies; and players with poor technique can get by.

I wince when I watch some games. Control and touch are often poor, passes are stabs in the dark, movement off the ball is statuesque and sometimes the only rhythm is provided by the music at half-time. Yet the whole is wrapped up with so much pace and soaked with so much sweat that there is general approval.

Pace is essential, of course, especially in attack. It imposes pressure, it enables a player to go past or away from an opponent, and it enables him to engage and cover and take on responsibility. But pace doesn't mean running around like an excited Yorkie for ninety minutes. Pace can also be represented by quickness of mind, the immediacy and accuracy with which the ball is passed and also, simply, in variation of movement. Change of pace is more effective than full pace.

My main argument with the way so many sides employ pace for its own sake is that speed of foot takes the place of speed of mind – and this brings me to my central belief about the game. Football is a battle of wits or it is nothing at all. A particular system gives a side its shape, while tactics add an edge, but all that is premeditated. Football is essentially a thing of the second. One set of players must out-think the other, make openings, recognise opportunities and then force mistakes and punish them. Instant decision and action are the core of the game.

A manager may send his players out with countless ideas and possibilities running through their minds but he can't tell any of them how things are going to look on the field. Each player must see for himself and react with intelligence. An example: West Ham were playing Spurs' famous 'double' side and we were given a free kick on the edge of their penalty area. Danny Blanchflower knew us well and spent a long time organising his defensive wall – pushing, pulling, adjusting and giving orders. He eventually got it to his satisfaction: Bill Brown crouched, while Maurice Norman, Dave Mackay and the rest of them, chaps who knew what they were doing, steeled themselves on their toes. Johnny Byrne was taking our kick and there were any number of well practised variations he could have tried. But what happened? He trotted up to the ball and whacked it straight into the net.

'How come?', I asked him afterwards. Budgie smiled: 'They were all so worried about what we might do, what stunt we were going to pull, that they didn't cover the obvious. There was a big hole.' That goal was all Byrne. Only he saw the chance. It was a marvellous bit of opportunism, which is the key to successful football.

It does not really matter what defensive system a side employs: the advantage is always with the attacking side. There is no lock that can't be picked and no door that can't be broken down. It is the same with bridge and chess and any game that fully engages the intelligence. Everything else stems from this belief, although I am not, heaven forbid, decrying the art of defence. Indeed, if there was a weakness in our make-up during my years at West Ham it was that we did not always have the players to counter the bright ideas of others. We were good at doing our thing but not so hot at stopping others doing theirs.

But even defence is double-headed. In the first place it means protection but then, the ball won, defence becomes the first line of attack. A side must earn the ball before it can use it and every player should be capable of winning or at least stealing possession. As Eddie Baily used to say: 'Be first. Get your foot in.' Spare me the prima donna who won't scuffle a bit. For that reason I have always loved players with an answer for everything, players such as Peter Doherty, Neil Franklin, Danny Blanchflower, Dave Mackay, Bobby Moore, Franz Beckenbauer, Johan Cruyff and, yes, George Best, who could really tackle. They could win the ball as well as use it. Each was a two-edged sword.

It is a fact of life, of course, that a club manager must live with the players he has. Some managers buy, some discover new talent and help it mature, while others just do their best with not very much. But, be a club big or small, the manager's future is in the players' hands and there is a limit to what he can do with them. Above all a manager cannot give a player character – and 'character' is a word that is going to crop up regularly in this book. From character comes the fire that makes a player a competitor, the courage that takes him into the heat of the action and the determination that makes the apparently impossible possible. It comes from within a man and it so often separates winners from losers.

All a manager can do is help his players do the best for themselves. He can get them fit, lift them mentally, polish up their technique, impose an overall method that enables them to relate to each other, he can give them ideas and variations and open their eyes to possibilities. He must then point them in the direction of the pitch, put his backside on a seat and keep his fingers crossed. Only players play: that is *their* business.

It is fair to ask, then, what blame managers must accept for the overall standard of our game. The answer is a great deal. When I was chairman of the League Secretaries and Managers Association we reached a point where a thousand managers had lost or left their jobs since the war, and I recall saying at the time that five hundred of them deserved the sack because they didn't know what they were doing, and that the other five hundred might have done well given time and support by their directors.

Some managers do not stand a chance. They have such limited experience and their minds are so closed that they don't know enough to realise how little they know. Some played under poor managers themselves so their eyes have never been opened. They have nothing to draw on and nothing to give. Some have their priorities all wrong: they say they have 'too much to do' to spend time with their players. There are even young managers whose first action is to appoint a coach who is even younger. They never put on a track suit, never work with their players and confine themselves to arguments about money and a Friday team-talk. There are also managers who are simply idle. They are part-timers in a job that should fill their days.

Too many managers are simply not right for the job but those with a nice turn of phrase and a good coach sometimes get away with it. They project the club in one sense but most of all they project themselves. I can understand why this kind of manager keeps well away from the training ground. He can't hold his own with his players . . . and players spot phoneys quicker than anybody. There are other managers who travel abroad only when they go on holiday. Do they still think that the continentals are a lot of fancy dans who won't tackle and can't shoot, and that real football stops at Dover?

The managers I feel sorriest for, however, are those with directors who can't see further than the end of their cigars. These directors want success a little quicker than immediately – an attitude which is self-defeating. A manager with masters like this knows his job is always on the line. And it shows in his side's football and usually in their results. Directors, too, are to blame for poor appointments. When they sack their manager they are holding up their own hands in guilt.

There is much to be said for the German system of licensing a manager or coach before he is allowed to get his hands on a football team. Courses are a short cut to experience: they make people more aware. Obviously a bit of paper won't turn a man into a good manager but it does mean he has been given a push in the right direction. How far he goes will then depend on his intelligence and personality.

Yet there are many first-class managers and coaches in our professional game. They've come through the ranks, hit or miss. Many were not outstanding players, a few did not even play League football themselves, but they think about their game and they study it. They keep their eyes open, and they know enough to realise that there is always something new to learn. The windows of their minds are open and they are receptive to change and innovation.

Many managers do not share my own admiration of continental football but that does not matter. There are a thousand ways to play this game and the trick is always in playing to your strengths. The British way works very well at its best. For proof we need look no further than the success of Liverpool, Nottingham Forest and Aston Villa in the European Cup: they won it, between them, for six years in succession. Some did not like their style, but style is largely a matter of taste and instinct. There was, for example, enormous and even vitriolic criticism of the way Watford played in their climb from the Fourth Division to runners-up in the First. Yet I thought they were brilliant. The long ball was the basis of their game and quick, constant pressure was their object. It is not a style I would employ by choice nor would I like to see every team using it. It is not a method, either, that should be imposed on youngsters who are still learning the game. But in the League there is room – and a need – for individual styles. We should be grateful to Watford's manager, Graham Taylor, for trying something different. His side made people think and a season later, in any case, a few new faces gave Watford more variation and set them off on their notable run to Wembley in the FA Cup. It is variety that gives football its appeal.

Those managers who don't like Watford's style should do their darnedest to find ways of proving it wrong. That is the best criticism of all.

Wolves under Stan Cullis used the long pressure game thirty years before Watford did. Elaboration was a capital offence to them. They destroyed bad defenders but then, in the European Cup, they met Barcelona who had good defenders. The Spanish side swallowed the long balls and spanked Wolves hard: four goals in Spain, five at Molineux. Wolves' percentage game suddenly looked poorly.

Push-and-run caught everybody out when Spurs, under Arthur Rowe, started using this method not so long after World War II. It was marvellous to watch and proved very successful. But opponents learnt to counter it. They ran with the man and not after the ball: push-and-run's number was up.

There is a world of difference, of course, between practice and theory, between men who see the game for what it is and men who open folders, produce diagrams and quote statistics. The realist relates everything to what he knows will or might happen on the field. He draws on his experience and knowledge, makes some informed guesses and doesn't forget that two sides are always involved. There are two reasons for everything that happens in a game. Your reason . . . and their reason.

Charles Hughes, the FA's assistant director of coaching, is a champion of the long ball, whatever the match and whichever players are involved. He can produce figures to prove that eighty per cent of goals are the product of movements involving four passes or less. I am not surprised. Many British sides spend ninety per cent of their time thumping the ball high into the opposition penalty area and so, inevitably, most of their goals come this way. Statistics like this can prove anything and nothing.

I am not knocking the long pass, though. It can be devastatingly effective and all the best sides in the world use the technique, but only when the moment is right and only as a single part of their armoury. It is no coincidence that while the Brazilians, Dutch, Italians, Germans and Hungarians all have different methods and tempos they still, by choice, keep the ball on the ground. It has been the same with the finest post-war sides in England: Bill Nicholson's 'double' side, Liverpool in the 1960s and again in recent years, Leeds in their later period under Don Revie. The basis of their game was controlled possession. Stanley Cullis's Wolves have been the only long-ball winners of note since the war. They believed in their method and they were good, but their way was never championed as the only way.

There is no doubt, alas, that football's professors of theory are on the march. I attend courses in Europe and hear so much 'scientific' rubbish that I wonder if we are discussing the same thing. The Iron Curtain countries are some of the worst culprits. I got a letter from Russia soon after the 1966 World Cup asking me for all the vital statistics of Bobby Moore, Geoff Hurst and Martin Peters – they wanted height, weight, measurements, colour, the lot. I wondered if they were set on finding three look-a-likes, putting boots on them and pointing them in the direction of a pitch. The beautiful game? These scientists wouldn't know what that meant.

Doctrine and statistics to the second decimal place are a menace to football. It would be disastrous if such theorists got their hands on our game. Bless them, of course: we do have free speech. But they must not be taken seriously.

There is no mystery or mystique about football. There is nothing about the game that can't easily be grasped by the chap on the terrace. Its techniques and patterns can all be described in plain, honest words. As in everything there are degrees of knowledge and experience; some learn much from a little, others little from much. But the joy of the game is its dramatic simplicity.

I doubt if there is much that is new waiting to be discovered about football. Wingers come and go, forwards push up or hang back, the middle region expands or contracts, full-backs improvise or mind their own business and sweepers, screeners, markers and free-wheelers join the queue. Almost everything is now a variation on an old theme, even when the basic idea is borrowed from another sport.

Basketball, for example, was the source of 'the press' which Rinus Michels introduced to Dutch football during his Ajax days. This simply means that when the ball is cleared a side pushes forward and closes down fast on the opponent in possession. Four or five press on the man with the ball, putting him under pressure, blocking all his avenues; the idea is to force an error and then attack from an advanced position. Essentially it is an attacking ploy but many have copied it and changed its original aim. They use the move as a defensive strategy, with the off-side game built in as extra insurance.

I have seen variations of this idea all over the place but it took a team of youngsters in North Africa to make the biggest nonsense of it. I was watching Uruguay play Honduras during the 1977 World Youth Cup in Tunisia, and Uruguay kept pressing forward, quickly and blindly, making life difficult for their opponents and very tedious for the spectators. Once they did this with such slavish enthusiasm that they all ignored the Honduras player with the ball and rushed straight past him – and he was in his own half of the field! That was one of the most astonishing things I've ever seen on a football pitch. The ball ceased to matter. Theory ruled. The poor Honduras player was flabbergasted: ten Uruguayans were all behind him, an empty half and a distant goalkeeper were in front of him. It was too much for the lad and he made a mess of his opportunity.

British football prefers old ideas that come in new wrappings but I wish some of the major clubs would give a decent trial to the sweeper system. In this we are out of step with the rest of the world. Surely we alone are not right?

The sweeper – or *libero*, a better term – is simply a player who takes a free role at the back. He provides essential extra depth and cover, enables the balance of the side to change easily and is a first point of attack. But he must be right for the job. He must be a good footballer, a man with a cool head and broad vision, a man who can tackle but also initiate, a man who is comfortable in possession and not afraid to put his foot on the ball. A *libero* should lead from the back and that is why it is a specialist's job – a job that wouldn't be wasted on the best player in any side. Franz Beckenbauer was the first and finest. He saved many games for West Germany but he won them even more. Beckenbauer at work, elegantly manipulating all the reins, was a delight.

It is not a job that can suddenly be thrown at a player or his side. Everyone must know what is involved, and this is one of the reasons why so very few of our clubs have taken up the challenge. Managers whose football education has been strictly British are suspicious of the idea. They are reluctant to commit one of their best players to the role – which means they don't really understand or believe in it.

A good sweeper changes the whole make-up and chemistry of his side. Full-backs can push up without too much conscience, knowing that one or two markers plus extra insurance are still behind them. There is extra width and new options with the *libero* himself always there to carry the ball forward and link up in midfield. The pattern of play is more fluid and therefore less predictable and yet the capacity for defence is improved.

A *libero* is almost essential in international football. I would have given anything for one during the 1982 World Cup finals in Spain but I did not have any players used to the role and it was hardly the place or time for initiation. Bryan Robson would be ideal for the job but his goals and more forward influence for England and Manchester United have become so important that any switch at this point in his career would be difficult. I flirted with the plan once or twice in my five years as England manager and everybody started saluting it as something new. This was embarrassing because almost every good team in the world has been playing it for years. British football is simply behind the times here and I don't think this will change until some of our top clubs give a positive lead. Too many managers in this country only imitate. It would need a side with a *libero* to win the championship to make them sit up and take notice.

Ability and intelligence are central to everything in football but they rarely add up to much without practice and experience. I don't think a lot of professionals believe this. They will spend hours on a golf course, grooving their swing or rolling in three-footers, but they are loth to spend an extra thirty minutes working on their weaknesses in the game that gives them a very good living. This is often the difference between those who make it and those who don't.

Kevin Keegan is a perfect example of a 'self-made' footballer. His natural ability was not of the highest order but he made himself into a rare player by working hard and systematically on every aspect of his game. He got much because he gave much.

Keegan's attention to detail came home to me forcibly during an England training session at the time he was with Hamburg in West Germany. We were playing a pig-in-the-middle game involving a ring of players around the centre-circle and four in the middle. Three of those in the middle were 'defenders' while the fourth linked up with those on the outside, dribbling, bouncing off passes, with the usual aim of keeping possession. Trevor Brooking was so brilliant when he became the extra man in the middle that the other lads would start shouting '*Olé*'. Yet others would find it almost impossibly difficult. Anyway, on this particular day, Keegan was one of the 'defenders' and Steve Coppell was the extra man. Suddenly I noticed Kevin sticking to Steve closer than a shadow. Steve couldn't shake him off. Afterwards I asked Kevin what he'd been doing. 'Well, everyone marks man-to-man in Germany, even the forwards when they haven't got the ball' he said. 'They tell me I'm bad at it but, I'll tell you what, this is a great exercise for helping me get the hang of it.' Keegan had turned even a routine exercise to his own advantage. That was Keegan: he didn't miss a trick.

Keegan's finishing when he was at his best was lethal. He had the right kind of composure, didn't snatch at his chances and could tuck them away no matter what the height and angle. But, once again, he wasn't born with this ability. He was always demanding practice. He delighted in it and would carry on much longer than anyone else. He would devote a whole session, for example, to hitting crosses on the turn – and he wanted those crosses cut back at him low and hard. Most players tend to lift these over the bar because they lean back on the turn when they shoot; but the secret is in the angle of the body which should be almost parallel to the ground. It is a very difficult art to acquire but Keegan worked and worked until he got it right.

Overhead kicking in the goalmouth is another awkward business and I once saw West Germany's Klaus Fischer devote a long session to nothing else. He used a mat to land on, centre after centre was knocked into him and, as the non-stop practice went on, he got better and better. Technique, timing, direction, selection . . . they all improved. Yet when people see a forward whirl the ball into the net they put it down to a moment of inspiration rather than hours of hard work. Practice like this is a repetitive and even painful business but there is no substitute for it. It is the only way.

So much goes into the making of a good team and a good game. The professional obviously sees more than the spectator who concerns himself mainly with results, goals and near-misses, and moments of unusual skill or obvious stupidity. A committed fan is only really conscious of one side, his side, and this struck me more than ever after I became England's team manager. In boardrooms and guestrooms I would listen to two entirely different versions of every game. A winning goal was always brilliant, great or unbelievable, a losing goal bad, shocking or diabolical. Victory and defeat were as life and death. There was nothing in between.

The average fan sees a game as a picture he likes or doesn't like. The professional notices canvas, brush-work, composition and light and shade. Great talent is easily recognisable but most players are little details who help make up the whole; every performance is related. No one player is in possession for more than a minute or so in any game and even then he will make a lot of mistakes. The men without the ball are equally important and a good defender can run himself into the ground without making much contact. He is being effective because he is back and facing, or he is being effective because he is forward and supporting. He is doing two jobs in one – and the distance between the two can be fifty yards in double-quick time. How much credit is he given?

The only people I never watched closely in a game were the referee and his linesmen because I could not influence them in any way. Their decisions were a matter of fact; like the weather or the ground conditions they had to be accepted, and that is why I never criticised them.

I wonder if fans even notice the difference between the worst and the best of British football. At its worst there is no space on the field. Every door, window and shutter is closed. When a goalkeeper has possession, for example, both defences will flatten and push up until twenty players are sandwiched into a few yards either side of the halfway line. The goalkeeper then clears the ball into an area that looks like Piccadilly Circus in the rush-hour. Even breathing is difficult.

Compare this with, say, Liverpool at their best. Their measured rhythm comes from understanding and good technique. They vary their pace and point of attack, they build from the back and they use the whole width of the field. One moment they are playing within themselves, creating space and passing beautifully, but then down goes their collective foot and they are looking for a kill. Their game, basically, is all about angles and space. They move the ball at a pace they can work with, a pace that enables them to play it off first time. Their running opens up alternatives for the man in possession and the angle of their passing is excellent. The ball is always going between or away from their opponents. They play with patience yet give an illusion of pace. And they always have something left under the bonnet. It ought to be added that Liverpool also have a lot of very good players.

Certain factors are common to all good teams: intelligent running off the ball, a proper understanding of space and an ability to let the ball share the work. Good running demands awareness, imagination and determination. It involves constant improvisation, leaving defenders, taking defenders, overlapping, checking and changing direction, little scissor combinations and getting into a movement for a second or even third time. Good running pulls defences apart and is the best way to break down man-for-man marking.

The space opened up by this skill then has to be used – and space, remember, is simply an open area between two colleagues. Move into it too soon, a defender will follow and it no longer exists. Ideally man and ball should arrive together and this will be easier if the angle and pace of the pass are right. A safe angle is better than a tight one and a ball played off first time is better than one in which two or three touches have wasted split-seconds and perhaps signalled your intentions. But remember we are talking about control under pressure, players have different levels of anticipation and opposition defenders are not always mugs. Good habits can be countered by good habits, hard labour by hard labour. The game then becomes a battle of skill and wit . . . as I have said, football at its best.

The only statistic I would love a computer to come up with – and there is no way one could – is the number of decisions a player has to make in the course of a ninety-minute game. One decision runs into another: he makes a new one almost every time the ball is touched. It is a never-ending process of assessment and reassessment, and if a player isn't mentally as well as physically tired when he leaves the field he probably hasn't been doing his job.

But one thing above all is constant now. No team has a hope of competing successfully unless its players are all twentieth-century athletes. The modern game demands this. Unless a side is right up to the mark in this respect it will be short on everything else. Athleticism, power and stamina were always important but now they are absolute essentials.

In the years before and after the last war clubs would get their 'heavyweights' to report a week or so before the rest at the start of a season so that they could work off their surplus weight. Now, though, the fleshy professional is almost a being of the past. The new breed is wirier, slimmer and even the bone structure seems a little different. They also know that a few extra pounds would make it difficult for them to get into their trendy clothes.

The game is always changing because it mirrors the day and age. Liberation back in the late 1940s was reflected on both pitch and terrace and the game had a wonderful boom. Nobody had much money but it didn't matter. In its own way the game stood for freedom. But now, although players are getting paid more than ever before, every club is short of money, dole queues lengthen, turnstiles are slowing down and the game itself is going through a bad patch. This is man's fault not football's, however, and I am totally opposed to any attempt to change the laws of the game in an effort to brighten it up.

My feeling on this goes back a long way. Soon after the 1966 World Cup I attended a meeting of FIFA's technical committee in Paris at which Alf Ramsey, Helmut Schoen of West Germany and Portugal's Otto Gloria, three of the semi-finalists, were also present. Sir Stanley Rous, president of FIFA, said the game was becoming too defensive and that he felt the time was ripe for a change in the off-side law. I waited until last and then told the meeting that it would be ridiculous to change the laws just to make things easier for people without invention. 'Only imagination will improve the game', I said. 'Every defensive idea is a challenge and it's up to us coaches to find new ways of breaking them down. The laws of the game have stood the test of time. Change them and you change nothing because it's people who are at fault.'

The subject came up again just before I retired as England's manager. This time I described two games I had seen in Spain, Real Sociedad against Real Madrid in San Sebastian and Barcelona against Real Madrid in the Nou Camp. I told the meeting: 'Both were wonderful games, full of adventure, but there weren't more than a couple of off-side decisions in either. Yet here we are in London talking about changing the small print. People in Spain wouldn't understand what we are fretting about.'

There is nothing wrong with the off-side game in moderation. If a couple of steps in the right direction are going to catch out your opponents then only the naive won't take them. But some sides over-play the technique because they are short of ideas while others, like Queen's Park

Rangers, essentially a creative team, use it to punish stupidity. They would all have to think twice if their opponents began to give them the slip. Smart sides can turn the gambit to their own advantage.

In the end the quality of our players and our game stands or falls on the standard of its teachers, coaches and managers. They shape the future and they will only succeed if they are men who believe in the game and are not merely mercenaries. They must have knowledge and the expertise to pass it on, and they must have time and facilities.

I am often asked if I think coaching has ruined our game. I reply that bad coaching hasn't helped, but then I ask the questioner what he does for a living – and I follow up his answer by asking if he became a finished product overnight, the moment he left school. It is my way of emphasising that footballers need to learn their trade in the same way that accountants and surveyors or carpenters and electricians have to learn theirs.

The truth and the crime, alas, is that we teach our youngsters to win before we teach them to play. They are brought on like hot-house flowers and the blame must be shared by over-ambitious parents and impatient, short-sighted clubs. Little chaps of eleven or twelve are sent out to battle for medals and cups before they understand what the game is all about. They are encouraged to compete to their limits rather than enjoy the game for its own sake. Size is more important than ability and aggression of more value than technique. Their bodies are stressed and their natural pleasure in the game is squeezed out of them.

The pressure on the better youngsters then increases. Football starts to fill their lives. They can find themselves playing four, five or even six games a week with training sessions in between. Parents push and demand because they can see their sons earning fame and fortune in an England shirt, while coaches and clubs push and demand because they have tunnel vision. The kids become robots. Present them with a situation on the field and click, click, there is a programmed response.

I was very aware of this danger during my West Ham days. I would say to our youngsters before they went out: 'Our aim today is to make you good enough footballers to play with Bobby Moore, Geoff Hurst and Martin Peters.' I wanted them to think about their game and to do the right things for the right reasons. I wanted them to express themselves and enjoy their football. And I found that if they remembered this they usually won as well. I once asked Rudi Krol what would happen at Ajax when a new manager with new ideas took over. 'It doesn't matter' replied that brilliant Dutchman. 'We were taught correctly when we were young. We will always be able to play.' What price can be put on that sort of upbringing?

John Cartwright did a fine job during his three years as England Youth coach and, slowly and only in some quarters, there is now a more enlightened attitude. He helped improve the relationship between League clubs and schools but this has always been a prickly one. Some have got it right but there has been awful mistrust between others. Many clubs have cheated for years, sweet-talking and sweet-giving parents into letting them take their boys away from school without a thought for the youngsters' future. The lads who didn't make it as footballers were left with nothing.

I always insisted boys went through with their education because I felt the game owed them something. Trevor Brooking was just one who did well. Spurs and Chelsea were keen on him and wanted him to sign as an apprentice immediately. We agreed to let him carry on with his studies for a year and, even after he signed, he went to day classes. He finished with eleven 'O' Levels and Economics and Accounts at 'A' level. It didn't seem to do him any harm.

There is no doubt in my mind that one of the best-paid men in any club – perhaps even the best – should be the youth coach. His job is investment. His responsibility is the future. It is not a position for a faithful Tom, Dick or Harry or for somebody who is cutting his own teeth. A learner teaching learners is not a sound idea. But this is what happens at many clubs and it has ruined many promising youngsters. Clubs haven't got the foresight, or the money, to employ good, experienced men at this level. But it is poor husbandry and, in the end, they and English football are the losers.

When I went to the FA in 1977 I talked with Allen Wade and Charles Hughes about an idea I'd had in mind for a long time. I wanted 'schools of excellence' to be established around the country. Once a month they would bring together carefully selected boys under the best coaches we could muster. Some boys would fall by the wayside but others would take their place and all would be better for the experience. Sadly, I discovered there was a poor, thin relationship between the coaching and international departments of the FA. There were personality problems and wrong attitudes but, most of all, the difference was one of ideology. Football meant different things in different rooms at the headquarters of the English game. The result was that my idea never got off the ground. I was told no money was available.

But now Bobby Robson has taken over as national coach as well as England team manager, certain basic problems have been removed and there is some uniformity of approach. A residential school of excellence has been established at Lilleshall, properly organized and handsomely sponsored, and it is going to be fascinating to follow its progress and output over the next few years. Problems will arise because a football school is not like a school of ballet or music. The game is not a precise art and success in it depends on so many factors. There are no guarantees and no one can yet say whether the school will be a success.

2

England: a Cause

Somebody once asked me whom I was answerable to as team manager of England. 'Nobody' I said '. . . except the nation'. It is a one-in-fifty-million job. I was my own boss but everyone's Aunt Sally.

There was neither interference nor pressure from the people who gave me the most important position in our national sport. The Football Association let me pick and mix as I chose. I did the job my way, rightly or wrongly, though everyone believes he can do better than the chap in charge. Advice rolls in like a huge tidal wave, by way of the newspapers, radio, television, letters, telephone calls and even comments in the street. Fellow football managers are often at the head of the queue.

Bobby Robson will forgive me if I remind him that even he told the nation where I was going wrong. He definitely knew better. Then, of course, he got the job himself and suddenly he had a new tune.

'This is such a roller-coaster of a hot seat that the only people with any conception of what it's all about are Alf Ramsey, Don Revie, Ron Greenwood and now, to a small extent, myself', he announced. 'Others like Brian Clough and Ron Atkinson may think they know, but they don't, any more than I did. When I took over I was a million miles away from understanding the unique demands.'

The problems come in all shapes and guises. Most didn't bother me, others I learnt to handle, but a few wounded me deeply.

I did not mind receiving three hundred letters demanding that I pick a young West Bromwich player called Bryan Robson, who was already in the England Under-21 side: the writers simply confirmed something I had noticed all by myself, that the lad had talent. It was endlessly frustrating, on the other hand, not to be able to send out my best sides because of injuries sustained in a domestic system that drained and smothered. It was not very pleasant being followed back to the Wembley dressing-room by chants of 'What a load of rubbish'. It was acutely distressing when deliberately unkind comments, made for effect on television and heard by millions of people, upset my family.

The big difference between club and country for a manager, though, is in the weight of responsibility. A club manager works inside parish boundaries. Failure is a matter for private grief. Cats will be kicked in Ipswich or Leeds or East London if the local side goes down but who else cares? But if England lose it is a national disaster. Victory is a slice of heaven and defeat a step towards the fire below.

I very nearly retired during the qualifying stages of the 1982 World Cup after our traumatic defeat in Switzerland and the consequent awful criticism and rumour. Then we beat Hungary in Budapest, a famous victory, and on the plane home the players themselves talked me into changing my mind. That is a story for later.

Yet, despite all the heavy responsibility of the job, my five years as England's manager were wonderfully rewarding and always stimulating. It is a privilege to play for England . . . and an equally great honour to manage England.

I felt my whole career had somehow been leading up to the appointment. I was convinced I could succeed at a time when the game in this country was on its backside. Don Revie's defection to the Middle East had kicked the feet from under everybody. Players, fans, officials and media all felt it, and so did I. My appointment also came at a time when I had almost fallen out of love with football. My spirit – and the game's – was low.

When the call came, everything changed. I was fifty-five and faced with the biggest challenge of my life in the last years of my career. But I saw my task quite clearly. I had to help restore faith in our game and I had to prove to the world that we could still play a bit. I choose to think I succeeded. I can't prove it by pointing to ultimate victory in the European Championship or World Cup but we did reach the finals of both tournaments as well as winning the European Youth and Under-21 Championships and the British Home Championship three times. We played 55 games in my five years as manager, won 33, drew 12 and lost 10. We lost 3 of our 24 home games – all 3 defeats coming in the space of two months in 1981 – and 7 of our 31 away games. We scored 93 goals in all and conceded 40.

I was certain we were going to do well in the European finals in 1980. Two months before we went to Italy we had a stunning win over Spain in Barcelona with Tony Woodcock and Trevor Francis scoring our goals. They were the sharp cutting edge of a side that was an excellent blend of flair and efficiency. One Spanish paper said our football was 'out of this world'. Another suggested Spain's players should be given a grant to go to England to learn what the game was all about. People saw the match on television all over Europe and Kevin Keegan came back from Germany to say everyone was scared of us. My good friend, Enzo Bearzot, Italy's manager, said we were 'logical favourites'. Our qualifying record, seven wins and a draw, was the best in the championship and I felt we had a side capable of beating anyone. Then, tragically, we lost Francis through injury and the balance of the team was critically altered. We drew 1-1 with Belgium in Turin, in a match flavoured by an English riot and tear gas, we lost 1-0 to Italy on the same ground in a game that was more about competitive strength than skill, and finally we beat Spain 2-1 in Naples. We were out of the tournament without having begun to do ourselves justice.

My towering ambition, however, was to win the World Cup – and this was no impossible dream. We were unbeaten in Spain in 1982, winning our first-phase games against France, Czechoslovakia and Kuwait, a record matched only by Brazil; but then we were locked up in goalless draws with West Germany and Spain in the second phase. I believe, though, that if Keegan and Brooking had been fit we would have gone all the way. I am certain this pair would have been our key to the semi-finals, and once there we would have been difficult to stop. Once again, we had more under our bonnet than we showed.

My minimum target, the very least I would have settled for, was a place in the final stages of the two tournaments. I believed this had to be achieved. England had not joined the game's best since Alf Ramsey's team played in the 1970 World Cup finals in Mexico, and for a country that took such pride in its football this was terrible. We desperately needed to appear on the big stages of the game and I was determined we would. We made it, and, although I was not satisfied with what we eventually achieved, I think our credibility at international level was restored.

Success in the finals of a high quality tournament never comes to order. It depends on so many things being right, including fitness, confidence and the run of the ball. Everything needs to fall into place like the pieces of a big, complex jigsaw puzzle. Sometimes the plan can go wrong through circumstances beyond anyone's control. This is no sort of excuse. It is just the way it is.

I sometimes wonder how I would have coped if I had been given the job seventeen years earlier when it was first mentioned that I might become England's manager. I was manager of England's Under-23 team at the time, during my days as coach with Arsenal, and the subject cropped up on the way to a match at Norwich. Walter Winterbottom was the England manager then and he had high hopes of succeeding Sir Stanley Rous as secretary of the FA. Walter asked me, quietly, how I'd feel about becoming England manager if he got the FA post. 'I'd be delighted' I replied, and no more was said. But Walter did not get the job – Denis Follows did – and Alf Ramsey eventually took over as manager in 1963.

That was, with hindsight, a blessing in disguise because it is a job that demands experience. I was not ready for it then while Alf Ramsey certainly was. I admired Alf. He had done a first-class job with Ipswich, winning the Second and First Division titles in successive seasons with methods that were original and efficient, and he was a stable, positive, deep-thinking person. He knew where he was going and how he was going to get there. He was the right man, and he proved it in the best way possible.

Alf undoubtedly had a big hand in shaping the job I inherited; but so did Walter Winterbottom and even, in his way, Don Revie. Walter created the position and set up our national coaching system, Alf ensured that the manager was the unchallenged boss and Don Revie took the overall organisation a stage further – as well as reminding the country that even England managers are not perfect.

Revie's sudden and secret decision to throw in the England job for Arab dollars was a bolt from the blue. I was not close to him and I have no idea of the real reasons for his action. He made mistakes, as we all do, but I do not know if the job was too big for him. I do not want to judge him as man or manager, but the cloak-and-dagger manner of his going was beyond all excuse and I reacted like most people when I heard the news. His defection undoubtedly damaged the reputation and morale of our game and that was unforgivable.

I was acutely sensitive to all the repercussions because I had become very disenchanted with football. Partly this was a problem of my own making, going back to my decision to hand over control of the West Ham team to John Lyall in 1974. I needed close contact with players and, after becoming general manager, I was divorced from the one aspect of the game that really mattered to me. I suppose I was suffering withdrawal symptoms.

My depression had been getting worse for two or three years and even when West Ham won the FA Cup in 1975 I stayed down at Brighton on the Sunday morning instead of joining in the celebrations. I went for a walk along the sea-front with my wife, Lucy. John Lyall didn't want it this way: I deliberately cut myself off. I felt blue about football, about my own lack of involvement and about the way the game in general was going. I didn't even like myself very much.

I needed something to fire my enthusiasm again; and the challenge I needed came in the summer of 1977. Along with Walter Winterbottom, I went to the first World Youth Championship in Tunisia, as a member of

FIFA's technical committee, and I thoroughly enjoyed it. I saw some marvellous youngsters in action, full of skill and adventure, and I drew great hope from them.

It was a busy period and shortly after returning home I was due to fly off again with West Ham for a tournament in Majorca. During those few days between trips, however, I got a call from Reg Pratt, West Ham's chairman, who said Professor Sir Harold Thompson, the chairman of the FA, wanted to speak to me urgently. 'I think they're in trouble after Revie', he said, 'and if they want you to help that's all right with us'. Sir Harold then called me and, without beating about the bush, he said the FA would like me to stand in with England until they made a new appointment. I told him there was no problem but asked if I could give a definite answer when I returned from Majorca in a week's time. I kept quiet about the matter in the sunshine, only mentioning it to John Lyall near the end of the week. There were no doubts in my mind, however. I arranged to meet Sir Harold at the FA as soon as I got back. But when I walked into 16, Lancaster Gate, he said immediately: 'We'd better get out of here and find somewhere quiet.' So we went to the Park Court Hotel, just down the road, and wandered from room to room looking for somewhere to chat.

We eventually finished up in the basement and there, right on cue, we were joined by a gang of workmen. They started thumping away but – it was silly really – we decided to stay put. 'We've a bit of a situation', said Sir Harold, 'and we haven't made up our minds about anything'. Bang, bang. 'We don't know what to do.' Bang, bang. 'We're wondering if you would take over as caretaker-manager for a while.' Bang, bang.

It didn't occur to me at the time that I was arriving with a bang but I said I'd be delighted to help. I had been manager of the Youth and Under-23 sides, so why not the first team? But it did occur to me that I was getting the job because I was the only man available. A new season was approaching, clubs had hardened their plans and the FA would not have been very popular if they had pinched someone's manager that late in the day.

The formal announcement followed on 17 August, 1977:

'The Football Association has invited Mr R. Greenwood of West Ham Football Club to act as team manager for the next three internationals, until December next, and subject to the agreement of his board of directors he has accepted the invitation.'

I was under no illusions. 'We're going to advertise the job so no promises' Sir Harold had told me in our basement workshop. 'But the image of the game is all wrong and we need a firm, stable hand immediately. Everyone is being roasted, including myself and the rest of the international committee, and we don't like it. See what you can do.'

It was up to me. I did not know how long I would be wanted but that did not matter. It was enough that I had a chance to help. The point was made by some that my image was right. Others disagreed. But I could feel the fire rising in me again. I decided to find out what needed to be done and to have a go. I was going to restore faith in our game and to help give it back its dignity. I had a hope, too, that my ideas about football might be better suited to the international game. I was not sure about this because I needed time to put my principles across – and time is always the enemy of the England manager. But against this I knew I would be working with our finest professionals. I had the pick of the lot and every manager believes he can do something in this position. Bobby Moore and Johnny Byrne once told me they thought I was ideally suited for the England job. That notion was now to be tested. A dream had become reality.

The players themselves, I believed, would be the key. If England started to win attractively the game's more general problems would be seen in a different light. Everything might start to fall into place. I decided to go on a grand tour and meet every player who had turned out at full international or Under-23 level in the previous two years. I knew most of them only as opponents and I wanted to talk with them as component parts of my own immediate future.

There was only one starting point. Liverpool were the standard-setters. They had just won the European Cup in impressive style in Rome, beating Borussia Moenchengladbach in the final, and they had a strong, exciting backbone of English players. I rang Bob Paisley and he immediately invited me to join them for their opening game of the season at Middlesbrough. I went up on the Friday and met the players on the Saturday morning. There was Ray Clemence, Phil Neal, Phil Thompson, Ray Kennedy, Emlyn Hughes, Jimmy Case, Terry McDermott and Ian Callaghan: there were so many there it felt like a team meeting. Bob Paisley, Joe Fagan and Ronnie Moran, Anfield's celebrated 'boot-room' trio, also joined us and I realised they were as keen to get a new slant on me as I was to get one on them.

My intention was to listen rather than talk. I wanted to find out what *they* felt about the England situation, what *they* felt was going wrong and what *they* thought were the answers. It was their business and their game as much as mine. I had a lot of ground to make up and I aimed to draw on their collective experience.

I also wanted to know what they felt about me and, in fact, Emlyn

Hughes was to tell me they half-expected me to walk through the door with a mortar-board on my head and a gown over my shoulders. They had heard those old and ludicrous rumours that I was a footballing egghead. This always amused me because I have never used a blackboard in my life. The only worthwhile work in football is done on a pitch. Football is essentially a practical subject. The only props that count are a ball and a few square yards of grass.

No blindingly new truths emerged from our chat but it still proved immensely valuable. The Liverpool men told me they didn't like playing at Wembley, for example, because the crowd became impatient too quickly. They were sick of getting the bird. Wouldn't it be possible, they asked, to play at Anfield or Old Trafford? I told them this was ridiculous. Half the players in the country would *walk* to Wembley to play there – and there was nothing wrong that a good win or two wouldn't put right. Bob, Joe and Ronnie said they would like to be involved more, along with other managers and coaches with something to offer.

Above all, I was impressed with the sincerity and modesty of these men. They were our top players. They had just won the European Cup. They were folk-heroes on Merseyside. But they were so attentive and polite you wouldn't have thought they'd won so much as a local hospitals' cup. It was the same with their management trio. There was no swank or side at all, and I felt that if they were typical of England's footballing people then there wasn't much wrong with our game. They were men after my own heart.

I went everywhere to meet players – including West Ham, where I talked with Manchester City's players, Dave Watson, Joe Corrigan, Mick Channon and company, in the familiar little boot-room there. And down at the Dell, where I had words with Alan Ball and the Southampton players, I incurred the wrath of an Irishman. Lawrie McMenemy told me that Chris Nicholl said: 'Don't – – – – – worry about England. We've got a game to play here.' Even throwaway lines proved helpful, like Trevor Brooking's comment: 'When we go to West Lodge Park before games we don't half eat well and I reckon those who aren't playing go back to their clubs a few pounds overweight.'

Now I was getting a clearer picture. One of the things coming through was that there was a lack of collective spirit, a factor emphasised by Don Revie's departure. Players had been hurt by that almost more than anyone. Life at the top had been going wrong for two or three years but I did not want to talk specifically about Revie – this was no time for recriminations. I was only interested in the future.

One thing many players wanted was someone of similar age, someone they could get close to, to act as a bridge between themselves and the manager. I acted on this immediately by turning to Geoff Hurst, one of my old West Ham stalwarts, who was then managing non-League Telford United. He was a man I trusted and admired, a man with the right pedigree, and I knew he would bring enthusiasm and honesty to the job.

Geoff made a handy contribution straight away. I asked him how he had preferred to prepare for an international and, although he was a little nervous in his new role despite all he'd achieved, he said emphatically: 'I always liked to prepare for an England game in the way I prepared for a club game. I liked things to have the same pattern.'

His comments struck a chord. Other players had said they wanted to be regarded as individuals. At work or play they hadn't liked being pushed into rigid, unfamiliar routines. They'd been obliged to do everything together. They hadn't been trusted.

I decided immediately that my West Ham methods would do for England. If players wanted to go to the pictures, that was fine by me. If they didn't, that was equally all right. If they wanted to go out for a drink, why not? And if a player was used to having tea in bed, instead of getting up, on the afternoon before a night game, then that was best for him. They were grown men and experienced professionals, not a party of schoolchildren who had to be led by the hand or rapped on the knuckles if they broke step. Self-discipline is the best and surest discipline of all. In fact when newcomers joined the squad their card was always marked by the rest. 'Don't mess anything up', a new man would be told. 'If you do you'll be letting us down and you'll be letting the boss down.'

My temporary appointment spanned three matches: a friendly against Switzerland at Wembley and two qualifying matches for the 1978 World Cup finals in Argentina – away to Luxembourg and at home to Italy. We had lost our crucial game in Italy a year before and as they had a better goal difference our chances were slim. But all was not lost: not quite.

The game against Switzerland came after a run of five without a win and just a month after I took over. I had little time and no magic wand so I decided to go along with Liverpool. I imposed their proven method on the England team by picking six of their players, Clemence, Neal, McDermott, Hughes, Kennedy and, after a lot of thought, Ian Callaghan. He was thirty-five and he hadn't played for England for eleven years but I felt if I was putting my faith in Liverpool I had to go all the way. He was fit, an all-purpose man who would give us width, and he was important to the overall balance.

I was giving the team an instant identity and with Kevin Keegan – an Anfield old boy – also in the side I knew that no introductions would be necessary. Keegan linked up with Mick Channon and Trevor Francis in front and, on paper, things looked highly promising. On the Wembley pitch, though, it didn't work out too well. Keegan, Francis and Channon filled each other's space, the right kind of room wasn't there and we couldn't score. The Swiss were good technicians, they played cannily and the outcome was a rather dull goalless draw. But it had been an interesting experiment, one worth trying again, and I was not overcome with remorse.

One or two little adjustments were necessary for our game in Luxembourg. I didn't pick a right-back, playing just Trevor Cherry, Emlyn Hughes and Dave Watson at the back, with Ian Callaghan on the right side of midfield, Paul Mariner in front and Gordon Hill wide on the left. I thought the players would enjoy themselves but although we won with goals from Kennedy and Mariner we didn't impose ourselves on the modest opposition. A few more goals would have been priceless.

Keegan might well have made a difference but we had to leave him out for this game. He was having some difficulty in settling down with Hamburg in West Germany and when he joined us before the Luxembourg trip he looked terrible, really ill. Peter Burrows, our doctor, decided he couldn't do anything to help so Kevin went back to Germany and we went off to our unremarkable win in the Grand Duchy.

I had no idea how long I would be England's manager but I was now totally engrossed by the challenge. I decided that as long as I was in the driving seat I might as well make all the progress I could.

My first request was revolutionary in terms of English football but an old and trusted formula on the continent. I said to the FA's International Committee: 'What we must do, no matter who gets the job I'm doing now, is to appoint a team of managers and coaches to run our international sides at all levels. It will give us something we've never had before – continuity. You will work with them and be able to assess them properly, their character as well as their ability, and that will mean you won't have to make any more one-off, on-the-spot choices as you did with Don Revie and then with me. You'll be able to make a good, objective choice. We know the system works because it works in other countries, including West Germany. I feel very strongly about this because it should have been done years ago.'

They agreed; and I didn't waste time. I knew the men I wanted. I kept Bill Taylor and Geoff Hurst with me at full level, Bobby Robson and Don Howe took on the England 'B' side and Dave Sexton, Terry Venables and Howard Wilkinson had the Under-21s. For the Youth team I turned to a man who'd rung me soon after my temporary appointment.

'Congratulations' said Brian Clough 'and if you ever want me to do anything for you just call me. I'll even carry the bloody sponge bag for the Youth team.'

I believed what he had said and decided to take him at his word. I offered him the Youth team and his immediate response was promising: 'I'll crawl all the way to Lancaster Gate just to be involved' he replied. He said he would also like Peter Taylor with him. This posed no problem and I had great hopes of the partnership. I admired Clough for the way he got the most out of his players and I felt our youngsters would be stimulated by him.

I thought the whole 'team' had a very strong look about it. The chosen men were excellent coaches, had strong personalities with a super sense of humour, and all bubbled with enthusiasm. I asked them at one meeting, in Manchester, to jot down the England side they would like to see play in our fast approaching game against Italy. I don't think any selection matched! The differences were not profound but I found them interesting because here were men of great experience, men whose opinions I valued, and even they couldn't agree. It emphasized the problem I faced. Only one of our 'A' team refused to write his side down. That was Clough. He refused to show his hand. I found this interesting, too.

Now we faced Italy at Wembley; and Keegan, I knew, would be raring to go. He was the man I felt I could build the side around but after two games I was a long way from having either a team or a formula that satisfied me.

I decided eventually that simplicity was our best bet. I would have the players for only three days before the game and this was not long enough to do any serious work. We needed to fall back on a basic pattern that was immediately understandable. Simple jigsaw puzzles can still produce splendid pictures.

Our answer was to use two wingers with an orthodox English centre-forward in between them and Keegan, just behind, filling the hole, playing off him. We used just two men in midfield and four at the back. This left a lot of space in midfield but it meant our pair here had wide options in front and would be able to play their way out of trouble. There would be plenty of targets and the business of selection was simplified for them.

I picked Steve Coppell and Peter Barnes as our wingers and Bob Latchford as the centre-striker – a first cap for each of them. Their inexperience did not worry me because I thought they had the right qualities and character for the job. Coppell of Manchester United was small, busy and elusive, a ferret of a player who worked the whole of the right touchline. He was perfectly balanced by Barnes of Manchester City who was a natural – pacy, tremendous at going past defenders, a potential match-winner. He had deficiencies but I was more interested in his strengths. Latchford of Everton was tall, strong, aggressive and bang on form. And behind them, beside them and in front of them we had Keegan, to draw the strings together and pick up the bits and pieces.

I asked the players for their opinion of this plan. They had to make it work: I wouldn't be playing. Everybody joined in the discussion and one thing we decided was that Dino Zoff, the evergreen Italian goalkeeper, should not be allowed the time he liked to build from the back. Italy's best moves often started from deep positions from one of his throws. They would establish their rhythm from there and get their one-twos going, and they were at their most dangerous once they had been allowed to set the tempo of the game. We decided to push up on Zoff and his defence and force him to kick. This, in turn, presented us with a problem or two. It sounded a bit like suicide to play with only two men in midfield, so I reminded Trevor Brooking and Ray Wilkins that keeping possession would be a key factor. 'When we have the ball let's hold it. Let's regard it as something precious' I said.

I also asked Dave Watson and Emlyn Hughes if they were happy to accept one-for-one responsibility at the back. Em always liked someone in front of him and pointed out the risk involved but he said the overall plan sounded good and he would have a go. The important thing was that everybody understood what we were doing. It was an idea tailor-made just for this game, but the players believed in it.

Enzo Bearzot did not know how we were going to use Keegan and I did not help him by leaving the announcement of our side until the last minute. We caught him out. Enzo played two hard characters in midfield, one of them Benetti, the toughest of nuts, because he thought we would have three men in this area. As it was they found it difficult to engage. Benetti was almost isolated and Brooking and Wilkins, with plenty of space to work in, kept the ball going. Zoff was being forced to kick so the Italians couldn't play through their midfield as often as they wanted.

We needed to score ourselves, of course, and it was the Keegan-Brooking combination that eventually picked the lock. First there was a craftsman's ball from Brooking that just took in Keegan on the way, perfect pass, clinical finish, and then Keegan returned the compliment and sent in Brooking for his first goal for England. Keegan and Brooking: what a pair they were. They cooked up goals for England that suggested telepathy. There was a special relationship between them on the field that springs from familiarity, confidence – and something beyond my ken.

There was some pain involved, inevitably, in our win over Italy. Keegan sometimes let Benetti get too close, with nasty results, but what a revelation the little man was that night. It gave him a lot of confidence and me a lot of hope.

The only disappointment for me was that some people promptly suggested Italy had not been trying. What miserable rubbish! Few had given us an earthly beforehand but when we won, squarely and convincingly, these people tried to diminish our achievement. We were out of the World Cup it is true, but Italy pipped us only on narrow goal difference. In any case, without exception, all opponents do their best at Wembley.

Nevertheless the victory was a wonderful shot in the arm for us and I could see promise in the method we had used. I felt if we could keep it going it would mature into something really good. Variations and subtleties would come with time.

Coppell and Barnes were essential to the pattern and I believed they were part of England's long-term future. They gave us width and flair, they were the edge to our blade, and I would have kept them in the team as long as I was in charge. Coppell fulfilled all my hopes: he was a little jewel, consistent, brave, a thinking raider, one of the names I always put down first. What a tragedy it was when injury cut short his career.

Barnes, sadly, did not keep going. Poor Peter seemed to get knocked sideways when he left Manchester City. He was a Manchester lad, through and through, and had he stayed in his home town I think he would have got better and better. He needed people to believe in him. His ability was given its point by confidence, and when he lost his conviction he was not the same player. It was not the sort of problem the England manager could do anything about.

I had no worries about my defence, especially in the key positions of goalkeeper and centre-half. Ray Clemence and Peter Shilton were two of the best 'keepers in the world – *the* best for all I knew – while Dave Watson was a straight-up-and-down minder of the highest quality, very powerful and very good to have around. His long legs intercepted everything and he loathed letting the ball into the danger zone behind him. He was also a better footballer than many gave him credit for.

Emlyn Hughes was a wonderful skipper. Kevin Keegan had been captain but I felt that it was better generally to have a captain at the back; and, in any case, Kevin was based in Germany and I didn't want our captain away from home all the time. Em was just right for us. I had great confidence in him. His enthusiasm was unbelievable and it rubbed off on others. But when Emlyn's international career came to an end – even he couldn't go on forever – then I gave the job back to Kevin who became an inspirational figure. I noticed that when Kevin returned from Germany the whole place lit up. He excited the crowds and lifted his team-mates. He put his stamp on every occasion and I cannot speak too highly of this man in terms of his application, sense of responsibility, personality and ambition. He is a rare and brilliant little chap.

The Italian win did my chances of getting the England job permanently no harm at all, of course, and although I wasn't supremely confident I thought I stood a very good chance. I rested my case on what we had achieved. Results had been promising, a real team was emerging and the spirit was excellent.

The Football Association invited applications and, in alphabetical not interviewing order, Brian Clough, Ron Greenwood, Lawrie McMenemy, Bobby Robson and Allen Wade all saw the International Committee. I was with Bobby, keeping him company in the office of FA secretary Ted Croker, while he was waiting for his turn. I had already appointed him England's 'B' team manager and we chatted easily before his moment came.

Allen Wade's ideas were interesting. The FA's Director of Coaching, together with his right-hand man, Charles Hughes, wanted the England set-up to be run by all their area coaches who are in touch with every level of the game. I didn't see it like this. I wanted professionals from the League clubs to run things, men in close contact with all the top players and men with experience of the game abroad.

One or two papers ran a poll to see who their readers thought should get the job and Cloughie seemed to be 'the people's choice'. That was fine. It was a game within a game and a bit of fun, but the polls had nothing to do with what was really happening, or what really mattered.

Lawrie McMenemy was later to state that all the runners were interviewed except me. Lord knows where he got that idea. I had an office in Lancaster Gate and I certainly took the few steps into the interviewing room. My interview lasted about half-an-hour, it was friendly and relaxed and I put all my plans and hopes to the committee. Peter Swales, the chairman of Manchester City, asked me what I would do if I didn't get the job. I said: 'Retire'. I meant it, too. I had no intention of going back to West Ham. I could see no purpose in returning. John Lyall had taken over the team and it would not have been fair to him. That chapter of my life was closed.

The day on which the appointment was to be announced formally happened to be a day off for me. I still took it. I stayed down in Sussex and took Lucy out for lunch to our favourite restaurant at Alfriston, halfway between Brighton and Eastbourne. We sat in our car outside to catch a bulletin on the radio and, towards the end, the news came that I had got the job. It was mine until the end of the European Championship which, if we reached the finals, meant about eighteen months. Then the position would be reviewed.

I did my best to keep cool but I cannot express the delight that I felt. I cared about the game, my profession and my country, and now I had the chance to do something for them all. I felt so good; and no lunch ever tasted better.

The FA eventually got hold of me to confirm the news and next day, without a change in step, I went into the office as usual. There was a news conference in the main chamber, cameras, microphones, notebooks, a million words and plenty of optimism, but my main immediate thought was simply to keep the ball rolling. I believed we were heading in the right direction.

The first thing I did was appoint John Cartwright as England's first full-time Youth coach. He was a former West Ham player who in his young days had shown really outstanding ability but then spoilt things for himself because his attitude was wrong. He matured into a splendid, highly-responsible coach, however, and I wanted him to be involved in everything – from internationals at Youth level right through to the schools. It was a hard and complex job: one of the toughest of all.

John said he would be happy to work with Brian Clough and Peter Taylor whose main impact so far had been on an international Youth tournament in Las Palmas. Their impact was eventful to say the least. The fact that Brian and Peter were even involved meant the tournament got a lot of unexpected publicity: it was almost news when they blew their noses. They were figureheads, really, and didn't do a lot of work – but when England won the tournament it was immediately attributed to their inspiration. The problem was that they upset everybody in the process. Frank O'Gorman, the doctor, and John Bayliss, the administration secretary on the trip, came back steaming and Ken Burton, our part-time coach, was so dismayed that he resigned. I tried to talk him out of it but his reply was emphatic: 'I can't put up with that. I'm sorry.'

Clough and Taylor were my appointments so I had to stand by them, but it wasn't a satisfactory arrangement. Nottingham Forest were hitting their peak and were on their way to the championship, a superb achievement, but this obviously meant the two were not very involved with England's youngsters. They were never available which was not very helpful to anyone. This was why I chose John Cartwright as coach: he is a man with definite values and ideas. Soon after, I bumped into Cloughie at a game and he asked for a word. He said he didn't think Peter and he would be able to carry on with England because of their commitment to Forest. It was, we agreed, an impossible situation.

I still feel that what happened was a pity, because Brian Clough is a man with rare gifts and I sincerely thought his personality and drive would be good for the youngsters. But he is an enigma. Nobody knows him well. I am not even sure how well he knows himself. But he is successful – and that matters.

The two games that followed my confirmation as England manager were the finest tests possible. They might have been arranged in heaven: first was West Germany in Münich and then Brazil at Wembley, Europe's best followed by South America's best, world champions both. We lost 2-1 in Germany and drew 1-1 with Brazil, not very impressive on the face of it but those two games were an important part of our education.

A real German winter greeted us. There was snow upon snow and our party even got split up on the way to our hotel in Münich. The players' coach arrived first with the help of a police escort and, instead of waiting for Alan Odell who usually looked after the room arrangements, I took hold of the list and sorted things out – registrations, room numbers, keys and so on. A group of German journalists watching us were clearly surprised at something and later I asked them what. 'We have never, ever, seen Helmut Schoen hand out keys' they said. 'Old habits' I replied.

We had two games to play, a 'B' international in Augsburg and the full international in Münich's Olympic Stadium. The pitch in the local stadium in Augsburg was covered in heavily rolled snow and Phil Thompson came back into our dressing-room after a warm-up saying: 'What a load of jessies. They've all got black tights on. We'll beat this lot, no trouble.' The Germans dressed for the conditions, sensible people, but Thompson was right about the result. It was an awkward game in tricky conditions but we achieved an honest win: West Germany 1, England 2.

This did our confidence no harm for the next night's game in the ultra-modern Olympic Stadium. Helmut Schoen went down with 'flu, and Jupp Derwall, his right-hand man and eventual successor, did not enjoy the first hour. We played well on a pitch that had been properly cleared, Peter Barnes gave that gutsy and knowing little full-back, Berti Vogts, a real running, and a Stuart Pearson header gave us the lead. But the man at the heart of our performance was Kevin Keegan who had been arbitrarily suspended for eight weeks for a flash of temper in a friendly. He kept himself fit, though, and he was obviously busting to play so I decided to take the chance.

Keegan was up against Rainer Bonhof, a good marker but also a strong and sometimes devastating runner, and the pair had a splendid battle. They romped all over the place but Keegan, no doubt, had the better match before I pulled him off near the end. He was looking exhausted after his long lay-off with Hamburg and I felt I had to be fair to him. As he walked off the big crowd gave him a handsome standing ovation – and from that night on his fortunes changed in Germany. He'd been struggling a little before but after that he went from strength to strength.

West Germany had equalised by then after sending on Ronnie Worms as a substitute. He was another powerful, mobile chap who'd actually played and scored against us in Augsburg the previous night. He started charging around all over the place, putting us under a bit of pressure, and then he pinched the equaliser. A draw looked likely but then West Germany were awarded a free kick on the edge of our area and Bonhof stepped up to take it. Keegan would normally have marked our card – he was full of information about German players – but we knew Bonhof was one of the best dead-ball kickers in Europe. We took a lot of time getting our defence right but then Ray Clemence signalled Mick Mills to go wider on the end, Mills started to move but was then pulled back, and that was the moment the patient but quick-witted Bonhof chose to strike. There was a gap, his shot struck Mills and the ball was in the net. We had lost our concentration at a critical point and the bill was a heavy one. It cost us the game, my first defeat as England's manager.

Bonhof did not try to be too clever with his free kicks. Like the Brazilians, he tended to whack them or bend them. Hungary's Ferenc Puskas did the same thing. Sometimes their kicks would go gruesomely wrong and everybody would say what a mess. But often everything went right and the hours spent in practising these kicks would seem a first-class investment. Brazil's players get their curl and trajectory right with the help of wooden cut-out figures. The rewards are there for all to see.

Our game against Brazil taught us never to take anything for granted. Five of their players were booked and a lot of things went on that had nothing to do with the kind of Brazilian football that won three World Cups. They were nasty. Claudio Countinho was their manager at the time and he believed his players would never reach their full potential until they matched Europeans – and especially the British – in the physical side of the game. Much of their tackling and blocking was crude which disappointed me, because they were not being true to themselves. That is almost the worst sin of all.

Our team was depleted because no Liverpool or West Ham players were available and, early on the day before the match, I found myself with only seven fit players. We patched and adjusted and earned our draw – but the problems of my job were suddenly coming into focus.

England took the British Championship, winning all three games nice and tidily, and I felt our victory over Scotland at Hampden Park with a goal by Steve Coppell was particularly important. The year before the Scottish fans had come to Wembley and smashed the place up and I thought our win up there returned things to an even keel.

I could see shape and promise in my squad: it had balance and healthy cover and this was handsomely confirmed when we beat Hungary 4-1 at Wembley just before they went off to play in the 1978 World Cup finals in Argentina. Our side was the best we could put out: Shilton: Neal, Watson, Hughes, Mills; Wilkins, Brooking; Keegan; Coppell, Francis, Barnes. It did not have an orthodox British centre-forward but Francis and Keegan gave us pace and high mobility in the middle, Coppell and Barnes provided essential width and Brooking and Wilkins had the ideas and patience to keep the whole machine ticking smoothly. Francis was given a lot of room that night and made excellent use of it. I told him afterwards it was one of the best games I'd ever seen him play.

But what pleased me most of all about that night was a comment from Gustav Sebes, who managed the great Hungarians in the early 1950s when they had shown England and the rest of Europe how the game should really be played. Gustav told Sir Stanley Rous, who was there as honorary president of FIFA, that 'England played like Hungary at their best'. There was a degree of courtesy in the observation but it was still good to hear. Hungary went off to the World Cup, where they were beaten by Argentina themselves, Italy and France in the strongest group of all, and we looked towards our qualifiers for the 1980 European Championship finals in Italy.

One other 'team' must be mentioned: my close friends and colleagues at Lancaster Gate. Harold Thompson and then Bert Millichip, the two chairmen of the Football Association during my time as manager, and Dick Wragg and his international committee all gave me wonderful support. They were always with me when the going was sticky. I had an excellent rapport with Ted Croker, the FA secretary, and – as I'd discovered with Eddie Chapman at West Ham – a good relationship between manager and secretary is of paramount importance.

Administration was always made very easy for me by Alan Odell, the secretary of the international department, who took many tasks off my shoulders. Right the way through I had great respect for the FA staff. They knew their jobs and I knew where I was with them.

3

Europe: Highlights and Lowlights

The European Championship finals in Italy in 1980 should have been a show-piece for football but they proved to be perfectly in tune with the modern game. They were dull, wretchedly supported and coldly undermined by live television. We travelled in high hope and returned with empty hearts.

The football was functional at best and instantly forgettable at most other times. There was a chronic shortage of originality which depressed me because it seemed to be a signpost to the future. The matches were an indictment of the game rather than a celebration of it. Football is what men choose to make of it and Europe's best players made a pig's ear of this tournament.

The Italians only stirred themselves to watch their own team, saw them score just two goals in four games and ignored almost everything else except West Germany's victory over Belgium in the final in Rome. England's defeat by Italy in Turin was watched by sixty thousand but only around fifteen thousand mustered to watch us draw with Belgium and beat Spain. The rest of Europe sat and moaned in their armchairs.

The dangers of live television coverage were spelt out in big letters during that Italian summer, and this is a fundamental problem for football. It has got to be faced and I only hope the right conclusions are drawn from the right facts and figures when the live experiment with our League and Cup football is finally evaluated. I agree that television gives the game an interesting extra dimension and generates valuable income. But there is a very fine balance to be maintained – for where television is given its head it can take over and destroy.

Football cannot eat its cake and still have it, and I fear the game is in danger of selling its future in order to pay its current bills. What is the point of professional football unless there are backsides on seats and feet on the terraces? Fans give football much more than their money. They contribute to the game; they are part of it because players feed on noise and atmosphere. It lifts and inspires them. Great performances are never given in empty theatres. Football is a spectator sport – not a television entertainment where we all put our feet up, watch a replay or two and become instant experts. There are kids today who will eventually put football in the same category as *Dallas* and *Coronation Street*. Is this the game's future?

I did not conjure up any excuses or hard luck stories about England's modest achievements in Italy because in a short, high pressure tournament like this a side either gets it right or it doesn't. Every nation has its problems but winners patch them up and still manage to peak. I thought we did everything we could to prepare our players for the job, and our build-up, organisation and spirit were right on cue. But, when it came to it, we could not make good the loss of Trevor Francis, who had severed an Achilles tendon just a month before, or the vital degree or two that was missing from Kevin Keegan's game following Hamburg's defeat by Nottingham Forest in the European Cup final and narrow failure in their League championship. Kevin admits he was well below his best and he looked a tired chap by the end of the finals.

Ray Wilkins said the players let me down, but I cannot agree with this. Not all played at their best but they all did their best. The truth is that we didn't have the penetration or range to win our first two games. A fit Francis and an in-form Keegan might have swung the balance because there is no substitute for quality. I am not talking about great players, because every team is short of these, but high calibre internationals. Our failure had nothing to do with luck of any sort, good, bad or imagined.

Yet, in all honesty, I must admit I was terribly disappointed. We struck the right notes so often in the qualifying tournament that I believed we were potential winners of the championship.

We twice beat Denmark, Bulgaria and Northern Ireland and the only point we dropped was against the Republic of Ireland on the Lansdowne Road rugby ground in Dublin. Our form and shape varied a little but the side retained a solid, basic structure. Dave Watson played in all eight qualifying games, Ray Clemence and Kevin Keegan in seven and Phil Neal, Mick Mills, Ray Wilkins, Steve Coppell and Trevor Brooking in six. And, after sticking with Peter Barnes for five games and Bob Latchford for four, the claims of Trevor Francis and Tony Woodcock, with their wider range and manoeuvrability at speed making us less predictable, interested me more. The format was simple but adaptable. We were solid at the back, an area which never lost me any sleep. There was variety and enterprise in the middle and going forward we had width and pace. The side was experienced, too, and could adjust and improvise to meet the unexpected.

Denmark pushed us hardest and provided significant evidence that many of Europe's smaller nations are climbing the ladder. We beat them twice, 4-3 in Copenhagen and 1-0 at Wembley, but their neat technique and quick thrusts from midfield stretched us over there while their defence frustrated us at home. The game in Copenhagen was like a typical West Ham affair, after Brooking had set up Keegan for a couple of well-timed headers. But Denmark were an expressive side who then punished us for one or two sloppy mistakes at the back. The crowd loved it but, as the errors and goals mounted, I almost wished I was a smoker.

A goal by Keegan beat the Danes at Wembley but again the side knew what they were doing. They had players from leading clubs all over Europe, including Allan Simonsen from Barcelona, Preben Elkjaer from Lokeren and Henning Jensen, Frank Arnesen and the young Soren Lerby all from Ajax of Amsterdam. I knew their best side would be sent out because some of the players had asked me in Copenhagen if the return match was going to take place at Wembley. They all wanted to play there because the old place still has a special status all over the world. Simonsen and company made sure they were released for our game, yet earlier half of them had not been available for the match in Northern Ireland. They were not so keen, it seemed, on Windsor Park and Belfast.

Northern Ireland gave us our two easiest games. We beat them 4-0 at Wembley, with Tony Currie coming in to enjoy himself in place of the injured Wilkins, and then overturned them with even more style by 5-1 in Belfast. We did play well on that wet Irish afternoon: Woodcock and Francis got two goals each with Pat Jennings, Northern Ireland's ageless and splendid goalkeeper, looking just a little reluctant for once to get in at the near post.

The Republic of Ireland took a point from us in Dublin because we fell for a sucker free kick – quickly played into space by Liam Brady for Gerry Daly to score. The crowd was big, noisy and totally one-eyed, the atmosphere was what is generally known as 'electric' and Brady's left foot kept finding some telling gaps. Brady was with Arsenal then, before his move to Italy, and he was at the heart of most of the Republic's best moments, a general who wasn't too obvious. He has good vision, a sharp, footballing intelligence, and a left foot that can clip, cut, push and spin to order. Around him he had a well-balanced side and we were pleased enough to win a point.

The Republic weren't so good at Wembley, though, where we beat them with a couple of goals by Keegan. I gave Bryan Robson his first cap in this game, and he almost marked the occasion with a goal near the end, but the performance that pleased me as much as any was by Kenny Sansom at left-back. It was his third cap and he was a natural left-footer in a position which had been shared by two men who preferred their right, Mick Mills and Trevor Cherry.

Sansom was brought along properly at Crystal Palace before he moved to Arsenal. He is full of good habits and although he lacks an inch or so in height he compensates by clever positional play. He is a good defender who isn't afraid of work and his skill on the ball means he is rarely caught in possession. He likes to go forward and keep on going and his pace often surprises his opponents. He is a very receptive player although – one fault – he seems to have no sense of history. He was once listening to talk of other left-backs when a name that wasn't familiar to him cropped up. 'Who is Ray Wilson?' he asked.

The victory which pleased me most, however, was our three-goal win over Bulgaria in Sofia in the summer of 1979. Even the home crowd cheered us off the field. The heat was terrible, really sticky, and Bulgaria were a fair side who played well through the middle; but we still out-classed them. We played within ourselves, setting our own tempo and keeping possession, and our finishing was excellent. It was an accomplished performance although oddly the incident I remember above all involved Keegan inside the Bulgarian penalty area. The Bulgarians took a quick, smart free kick and the shot that followed promised a goal. But somehow Keegan was back to stop the ball on the line. For a moment I thought he'd popped up through a trap-door in the ground. I have no idea how he got there. He also scored the first of our three goals in this game – and in the seven qualifying matches in which he played he scored seven goals. Keegan's value was boundless.

The one qualifying game which Keegan missed was Bulgaria's visit to Wembley, and that was hardly his fault. The game was postponed for twenty-four hours because of fog and Keegan, who was fit and raring to go on the Wednesday night, was then recalled by Hamburg for their League match that weekend. We had virtually qualified for the finals and, to keep Kevin's German connections sweet, I did not put up any argument.

It was the first time a Wembley international had been postponed but there was no alternative. I have never seen thicker fog. The fans wouldn't have been able to see the players . . . and the players would have struggled to see the ball. The decision to try again the following evening was taken before the turnstiles were opened but the embarrassing thing was that by half-past eight the fog had gone. The great, grey blanket suddenly disappeared. It was too late for second thoughts then, of course, but the postponement proved one very important thing.

I thought the crowd would be a smallish one on the Thursday evening, thirty or forty thousand perhaps, but I was very wrong about this. All the fans were there again. Coaches rolled up nose to tail, the car parks buzzed and trains were full: it was a wonderful response. Seventy-one thousand came back and I knew then that we had gone a long, long way to restoring faith in our national side. The way we were playing and winning counted once more. England mattered.

Keegan's absence meant that I was able to give a first cap to Kevin Reeves, who was then with Norwich, but it was another man new to the international game who caught everybody's eye – Glenn Hoddle of Tottenham. There had been noisy demands for me to pick him before but I waited until I thought the time was right for both him and us. The match against Bulgaria proved a good choice. Hoddle was given lots of room and he capped a stylish performance by whisking in the second of our two goals, a wicked shot struck with the outside of his foot from twenty yards.

Deciding when to blood a player can be a ticklish problem. Every case is different and every match is different. A good international is obviously a player with unusual talent but, equally importantly, he must have the temperament and footballing IQ to cope with high-order opposition, unfamiliar tactics and methods and the harsher pressures that come on the big stages. He must be adaptable enough to fit smoothly into a pattern that's very different from the one used by his club. He must also have resilience and patience.

Some players I had no doubt about. Others I was prepared to gamble on. A few made me think very carefully. Pick a player too early and he can be squashed. Push him into the wrong sort of game and his confidence in himself at this level can be permanently bruised. Timing is all important – and often more factors are involved than most realise.

Hoddle's case is a good example. Everybody could see tremendous possibilities in him from the very start and I certainly shared the general view. His ability is prodigious: there is no question about that. On the ball he is a delight. His control is of Brazilian quality. He is a living, breathing denial of the charge that British football cannot produce players with great technical skill. He also has balance and a feeling for the unexpected.

Yet there were good reasons why, despite all the squawks to pick Hoddle right away, I bided my time. I studied him closely. One problem with the younger Hoddle was that I did not think he was properly fit. There were periods in a game when he would duck out. His shoulders would slump and he seemed short of breath. I felt he should have done some commando training and built up real staying power because this would have improved his worth in all manner of ways. I am not talking about 'work rate'. I am talking about total involvement. A player needs staying power to keep looking for an effective position. The secret is constant movement, into space, then out of it, and then back in again at the right moment. A player must search constantly for a spot where his colleagues can't help but find him. And this needs mental and physical toughness.

Glenn was also tending to float into bad positions when I first started looking at him as a potential international. It was difficult for his teammates to reach him. He was creating space for himself on the ball but not off it. He had the ability to make room for himself, with a wave of a foot or drop of the shoulders, but this took time and limited his options. His best period with Tottenham was when he had Ossie Ardiles at his sharpest alongside him. Spurs found the little Argentine first and he would set up Hoddle. The basic service wasn't to Hoddle himself. Some players make space for themselves while others must have it made for them.

Hoddle was not as commanding as he should have been, either. He did not take a game by the throat, which may have had something to do with his personality. Glenn is a gentle sort of chap, and in those less mature days he was even a bit shy. The style is always the man and his character was evident from his play: he did not shape a side himself, it had to be shaped around him.

Often, too, Hoddle seemed obsessed with the long ball, rather like the Johnny Haynes of old, and this demanded a special understanding with the men in front. His passes were struck with cutting weight and direction but it was not always easy to be in an effective position to receive them. Sometimes these passes looked better than they were.

There were times when Hoddle moved into splendid positions just outside the opposition penalty area and he could strike the ball from there with stunning pace and accuracy. But usually he would be involved in a movement only once. He did not often drive forward to become an extra man. Such a move only partly depends on fitness: it is also dependent on hunger for involvement and ambition to be in at the kill. There is a limit to what even the greatest artist can achieve with just one stroke of his brush.

Sometimes a player's weaknesses can be ignored, his strengths override everything, but I did not feel this was the case with the young Hoddle. He was twenty-two when I gave him his first chance and, in fact, I did not pick him for the next game and continued to give him an outing every three or four matches. A football team must be looked at as a whole and I felt Steve Coppell, Terry McDermott and Phil Neal were the men likely to give us greatest strength down the right; and with Keegan *and* Hoddle in the side it was this flank which would have been disturbed.

Hoddle played whenever the match was right or whenever there was room for him. I could see he was learning from the experience and I picked him instead of Bryan Robson to complete our party for the European finals. I had no doubts about Robson but he was not fully fit at the time and I felt Hoddle's talent might just give us an interesting extra dimension; and, indeed, he did not let himself down in our final game against Spain.

It was towards the end of the following season, 1980–81, that I put more weight on his shoulders. It was a period when everything seemed to go wrong, at Wembley of all places. Hoddle scored against Spain but our young defence got caught out and we lost 2-1. I then picked him for successive home international matches. Wales held us to a goalless draw, an instantly forgettable exercise, but for the 'big one' – our home game against Scotland – I decided to give Hoddle absolute freedom. I told him simply to express himself. I had just seen Socrates play like this for Brazil and also Nyilasi for Hungary in a game against Rumania. Their involvement was total. They were fit enough to be at the heart of every move and their talent and wit did the rest. They were birds on the wing and, although I was not comparing Hoddle in my mind with Socrates or Nyilasi, both very experienced men, I thought it was a role that might suit him. I decided to let everyone else work for him against Scotland and then see if his skill on the ball and his passing could open doors for us. I wanted him to enjoy himself.

We tried Hoddle in this role in practice games and my hopes were genuine. But the fact is he did not even promise to take control of the Wembley match. He had fleeting moments of brilliance, the odd pass was out of a magic hat, the occasional dummy was a delight, but he lacked conviction. His influence on the game was minimal and, although we played well enough with a young side that also included Bryan Robson, Graham Rix and Kenny Sansom, we lacked authority, for which Hoddle took his share of the blame. We lost to a penalty by John Robertson.

Hoddle was still maturing, however, and I believed his time would come. But I have no regrets about the way I handled him early on. I did what I thought was best for him at the time and for the slightly longer-term good of England.

I was certainly happy with the quality and depth of our squad before the European finals; and I was equally pleased with the success of the squad system itself. Strangers off the pitch are also strangers on it and I introduced players to the squad before they were likely to be picked to make them familiar with the accommodation, training methods, atmosphere and the set-up in general. I wanted newcomers to get used to shouting at men like Keegan and Brooking and to receiving advice from coaches like Don Howe and Geoff Hurst. The system also helped create a club spirit. Laurie Cunningham used to come back from Real Madrid and, even though he could be rather a withdrawn character, he would breeze in and say 'Hi everybody' as if he had never been away.

Bobby Robson told me after he took over that he thought a squad of twenty-two was too big. 'It's not', I told him. 'You pick eighteen and five drop out and you're suddenly short. You've problems. But have twenty-two and you're still all right. You'll rarely find you've many spare.'

The squad system does not mean its regular members can take things for granted or form themselves into a protective clique. Nobody is a permanent fixture. There are always places available for players with the right kind of ability and character; and, when the moment comes, the step into the first team is made infinitely easier.

A first international is a testing time, but I would tell every new man: 'You are being picked for what you are and what you've done. Don't change. Be yourself. Be natural.' It would be criminal to ask a player to change his game, to do things beyond his compass or outside his experience, although once he has come to terms with the international stage then, obviously, he can begin to experiment. There are no formulae and no guarantees in international football. It is up to the man himself.

The run-in towards the European finals began with our 2-0 win over Spain in Barcelona. Trevor Francis and Tony Woodcock were the scorers and their pace, with skill and intelligent application all about them, undermined Spain's rigid man-for-man marking. I've already referred to the importance of this win and it undoubtedly served as a clear, strong warning to the rest of Europe. Our progress was then confirmed when we beat Argentina, the world champions, by 3-1 at Wembley. All the managers of the finalist nations were there that night, good judges taking a clinical look at us in action against the best in the world, and I felt it was vital that we did ourselves justice. Our confidence was strong but I wasn't sure it was bullet-proof: a convincing win against the game's champions would confirm it.

Argentina were a team I admired and enjoyed watching during the 1978 World Cup finals. They had some wonderful players but their attitude was aggressive, they hit off first-time passes without losing their pattern or control and their linking and supporting were that of a side in harmony. They also brought a sixty-five-inch tall celebrity called Diego Maradona with them. Here was one of the world's great players, extravagantly gifted and able to do everything at pace. He has almost animal reflexes and awareness and is one of the game's small and sadly diminishing band of genuine match-winners.

'We all know about this fellow', I told the players. 'But I don't want to upset our pattern by putting somebody on him because we'll get dragged all over the place. Let's remember one thing, though. He's not used to people coming at him from the back. Let's attack him from back and front. The nearest to him takes the responsibility. Let's put him under real pressure.' And it worked well: we closed Maradona in from all angles and he did not have a great game. He did not know where the next challenge was coming from. Even when he went past somebody he still needed eyes in the back of his head. We set the whole team on him rather than just one man although once or twice, inevitably, he rose above us and proved his greatness.

Dave Watson, a rock of a man, had a splendid game, and Dave Johnson scored two of our goals, the first a beautifully-timed header. Although we won well, I would have been blind not to notice that in one or two areas we did not match the Argentinians technically. Ardiles did not play because of his commitment to Tottenham and because Cesar Menotti wasn't sure he was part of their future, but they were a lesser force without the little man. He was a major reason for their success in the World Cup, a player of great vision and range.

Our attitude had seemed exactly right after beating Argentina but it proved to be all wrong for our first British Championship game against Wales at Wrexham four days later. I made half a dozen changes for this match because I wanted everyone to be in touch before Italy. Hindsight, that old friend of mine, tells me that was a mistake but it seemed a fair idea before the game. I particularly wanted to have a look at Larry Lloyd, who had been playing very well for Nottingham Forest and who I thought might be a possibility as our cover at centre-half. But he was one of several players who unaccountably believed the match would be easy. We were just humans being human. We had beaten the world champions, hadn't we, so Wales were obviously no problem! Alas for us, the Welsh players were hell-bent on impressing their new manager, Mike England, and they ran us off the park to win by 4-1. Wales proved once again that attitude is a major key to success in this game.

The Wrexham defeat presented me with a problem. Cohesion is important but it was a luxury I now couldn't afford, so more changes had to be made for our next game, against Northern Ireland. Watson, Hughes and Wilkins came in to restore stability and I also gave a first cap to Alan Devonshire from my old club, West Ham, a left-sided player of pace and variety who took the game to his opponents and who promised to be a better bet than Peter Barnes whose form had gone cold. It was a poor old match on a greasy Wembley surface, though, and a 1-1 draw was just about right.

We had beaten the world champions but, with one point from two games in the British Championship, we now faced Scotland at Hampden and the prospect of finishing bottom. Where would this place us as likely winners of the European Championship? I believed our wins over Spain and Argentina said a great deal more about us than our muddled performances against Wales and Northern Ireland. It was no time to lose faith.

The Scots, of course, made the most of our position. They had a big wooden spoon specially made and all ready to present to us, and there wasn't a doubt in the mind of anyone north of the border that we were there for the taking. I will not claim I have any deep feeling of rivalry when it comes to the Scots, because I know and like so many of them, but I can understand why their fans get so worked up about their games with England. The reasons are part of our island history.

Eighty-eight thousand people were at Hampden, their roar was like a long roll of thunder, and I think they saw us as Christians on a tray for the lions. What they had to suffer, in fact, was an excellent early goal by Brooking and another in the second half by Coppell. We looked confident and well organised, Coppell was splendid going forward and Brooking, McDermott and Wilkins did everything right in mid-field. I wasn't really surprised. I had sensed our attitude was right again – it was evident from the players' eyes and words before the game – and afterwards in the dressing-room I thanked them all for knocking the knockers.

England had got it right when it mattered, a vital knack in football as in most other things. Remember, too, that Keegan had not been involved in the British Championship because of his obligations to Hamburg. Northern Ireland won the title, which was healthy for the game, and we left that big wooden spoon where it belonged – in Scotland.

This should have been our last match before the European finals but one more cropped up which, with respect to a lot of good friends, I needed like the proverbial hole in the head. It was in Australia, a single, long-arranged match to celebrate the centenary of the game there, and although the side we sent out wasn't our best, for obvious reasons, the match was given full international status. Bobby Robson was in charge but Sir Arthur George, the president of the Australia FA, asked me to go as well and I did not feel I could refuse. The match was important to the Australians and to a few of our players as well, including Terry Butcher, Russell Osman and David Armstrong, because it gave them their first cap. Bryan Robson and Glenn Hoddle also played and on the way back, that endless night-into-day flight of meals and naps, I made the decision to take Hoddle to Italy rather than Robson. 'I don't want you to worry', I told Robson, 'because it's only a question of time before you're in'. Robson had a troublesome injury and he'd done well to play in Australia. I also decided to leave out Barnes and Cunningham, even though this left us with only one authentic winger in Coppell. The decision had to be made: Peter and Laurie were simply not on song.

The general mood when we finally came together for the European finals at our headquarters at West Lodge Park in Hertfordshire, a nice, rambling, comfortable old hotel, was just right. I saw no sign of worry or nail-nibbling, which was important. Tension scrambles the wits and taut bodies will never produce composed football. I let the players do much as they wanted and a few of our racing experts, Hughes, Mills, Thompson, McDermott and Johnson, even hired a helicopter and whirled off in style to watch the Derby. The value of taking things easy before a major challenge was always emphasised to me whenever I spent time in the training camps of other leading national sides, particularly the Dutch and Argentines, who saw relaxation as an integral part of their preparation.

We were even invited to a cocktail party at Number Ten Downing Street, an experience that did no harm at all because it perfectly reflected the interest and hopes of the country at large. Mrs Thatcher is a hostess who pitches her talk at just the right level and after the party she even proved she knows a bit about football. We were on the famous steps of Number Ten, posing for a happy send-off picture, when one of the photographers produced a ball. 'You'll be heading that ball unless you're careful', I said to our immaculately groomed Prime Minister – and Mrs Thatcher's answer bounced straight back: 'I think Trevor Brooking does that, doesn't he?' Trevor had just won the FA Cup for West Ham against Arsenal with one of his rare headers. It was a splendid party and a real honour.

Our next stop was Asti, a place noted for its sparkling wine, about an hour to the south-east of Turin and our first headquarters in Italy. We had done our homework thoroughly and I don't think anything could have been improved. We had our hotel, the Hasta, a lovely little place tucked away on a hill-top, all to ourselves. The training ground was next door, the staff knew their job and the food was excellent. Facilities, privacy, food, service and a scene that was easy on the eye; it was a super set-up.

We had won twenty and lost only three of the twenty-nine games between my taking over and the start of the European Championships.

It was a record I was hardly ashamed of but we now faced a new challenge, a high-pressure confrontation involving eight nations and lasting just twelve days. It was also the first time that any of our players had played in the finals of a major international tournament and this is why I was not worried that our average age was fairly high. I believed maturity would be a telling quality.

The eight nations were split into two groups of four with the winners moving on to the final in Rome and the runners-up meeting in a third-fourth play-off. Belgium, Italy, the hosts, and Spain were in our group. I had watched all three whenever I could in the months before and I felt we could do better than Alf Ramsey's team back in 1968 when England finished third – our last major success in this championship. The final stages then, by coincidence, had also been held in Italy.

I had no illusions, though, about the size of our task. Belgium were strong, well-drilled, ultra-competitive, and mixed their long and short game intelligently. They were also without much charity. Italy, though a familiar quantity, were forever unpredictable. They were technically excellent and could be explosive – a disciplined, experienced blend of high skill and muscle. A lot was expected of them as host country, however, and I wasn't sure how they would react to all the demands. Spain, I felt, we had the edge on. They were a very fair side at their best and sharp in counter-attack but they were not consistent and had limitations. I believed our win in Barcelona gave us an important psychological advantage.

A good start was of prime importance but I doubted if Belgium would allow the game to be a show-piece. Clemence was in goal for us, Watson with Thompson lying slightly behind him were the centre-backs, Neal and Sansom could be counted on to do their defensive job as full-backs but also give us width going forward; Wilkins and Brooking were in midfield with Coppell using the right flank, while Keegan was there to supervise, improvise and work to Woodcock and Johnson, who'd been scoring some important goals in the run-up. We had a big contingent of supporters in the Comunale Stadium, banners with familiar names were all over the place and when players and fans acknowledged each other before the kick-off I settled down feeling something more than just hope.

Yet Belgium caught us out. I had watched them five times before the finals and not once had they used the off-side trap as a calculated strategy. They used it very effectively on that day in Turin, however, and for a while we tumbled into it regularly. Woodcock had a goal disallowed and this proved crucial beyond words. It looked perfectly good to me and I would have been even more uptight had I realised just how significant the decision was going to be.

We still looked sharper than the Belgians but not always in the areas that counted and we didn't look like breaking them down until Wilkins produced something quite special. He turned the Belgians' off-side trap against themselves. He intercepted a clearance, lifted the ball over the top of the Belgian defence, who were coming forward like soldiers on parade, continued his run and picked up his own ball behind them. He then moved on smoothly to lob Jean Marie Pfaff in the Belgian goal. The move was a gem of skill and intelligence.

Belgium's off-side trap had been blown but, credit again to them, they equalised only a minute or two later. It was a marvellous goal from their point of view, an awful one from ours. We had plenty of time to clear a corner but no one took the right decision and Jan Ceulemans, a very talented, awkward customer who tended to play blinders or stinkers, moved in to score with power and gratitude.

It was then that the world seemed to lose its reason. Up in a corner behind the England net a small section of our supporters started fighting – their way of reacting to the goal – but the police moved in and, down on the touchline, we took a quick look and then returned to concentrating on the game. But the fighting got worse, the police started using tear-gas and clouds of yellow-black smoke began to spread and drift downwards.

The gas reached our goal and suddenly I could see Clemence wiping his eyes and signalling that he was in trouble. I didn't waste a moment. I trotted over to the match adjudicator on the centre-line and asked him to signal to the West German referee to stop the game and come over to our position.

'What's going to happen if a goal is put past our goalkeeper because he can't see?' I asked the referee immediately.

'It would count', he replied.

'In that case', I said, 'don't you think the game should be stopped until the gas has cleared?'

I don't think this had even occurred to the chap but, after a moment's hesitation, he agreed. The game was suspended for five minutes and when Clemence came over we could see he was in quite a bad way. His eyes were streaming and, with smoke everywhere now, one or two others were also affected.

The game never took off once it restarted. Stoppages always tend to unsettle because they break everyone's concentration. But I think we were bothered most of all because we were very conscious that it was our

supporters who had stepped out of line. The game was duly drawn and at
the end I put my arm around the shoulders of Guy Thys and just said
'Well played'. He replied: 'Yes, but you were the better side.'

My feelings were well above boiling-point. The disallowed Woodcock
goal still rankled, the silly way in which we had conceded Belgium's
equaliser didn't help and I felt we'd been worth more than a draw – but,
above all, it was the English hooliganism which hurt. It had been England's first game in a final tournament for ten years, since the 1970 World
Cup in Mexico, and in ten rotten minutes these imbeciles had spoilt
everything. I went on television – I didn't want to, but I'd promised the
BBC's Mike Murphy that I would – and suggested that the authorities
put all the hooligans back on a boat and then pull out the plug halfway
across. I was promptly criticised back home by a university sociologist
who said someone in my position should not make remarks like that.
What do people like this know of real life?

Not that I was the only one who sounded off. Mrs Thatcher, who was
in Venice for a Common Market summit, described the riot as 'a dis-
graceful embarrassment', while Sir Harold Thompson, chairman of the
FA, who never pulled his punches, said the louts were 'sewer rats'.

I have no answer to the problem but I do know that football itself
cannot cope. Hooligans have nothing to do with the game: they just use
it as a vehicle. Society produces hooligans and society, in the shape of its
law-makers and law-enforcers, must accept responsibility. Hefty fines,
prison, detention centres and even the birch are all handy deterrents but
unless *something* is done the trouble will persist. The problem will certainly not go away of its own accord.

Some suggested that we would be thrown out of the tournament. I
didn't believe this for a moment but we were fined £8,000 and I was
desperately worried that there would be further repercussions when we
played Italy in the same stadium three days later. The Italian press was
making a meal of it and the whole of Europe seemed to be looking at the
English as if they'd just crawled out from under a big stone.

The group was still wide open, however, because Spain and Italy had
locked themselves up in a goalless draw in the other opening match. It
was a familiar story. Nobody wants to lose the first game of a tournament
so the attitude is cautious at best and downright negative at worst. I tried
to use this to our advantage in the first game by sending out a team that
was positive in outlook but, alas, one or two things conspired against us.

One thing was now certain though: we had to beat Italy. They had
not been bettered at home for ten years and this, I felt, was our test of
tests. But I also believed it was possible provided we struck our game.

We had out-thought them at Wembley and, although they now had the best cards in their hand, I was convinced our task was far from impossible.

I thought long and hard about our team. We would be facing experienced opponents backed by a huge crowd. Obviously, I wanted balance, shape, a way of creating goals and a way of scoring them. I had to base my decisions on what I'd learnt from the previous game and what I felt might reasonably happen in this next one.

My answer in the end was to make two significant changes. I brought in Gary Birtles for David Johnson and Ray Kennedy for Trevor Brooking. I announced the team in the middle of our training pitch at Asti and I could see faces that registered everything from surprise to disbelief – all mixed up with a bit of sweat because it was a horribly humid day.

Birtles was obviously the unexpected choice, and I understood why, because his experience of international football amounted to just ten minutes as a substitute at the end of our game against Argentina at Wembley. I felt, however, that Birtles would be a better partner for Woodcock than Johnson against man-to-man marking. Birtles had just helped Nottingham Forest win the European Cup twice – the first time alongside Woodcock – and I thought their relationship could be important. He was a novice in international terms but no stranger to big, nervy occasions. Birtles was also an uncompromising type with underestimated skills and he was a determined tryer. He was quick on the turn, always important against a tight marker, and I felt he might give us better options than Johnson who liked the ball played up to him. There was, too, an element of surprise. I had a hunch Birtles might click and the decision was mine and mine alone. If Francis had been fit there would have been no problem, but he wasn't and I was faced with picking Johnson, Mariner or Birtles. Birtles was my choice.

I picked Kennedy instead of Brooking because I believed we had to hold our shape in midfield, particularly on our left where Franco Causio, ageing a little but still a demon for finding weaknesses, would be Italy's main threat. Trevor tended to float a bit, following his nose and instinct, while Ray's presence was more solid. I could see him filling our left area as he did for Liverpool. Brooking's drifting would leave Sansom too exposed at full-back. Kennedy's ample qualities would serve a dual purpose.

Enzo Bearzot had his own problems, of course. The Italian bribery scandal had lost him Paulo Rossi for a couple of years, Rossi a striker whose brightness and quick mobility impressed me enormously in Argentina in 1978. Enzo also had some worries about the form of Causio himself and their tall striker, Roberto Bettega. Inevitably, too, he was still fighting his battle against the suffocating philosophy of Italian football. He wanted his players to play.

The Comunale Stadium was a very different place this time. The crowd was sixty thousand strong, the place was buzzing with prejudice and expectancy and we'd discovered there was not much danger of our fans stepping out of line. There was talk of riot police with homicidal tendencies and keyless dungeons.

The game itself was also better. The Italians gave us some stick but we knew this would happen and we knew we would have to take it. Chances were scarce but we did make a few and Kennedy even hit a post, a clean, well-thumped volley with Zoff well beaten. But I had a feeling that one goal would decide everything and near the end Italy scored it. The goal was shaped by several factors – and we had ourselves to blame. Keegan was almost obsessed at the time with helping our defence, a responsible desire, but he overdid it. He was always dropping back, which meant two things: he was not helping us create much in front and Marco Tardelli, his marker who followed him everywhere, was being drawn into a critical forward area. The deeper Kevin dropped back the more Tardelli pushed up. He was constantly in a position to threaten us.

Then came the key to the Italian goal. Phil Neal sold himself on the right with a pointless tackle, a really desperate plunge, instead of just containing Francesco Graziani and allowing our defence to get back and face. We were exposed on that flank, Graziani was away like the wind, his cross was a good one – and Tardelli, quickly breaking away from Keegan, was the man who drove in.

Our hopes of winning the championship had disappeared but we still had a chance to finish as runners-up in the group and take third or fourth place in the tournament. This became possible when Belgium beat Spain in their second match which meant they and Italy had three points each, Spain and ourselves just one. But if we beat Spain in the final game and Belgium and Italy didn't draw then we still had chances.

I felt very sorry for Keegan because he had been burning to do well but a long, hard and eventually disappointing season was telling against him. His time and comments were in constant demand and there were always people around who could see profit in him. At Asti, for example, a couple of foxy photographers turned up with a girl and asked to speak to Kevin. It was a press day and Glen Kirton, our press officer, happily fixed them up. England's captain and the girl sat at a table and immediately she hitched up her skirt, showed some leg and posed for a picture that might have been embarrassing to say the least in the wrong paper with the wrong caption. It was all just a put-up job.

Kevin was in a spot of manufactured trouble once again when we moved from Asti down to Salerno, just along the coast from Naples, where we were to play Spain. He did an interview for radio in which he wryly observed that Italian teams at home always seemed to get a little help from referees. The interview was overheard by an Italian journalist and it obviously suffered, or improved, in the interpretation because the headline next day announced 'Keegan accuses referee'. This sort of thing only concerned me if it promised to upset a player because that, in turn, could upset his form. Otherwise I regarded such incidents as one of the prices to be paid for being in the public eye. Angry reaction merely provides a follow-up.

One or two players, among them Phil Neal and Phil Thompson, asked me if their families could join them in Naples and I agreed provided they stayed independently. But their wives found the hotel they were booked into wasn't so hot and I decided to let them join us at our hotel. It wasn't very satisfactory but they had been let down and I didn't think it would do any harm. Later, though, we talked about this and decided that family problems in the middle of a major tournament were not a clever idea. In future, wives would have to make sure they were dealing with reputable agents.

I still believed we had an edge on Spain, whatever team we sent out, so I decided to give everybody I could a taste of playing in the European finals. Viv Anderson and Mick Mills took over at full-back, Glenn Hoddle and Terry McDermott came into midfield and later I sent on Trevor Cherry and Paul Mariner as substitutes. That meant we had used nineteen of our twenty-two players.

The game promised to be more open than the first two so I brought the Keegan–Brooking–Woodcock triangle together again and waited with interest to see how Hoddle would play. I was not disappointed. We did not have an orthodox centre-forward but Keegan pushed up and with McDermott coming through strongly our method was not unlike the one we used against Spain in Barcelona. There was some composed football through the middle and in fact Hoddle, McDermott and Wilkins combined to set up our first goal for Brooking. Spain equalised with a penalty by Dani, a substitute, and they could even have taken the lead with a second penalty. Dani put the ball into the net again but the referee spotted an infringement and ordered a retake; and this time, although Dani changed direction, Clemence saved brilliantly. Our winner proved to be a beauty – Brooking angled a corner back to McDermott whose shot was parried by Arconada, a goalkeeper the Spaniards insist is better than Shilton or Clemence, and Woodcock fired in the rebound.

It was an entertaining game and an honest win but it counted for nothing. That evening we sat in our cliff-top hotel and watched Italy and Belgium go through the motions of a goalless draw. Belgium went on to the final, Italy to the play-off, and we were out.

West Germany were easily the best team in the other group in which Holland, their old stars fading and their great days done, were a big disappointment and in which Czechoslovakia lacked the character and spirit to complement their skills. The Germans work for their luck but I would never call them lucky. They earn what they win – and they laboured hard for their narrow victory over Belgium in the final in Rome.

If one thing more than another disappointed me in these finals it was the absence of outstanding forwards. Rossi, Fischer and our own Francis were missing but where were the young men to remind us of Cruyff, Muller, Kopa, Eusebio and, nearer home, Law, Greaves and Best? At least Karl Heinz Rummenigge of West Germany introduced himself with great credit, a front-runner with pace, courage and two lovely feet, who almost seemed to enjoy being tightly marked. He has since fulfilled all his early promise and is a very, very good player.

What was stressed during Europa 1980 was the importance of midfield players who can strike as well as create. Giancarlo Antognioni of Italy delighted me (except in their match against us when he just worried me) and nobody left a clearer print on the tournament than another West German newcomer, Bernd Schuster, whose mobility and involvement were dynamic. Life has become so difficult for strikers that goals from the men behind are a modern necessity.

I thought our own Ray Wilkins did marvellously well in Italy. I wouldn't claim he was a goalscorer – although he did get one of the tournament's finest against Belgium – but he proved, emphatically, that he would do very well on the continent; and now, of course, he has gone to Italy. I have heard people describe him as a negative player but I see him as a composed, mature innovator who draws other players into the game, slows things down or quickens them up to order and takes on responsibility. He has a quick mind, broad vision and hates wasting the ball. He also has character and patience and yet he is his own harshest critic.

We did our best in Italy and we failed because we could not break down Belgium's solid defence and because we did not take any of the four or five good chances we created against Italy. I make no excuses but I would like the privilege of a little 'if'. If only Tony Woodcock's honest goal against Belgium had been allowed to stand . . .

4

World Cup: the Road to Spain

I retired twice as England manager. The first time was after our defeat by Switzerland in Basle in May 1981, which threatened to torpedo our chances of reaching the World Cup finals in Spain, and the second time was after the 1982 finals in which we were unbeaten.

It was easy the second time because I felt I had done my job. I had taken England to the finals of the European Championship and World Cup, there was a hint of a smile on the face of our international football again and our set-up was a prop for the future. I was nearly sixty and the moment seemed right for change. Parting was sweet and the break clean.

But my first 'retirement' came during a period of failure and bitter criticism that made me feel I had somehow let the country down. I decided to step aside, halfway through our World Cup campaign, and only a heated, emotional appeal by the England players themselves, in a charter plane easing its way into Luton, persuaded me to change my mind. We were actually inside the airport, waiting for our luggage, when I finally agreed to stay on – just a minute or two before the Football Association was due to announce my retirement. It was a close thing.

The decision to call it a day capped an awful period for England and for me. Before our defeat in Basle we had been beaten by Spain, Brazil and Scotland and had drawn with Rumania and Wales, all at Wembley. We had five points from the first five of our eight qualifying matches in the World Cup and ahead of us, on our short summer tour, was the formidable challenge of playing Hungary in Budapest. The World Cup finals were a fading dream.

I was hurt and I had a feeling of shame, for I felt the fault was mine. Even ordinary conversation was difficult and I could sense people looking at me as if I had committed some crime. We had been badly hit by injuries but they were still my teams, playing my way, which had been failing. 'For God's sake, Ron, pack up' advised the headline in one paper. Life seemed on the darker side of black.

I made up my mind to go within a minute or two of our defeat by Switzerland, a sudden but firm decision which I kept to myself for a couple of days. There was still a job to be done and the following morning, back in Zürich where we were based, there was the usual news conference which I knew was going to be awkward. It was held in a large basement room and as I walked in there was a heavy silence. One or two voices said 'Mornin' Ron' but no one wanted to ask the first question. Eventually a voice from the back inquired 'Any injuries?'.

The embarrassment was understandable. Our football writers often go right over the top when England lose. Their harsh words are made to look even harsher by big and abrasive headlines. But I know these men and they care about England's fortunes as much as anyone. They would far rather write about victory than defeat. Many are good friends of mine and I know something about their job – not that this makes their opinions any easier to take!

I sat at the end of the long table, with concerned faces all around me, and did my best to put on a bold front. I even tried to break the ice by asking who was the latest tip to take over from me. Dick Wragg, the chairman of the International Committee, had joined us by this time and he broke in to give me a vote of confidence. 'Don't do that', I said, 'that's the kiss of death'. I answered questions about football as brightly as I could and stonewalled those about myself. It wasn't easy.

Nothing changed my decision and two days after the Swiss defeat, following a training session, I quietly took Dick Wragg and Ted Croker to one side at the team's hotel and told them. 'I think it's time for a change and I'm going to retire. Not resign, just retire', I said. 'But I'll tell you one thing. We'll win in Hungary. I'll make sure of that. This will be our ticket to the World Cup finals but then I'll just step aside and retire. This will leave you with room to bring in someone new in good time for Spain.'

Dick and Ted immediately said there was no reason for me to step down. 'Don't be daft', said Dick. 'There's no problem', added Ted. But I insisted our poor results were my responsibility and said my mind was made up.

Dick Wragg was about to go back to England, for the summer meeting of the Football Association, and it was arranged that he would meet us when we got back to Luton to make the formal announcement about my retirement. We even discussed financial arrangements and the whole thing was settled. We agreed not to tell anyone else for the time being and I did not even ring Lucy or mention it to Don Howe, Fred Street or any other member of our inner circle.

We stayed at Regensdorf, just outside Zürich, to prepare for the Hungary game, because the hotel and facilities were so good, and in the next few days we worked as never before. It may be that my determination to win in Budapest somehow got through to the players but, whatever the reason, their response was tremendous. We got right down to detail. We concentrated on such basics as movement off the ball, our service into the area and general passing. Not a second or a word was wasted. There was a special intensity about the way we worked and I realised everyone felt the way I did.

The mood did not change when we got to Budapest but, apart from training, I kept out of things. I shut myself up in my room. The Inter-Continental Hotel beside the Danube is enormous, a bit like a posh railway station, and I did not fancy joining in the usual chat which fills places like this before a big international. It was to be my last England game and I had enough thoughts of my own. But about one thing I was still very sure: I knew we were going to win.

Phil Thompson had joined us by now, fit again after helping Liverpool win the European Cup against Real Madrid in Paris, and I knew exactly the side I wanted to send out. I dropped Kenny Sansom at left-back because I wasn't sure he was in the right frame of mind. He had made a couple of errors which cost us dearly in Switzerland and he believed he was carrying the can for that defeat. He was deeply hurt when he was left out but I had a word with him and so did Don Howe, his coach at Arsenal, and we told him that what we felt we needed above all for this game was experience. It was the first time Kenny had met a setback at this level and, if nothing else, it taught him that nobody can take things for granted in international football.

I also dropped Ray Wilkins because I wanted more steel in midfield and I briefed Bryan Robson to look after Tibor Nyilasi because he was the best man for that job. Mick Mills switched to left-back to let in Phil Neal on the right, Phil Thompson and Dave Watson came together again in central defence, Trevor Brooking was there to boss the show in midfield, Steve Coppell and Terry McDermott gave us a good edge on the right and Kevin Keegan and Paul Mariner linked up in front.

Our side had balance and experience and was precisely shaped to beat Hungary, who had started well in the World Cup but still seemed to me to have limitations. I saw them play Rumania in the Nep Stadium and, although they won with style, I noticed they played with such depth that they conceded a lot of room in midfield. Their middle men didn't support much and I felt we could press up and almost isolate their defence. Mariner and Keegan would then be in a position to pull them about with their runs and dummies and this would leave holes for our men coming from behind, especially for Brooking with his ability to run with the ball.

It was a great occasion, with many of Hungary's golden oldies taking part in a waddle down memory-lane before the big game. Ferenc Puskas scored a hat-trick, the old left foot still a menace, and I wasn't sure which match most of the crowd had really come to see. We shall return to Puskas with relish later in the book.

The Nep was full, the din was oppressive, the big playing surface had been softened by a storm and I could not imagine a better theatre for my last match. The game, thankfully, matched the occasion – our performance was excellent, with the venerable partnership of Brooking and Keegan at the heart of everything. Trevor scored twice and Kevin added another from the penalty spot. Hungary 1, England 3. But there were some hiccups along the way.

I had warned our players to expect an early broadside but, oddly, it did not come and we took control earlier than I dared hope. We looked confident, we were composed on the ball and, according to script, the Hungarian defence allowed itself to be confined and stretched. Brooking got an early goal, a bobbly one after McDermott had got by on the right and cut the ball back, but Hungary equalised on the stroke of half-time through Garaba, a goal one or two of our defence took no pleasure in.

At that point the game was anyone's – and the Hungarians would have been even happier had they known what was going on in our dressing-room. Mills with a leg injury and Brooking with a groin strain were in real trouble and it was touch and go whether they would be fit for the second half. The result might well have been different without them: Brooking still had another goal to come, possibly the finest of his career, and Mills, a wonderful warrior, had been in the thick of the action. They were vital to our cause and Dr Vernon Edwards and Fred Street, our physiotherapist, worked hard on them on the table. We talked and cajoled but in the end, with our substitutes warming up just in case, I had to ask the two of them: 'Are you going to be okay?' 'We'll give it a go' they said. They were not concerned for themselves, just the team, and their decision said much for their character.

Brooking's second goal was a pearl. Neal found Keegan in space on the right and he picked out Brooking who was coming up to the box at speed. Trevor's left foot made perfect contact and the ball went into the net with such power that it forced its way behind a stanchion and lodged there. Keegan deserved a goal for that pass alone, and he eventually got one that was all his own. He was brought down by Garaba and, as the penalty was given, he kept hold of the ball, placed it quickly, picked his spot and put the game beyond Hungary's reach. Brooking was now signalling that his groin was giving trouble and we sent on Ray Wilkins in his place. Trevor's job was handsomely done.

I was first down to the dressing-room – I never hung about at the end of any game – and was there to meet the players and thank them one by one as they came in. But suddenly I realised Keegan and Brooking, who had been with us on the bench at the end, were not there. Doc Edwards said they had been snaffled by the television boys and this annoyed me because their place at that moment should have been with us and no one had asked my permission.

Our victory was, beyond doubt, one of the great moments of my life. We had made good all our errors and omissions against Switzerland and we had forced our way back into the World Cup. I had kept my promise to Dick Wragg and Ted Croker that we would win in the Nep Stadium and I was bowing out on a high note. And the fact that Hungary, the nation which shaped my thinking on the game, were involved simply added another coat of gloss. My cup was full, but I had not changed my mind about retiring and there were still things to do.

I went up to the press area and made the shortest speech I've ever given. I said: 'I'd like to thank you for your support over the years. Our win was a good one, well deserved, and it's given me great pleasure personally to beat the Hungarians. I don't want to answer any questions. Thank you.' I was curt but not rude. I simply didn't want to go on because I felt very emotional and I knew I would give something away if I started talking. Even so the story was there – in my thanks for support 'over the years'. It was a final statement.

The following day, Whit Sunday, our chartered Boeing 737, flight BA 9137, climbed smoothly into a blue sky and rolled gently in the direction of home. The England party was sitting at the front, the media at the rear. My job had meant so much to me for the past four years that I felt a bit tearful, I really did, as I sat at the back of our section with Don Howe and Geoff Hurst; but still I believed my decision was the right one. Only two people knew I was retiring and one of them, Dick Wragg, was at Luton waiting to make the news public. I felt I owed it to the players to tell them first, however, and we were about twenty minutes from touchdown when I stood up and pulled the curtain across to give us privacy. There was a microphone but I did not use it because my voice would have carried all over the plane.

'I'd just like to thank you all' I said. 'It's been great working with you and I've enjoyed every minute of it. I think we've more or less sealed our place in the World Cup finals now, by beating Hungary, and everything should be okay. But I have decided the moment is right for me to retire, and I'm telling you now because Mr Wragg's waiting at the airport to make an announcement. It's a personal decision and it will leave the way for someone to take over well before the finals. There are no problems.

There's been no pressure. It's my own decision. And it goes without saying that I wish you all the best of luck. Thank you again.' Then I sat down.

A second of silence was followed by hubbub. Heads got together in little groups, then in one big huddle. The next moment I was surrounded by faces all talking at once. 'What d'you mean, retiring? . . . You're joking . . . You can't mean it.' I stuck to my guns. I told them I'd intended to retire after the World Cup finals and all I was doing was bringing things forward a bit. We'd got seven points out of twelve, I said, and with a trip to Norway and a home game with Hungary to come the new chap would have a chance. 'You're out of order' said Kevin. 'We want you to reconsider.' Trevor, Millsie, Ray, Phil . . . they were all looming over me and it was getting noisy and emotional. 'Don't be bloody silly' said a voice. 'Think it over' added another. Then they left me alone for a while. Now I felt really screwed up inside, unbelievably touched that they cared in this way.

A few minutes later they were all back again. 'What are you going to do . . . c'mon!' But still I felt my original decision was right. The arguments carried on as we left the plane and walked across to the airport building. Millsie even came up to me while we were waiting for our luggage and said: 'If you retire I'll never speak to you again.' They kept at me and their general message was 'We started together, let's finish together.'

The luggage was rolling, goodbyes were being said, wives were waiting outside, I knew the press would soon be asking me for a final word and Mr Wragg was on his way in to break the news that I was calling it a day. But what counted most of all with me was the players' attitude. I had believed my decision was right for England and the man who was going to take my place. I was genuinely not concerned about myself, but if the players wanted me to change my mind *this* much then I decided, suddenly, that it was right to do so. They were the best bunch of lads a manager ever had. I was very close to them and what they thought counted with me.

'Okay then, all right', I said. 'I'll tell Mr Wragg I won't resign. I'll give it 'til after the World Cup.'

Half a dozen voices said 'Great'.

I spotted a pipe. Dick Wragg had come through into the baggage area. 'The players have got me to change my mind', I told him.

He smiled. 'That's good . . . because I was going to try and talk you out of it myself. They've saved me a job.'

The press conference followed. I gave it. It was business as usual.

Had I known what lay ahead of us I might have changed my mind a second time.

We did reach Spain but only by way of a defeat in Norway and an avalanche of criticism that made the knocking which had gone on that summer seem like three hearty cheers. I have said our victory in Hungary gave me some of the finest moments of my life. Our defeat in Oslo provided some of the worst.

In the end we owed almost everything to Switzerland, who took three points from Rumania, who had taken three points from us, and allowed us to hold on precariously to second place behind Hungary in Group Four. We helped ourselves by beating Hungary twice; but I knew whom we had to thank. I wore my Swiss tie for weeks.

The story of our wildly erratic and almost bizarre qualification began, however, in Zürich several months before. This was where we held our fixture meeting with the other four nations in our group, Hungary, Norway, Rumania and Switzerland. I always smile when I hear people asking why we chose, say, to play three away games in succession or two games in our off-season. I only wish they could attend one of these meetings themselves. It takes hours of argument and compromise to settle on a batting order because every manager arrives with his own preference and each is determined to get his way. The rest don't just sit back and say: 'After you England. Tell us where and when you want to play and we'll fit in with you.' The noisy bargaining seems to go on for ever.

Twenty matches had to be slotted into place and although Tor Fossen, Norway's bright and affable manager, was a good friend of mine, he didn't give an inch. He knew exactly what he wanted.

'You've asked to play us first at Wembley and that's all right with us', he said, 'but we'll only settle for that if England come to Oslo in September. This will be our biggest game, we'll get our biggest crowd and we are also at our strongest then.'

This was not so good for us because the English season would be new and our players would still be finding their touch. Yet Norway, on paper, were the weakest team in the group and if we had to play somebody in September they looked the best bet. The deal was struck.

The start of a new World Cup campaign is a time for quiet, firm reappraisal. We had not done ourselves justice in the European Championship but I believed that the core of an effective side was there. In fact, seven of the side that played in our first qualifying game against Norway also played in the World Cup finals in Spain twenty-one months later. They were Shilton, Sansom, Thompson, Robson, Mariner, Woodcock and Rix. Waiting in the wings, injured, not available, or simply not picked that day, were Keegan, Brooking, Francis, Wilkins, Coppell and Mills.

The problem is always one of balance. I had to pick a side to do a job in each qualifying game but I also needed to experiment whenever I could and, always, I had to keep the finals clearly in sight. A lot can happen to form and fitness over two seasons. I held the present in one hand and the future in the other.

Emlyn Hughes and Trevor Cherry, I decided, were part of England's past. They were wonderful players, great servants both, but I did not see them playing a major role in the tough months ahead. I rang them at their homes, explained that I had to look for younger men and thanked them with great sincerity for all they had done. I did say they mustn't assume they were finished for ever and they replied that they would do their best to fight their way back; but I knew they understood me.

I picked two new men for the Norway game. I brought in Eric Gates of Ipswich, a versatile little player who filled in neatly for the injured Kevin Keegan and who was used to playing with Paul Mariner, and I also gave a first cap to Graham Rix of Arsenal. Rix is a player with a lovely left foot and with Kenny Sansom, his Arsenal club-mate, behind him, I felt the two would produce some results on that flank. Rix told me he didn't like playing wide and forward on the left, so he was accommodated in an orthodox role in midfield on that side.

Norway gave us an easy ride on that September night in 1980. They had one or two players with clubs in West Germany and Holland but their defence didn't fill space very efficiently and they weren't decisive against free kicks. Terry McDermott got two of our four goals – one from a free kick nicely drawn into him by Rix. A good left foot is a treasure. We could have scored more, and I hadn't forgotten that three or four more goals would have sent us to Argentina in 1978, but it was a handsome enough start.

Our next game was in the August 23rd Stadium in Bucharest and this was a very different proposition. Rumania were an awkward side, Latin-European in style, technically sharp and good spoilers, and it did not help that we were again beset by injuries. I even had Justin Fashanu and Gordan Cowans from our Under-21 side on stand-by. Gates was under the weather and had to be replaced at half-time and, all in all, the day and the game ran against us. We lacked real craft in midfield and found difficulty in breaking Rumania down, but we had our moments and in the end it was a highly dubious penalty which gave the other side their 2-1 victory. Crisan, someone said, seemed to bounce off an imaginary force field around Sansom and the Swedish referee, Ulf Eriksson, gave the spot kick. Iordanescu was their penalty-man and, as I'd seen him take a few, I had told Ray Clemence exactly where he would put the ball. This time, of course, it went the other way! All credit to Iordanescu.

Brooking returned for the Switzerland game at Wembley but we were still without Keegan. Thompson was also unfit so I tried an important experiment. I played Robson as a *libero* with Watson as our central marker and Mills doing a holding job just in front. One or two critics said they didn't like Mills in midfield but they missed the real point. Mills was there to provide cover for Robson when he broke from the back. When Robson went forward Mills filled in: they rotated responsibility. The plan worked very well, too, with the shape and line of our attacks changing all the time. We took a two-goal lead, Coppell forcing an own goal and Mariner heading in from a Brooking free kick, but a game of football can turn on the slightest thing. One of Brooking's heels altered the shape of this match.

Robson had been breaking from the back, playing his way out of trouble and then into attack with little one-twos and he seemed to be in charge of the whole field. It worked so well that we got carried away and overdid the backing up. Robson went to play another one-two and Brooking somehow got in the way. The ball struck the back of his heel and bounced straight to the Swiss who immediately transferred to the other end where Rene Botteron, then with Cologne, went near to scoring. The Swiss nearly caught us out because we lost concentration – and, to make sure it didn't happen again, we then became a bit cautious. We began to give our opponents too much room in midfield, and this is dangerous against a side of their type. If you don't press up on them they start playing the ball around, which is exactly what they did. Botteron began to dominate, they pulled a goal back and we were hard-pressed to hold on for a 2-1 win.

This was Bryan Robson's fifth cap and already I had no doubts about him. Here was a gem of a player. There is more than a touch of Martin Peters in the way he knows when to go and when to hold back. Such a sense of timing is a priceless quality, especially in a powerful runner like Robson. He has direct pace, is hard to get off the ball and sees things through. He relates to the net and has the technique to finish well. But Robson's qualities don't end there. He is a clean, sharp tackler, passes well and reads the overall game intelligently. He is a very strong influence in all areas of the field and a man for any job – which is why I had no hesitation in setting him on Hungary's Nyilasi in Budapest. Robson is almost three players in one and even for one and a half million pounds, the sum Manchester United paid West Bromwich for him, he was a sound investment.

For a lot of valid reasons, however, I did not play Robson as a *libero* again, even though I would have liked him in the role in our next game, a friendly against Spain at Wembley, and even though Robson himself would have been happy about it. But when I talked the idea over with our players I found they weren't keen on it. It was outside their experience and they foresaw trouble. Their opinion mattered because they did the playing: if they did not understand the role and value of a *libero* and did not want to play with one then I felt the plan was best shelved. This was not conceding responsibility: it was being realistic. Watson and Thompson were not fit, moreover, and I was loth to give Terry Butcher the responsibility of being our lone marker in only his second international. So I moved Robson forward into midfield and chose Butcher and Russell Osman, the Ipswich pair, as our central defenders. They were caught flat once or twice and we lost 2-1 – our first defeat at Wembley since I had become England's manager.

Rumania visited us in the spring of 1981, for the second part of our argument, and they held us at arm's length to draw o-o. Their defence was spiky and tightly organised and we rarely looked like finding a key to the problem. That meant Rumania had taken three points from us, and with Hungary then beating Rumania in Budapest a fortnight later our prospects suddenly looked thin.

We had five points from four games and our form and confidence were wobbling dangerously. We plunged on with that awful run at Wembley, defeats by Brazil and Scotland following the one by Spain, and if pressed for reasons I will offer two. Firstly, obviously, we did not play well. Our sides were unsettled and short of experience in critical positions, our run of injuries right through the season were catching up with us. Secondly, and not so obviously, Lucy missed all three games. She never saw England lose at Wembley during my time as England manager – and the only games she missed in five years were those against Spain, Brazil and Scotland. I was as superstitious as the next man when I saw profit in it. I made sure she missed no more!

I wanted to win everything on tour, in Switzerland and Hungary, and with Keegan in touch again I convinced myself anything was possible. My feeling may have been a triumph of hope over reality but I knew I had to believe if others were going to. I made sure I said the right things. 'Four points from the two games will mean the rest have to worry about us' I announced. And when Liverpool won the European Cup I described their win over Real Madrid as 'a great lift for British soccer'. Once at least, though, I managed to say the wrong thing: 'For our second game, in Budapest, Phil Thompson will come into the squad and Brian Rix will drop out . . .' The English media team, with a little help from Bobby Charlton, Terry Venables and Howard Wilkinson, beat their Swiss opposite numbers by 5-4 after being four down – and I was assured this was another good omen.

Alas, everything that could go wrong then did so. The hooligan fringe spent the day in the squares of Basle drinking wine and got themselves on the front pages of Europe again, while on the pitch we made a couple of dreadful and decisive mistakes. There was not a great deal between the teams but our finishing was loose so I sent on McDermott for a weary-looking Francis and pushed Keegan forward. McDermott soon got a goal that gave us a chance but while we weren't bad collectively we still lacked teeth and conviction in front of the goal. That was the killer. I was told afterwards that it was Switzerland's first victory over us for thirty-four years: just the sort of fact I could have done without.

Paul Wolfisberg, the Swiss manager, looked the happiest chap on earth. I think I was probably the saddest. The road to Spain seemed to stop right there. The decision to retire was already forming.

Yet the doubts that filled my mind on that sunny evening in Basle were more than matched by the hopeless frustration that hit me in Oslo early the following season. Our win in Budapest had put us on the right road again and changed my mind about retiring; and with seven points from six games I was convinced that victories over Norway and Hungary at Wembley would send us to Spain. But we lost in Oslo's Ullevaal Stadium: 9 September, 1981 – Norway 2, England 1. We began brightly, scoring first through Bryan Robson, and we should have got more; but then Norway punished us for a couple of prize errors and, on a real high, stuck out to the end. That, briefly, is the story-line and there are a thousand reasons to explain it. But they don't mean a thing.

Yes, I made changes from the side that beat Hungary. Francis came in for Coppell, Hoddle for Brooking, who wasn't match-fit, and Osman for Watson whose time was running out. Yes, we relaxed for a few crucial minutes after a start that was almost too easy. Yes, the Norwegian fans lifted their team with tremendous support on a tight little pitch that cramped movement. Yes, it was early in our season and comfortably into theirs and, yes, we missed chances, made stupid mistakes and lacked a bit of luck. Hoddle started well but then began to hurry and muff things when the real battle started, and I replaced him with Barnes after an hour, and Osman made a mistake or two that stuck in the mind. But I certainly don't blame Glenn and Russell because around them they had most of the team that beat Hungary in Budapest. England's best would certainly have been too much for Norway's best; but in football you get what you deserve and we didn't deserve anything that day. As Tor Fossen, their manager, said: 'Our game hit the sky just because we were playing England – that's the price you pay for fame.'

What astonished and depressed me far more than the result was the reaction to it. The press and everyone else were perfectly entitled to have a go at us. We deserved that because we had allowed ourselves to be turned over by a country who had never beaten us before. It was a bad performance which looked like costing us a place in the World Cup finals, and how can one put a value on that in terms of prestige and morale? I was made to feel like Public Enemy Number One and I could even understand that. But what was ludicrous was the immediate accusation that England's footballers were mercenaries who cared only about their wallets – that bank managers mattered more to them than team managers. Everybody jumped on the bandwagon: television pundits, newspaper journalists, radio commentators, officials and administrators, managers and even politicians queued up to describe England's players as over-paid idlers. Money, it was claimed, was at the root of our troubles because our players went into every game wondering how much they were going to earn rather than how they were going to win. Some of the critical arrows came from people who don't think too deeply. Others should have known better.

I know how determined my players were before the start. I know how much they gave during the game even though one or two were off-form or over-confident. I know how desolate they were in our dressing-room afterwards. They put everything they had into that match and if it wasn't enough on the day, well, that is not a crime. They failed as players, not as human beings.

Not once, in my five years as England manager, did I feel that any player consciously gave less than his best. I would have come down like a ton of bricks on any man who let his team-mates and his country down like this, but it was never necessary. We lost in Oslo because Norway played out of their skins and because we did not do ourselves justice. These were the same England players who won in Hungary, yet after Norway there were people who said I should never pick any of them again. Utter stupidity!

Upsets like this will always happen in football, as in any other sport. Bournemouth will beat Manchester United, Walsall are going to beat Arsenal, Algeria will better West Germany and the likes of the United States and Norway will up-end England. Nobody has a right to win, and any side can win on its day. Not that thoughts like this made me feel any better after the game or helped me to answer some of the questions that were swung at me like sledgehammers. I did an interview for Norwegian television and their best-known commentator went straight for my throat. His first question was 'Will you get the sack tomorrow?' 'Will you get the sack tomorrow?' I countered. 'I don't know' he stammered back. 'And neither do I', I went on. 'Next question please.'

Next morning a Norwegian official who was seeing us off said his wife sent her apologies for 'that rude commentator'. And somebody else told me: 'We watched that interview in a restaurant and everybody stood up and clapped when you replied. He's always asking questions like that and everybody was delighted that you put him in his place.'

Our own place in Group Four, however, concerned me a thousand times more. We were still top, with seven points from seven games, but it was a painfully false position. Rumania, Hungary and Switzerland all had games in hand which could take them above us and our future was no longer in our own hands. There were still half a dozen matches to come, and there was a lot of calculating talk about goal differences, but realistically what we needed was a little miracle. And we got one. Switzerland, bless all their mountains, cuckoo clocks and financial gnomes, beat Rumania in Bucharest, lost in Hungary to spoil their own chances and then drew at home in their return game with Rumania. Our better goal difference meant a draw in our final game, at home to Hungary, would be enough. Our future was back in our own hands.

The game against Hungary, on 18 November 1981, was only a week away when we finally knew what we had to do and the prospect seemed to roll towards us, picking up pace and size, like a giant snowball. No one was in any doubt about what was at stake. The Football League cleared the previous Saturday of all but a couple of First Division games and we were able to have five precious days together before the match.

Norway, oddly, seemed to be forgotten. We hadn't played a game since our Oslo defeat and we were on the brink of the World Cup finals only because Switzerland had done us a favour. The players hadn't changed and neither had I but nobody was talking about greed and lack of commitment now. They were all ready to put us back on our pedestals, and in just five days ticket sales for the game rose from thirty thousand to a ninety-two-thousand sell-out. The general message was that life is all about winning and losing and for this one game I was happy to go along with that: never mind about the quality. 'If we don't go through now, we don't deserve anything', I told notebooks, microphones and cameras.

A lot of mileage was made out of the similarity between this game and the one back in 1973 when Alf Ramsey sent out an England side needing to beat Poland to qualify but were held to a draw on a night of hysteria, high drama and, of course, heroism by an awkward, long-armed 'keeper called Jan Tomaszewski. I made up my mind that it wasn't going to be a similar story this time. We knew Hungary well. We had beaten them once and believed we could do it again. We talked about composure and patience but also about a hundred and one different ways of putting the pressure on them. There was no need to motivate our players: the game, the prize and the hopes of the nation did that. As I said to the players before a valuable game against London FA at Highbury: 'We've been given a kiss of life – and now we've a great opportunity to show everyone what we're made of.'

Sadly, our coach, Bill Taylor, had to leave us in the middle of our build-up. He had survived a major operation the year before but now, feeling unwell again, he was advised to return home. He saw the game on television and, a loss we all felt very deeply, he died a fortnight later at the age of forty-two.

Bill was a lovely man whom I'd known since his playing days with Orient. He was a popular and steadfast person who was always ready with a smile and a kind word. Don Revie brought Bill into the England set-up and although he was a Scot, which meant he got some terrible ribbing, he had set his heart on seeing us through to the World Cup finals. Bill's coaching and training did help us get there. There is no doubt about that.

The space given to the game in the papers ran to acres, most of it buoyant and hopeful, and I can only recall one morning's reading that was less than pleasant. On the Saturday evening we had a meal together at the Swiss Centre, Leicester Square, and then went to see a show at the Whitehall Theatre. We had a hard training session at London Colney the following afternoon and I then told the players they were free to do what they wanted that evening. I knew nobody was going to be stupid and didn't give it another thought. Ray Clemence, who had moved from Liverpool to Spurs at the start of the season, Glenn Hoddle and one or two others went for a drink in a club at Tottenham. They were back at West Lodge Park by 11.30, our normal time, but somebody had seen them out and told the papers.

The press rang our hotel and were put straight through to the players' bedrooms. Instead of saying they were out with my permission, however, they denied the whole story – and the papers promptly made an issue of it. 'World Cup stars out drinking' and all that. 'Why did you deny it?' I asked Ray and the rest when I saw them. When the journalists questioned me I simply told the truth: the players had all been out with my blessing, and I hadn't cared where they went provided they were back on time.

There were a few cartoons and some righteous comments for a day or so but then the incident was forgotten. It had all happened four days before the game and I had no intention of shutting my players up like monks.

Neither Clemence nor Hoddle, in any case, were in the side I intended to play. Shilton, who had played against Poland in 1973, was the 'keeper in form and with Brooking fit there was no place for Hoddle. I also brought back Coppell for Francis and preferred Alvin Martin to Osman – Martin being a powerful central defender whom I had taken on at West Ham and who'd done well against Brazil earlier in the year. There were four changes from the side which lost in Oslo but only two from the one which won in Budapest – Shilton for Clemence and Martin for Watson. We were on the high ground and I was conceding nothing.

Everything went right on the night. It rained, but who cared? Hungary had already qualified and did not show much imagination. They made things pretty easy for us and although we only scored once the issue, in my mind, was never in doubt. These Hungarians had nothing to do with Puskas and company. Our crowd roared away happily, Mariner scored our winner after Brooking had poked in a shot and Tony Morley, the Aston Villa winger, a talented chap, came on for his first taste of the big time. He took the place of Coppell, who had been given some harsh treatment by defender Jozsef Toth. And that was the start of the knee trouble which was to put Coppell out of the game a couple of years later.

The road to Spain had been a long one which threatened to pitch us over a cliff-edge more than once. We walked down the grey tunnel towards our dressing-room at the end followed by *You'll never walk alone* sung by a choir of ninety-two thousand. There were times, I reflected, when we *had* walked alone.

Lucy had been there, I remembered. She had still to see us lose.

Next morning, eating toasted bacon and egg sandwiches with the press, life seemed very good.

'Mornin' chaps . . .'

5

Spanish Summer

I watched the 1982 World Cup final on television at my home in Brighton, seven hundred miles from the colour and passion of the Santiago Bernabeu Stadium in Madrid, with my wife Lucy, a cup of tea and that little word 'if' to keep me company. I was a former manager of England.

The high drama of the past month was still sharp in my mind on that warm Sunday evening in July. Wishful thoughts would not go away. If only Kevin Keegan and Trevor Brooking had been fit . . . if only we had maintained the form we showed in our first game against France . . . if only a couple of the chances we made in our last game against Spain had gone in . . . if only England and Brazil could have been there in the Spanish capital playing for football's greatest prize. My retirement, then, would have belonged to tomorrow.

But reality was on the screen in the corner. Italy and West Germany were on stage and when my old friend, Enzo Bearzot, walked slowly across the pitch at the end of a fine, well-won game to share the most wonderful moments of his life with his players, I knew exactly how he felt. His pleasure was my pleasure – and football was the better for Italy's success. At last Enzo had got his players to play; and, in doing so, he proved that the crime of defence for the sake of defence does not pay. I sent him a telegram of congratulation immediately.

I had returned to England six days before, on the morning after our goalless draw with Spain, and next to me on the plane was Bobby Robson. We shared a past that went all the way back to our playing days at Fulham but the future was now his. He knew some of the problems of the England manager's job as well as I did, but I knew there were many he would have to discover for himself. The experience would be painful. A day or so later, armed with a five-year contract, he returned to Madrid for the final. I watched and reflected in Sussex.

England were unbeaten in Spain and this was an achievement of which I was proud. We defeated France, Czechoslovakia and Kuwait in the first round and drew with West Germany and Spain in the second. We proved ourselves in the highest company and stretched an unbeaten run to eleven games. I told our players, more than once, that they had nothing to be ashamed of. I meant it, too. They played to their limits and no more can be asked. Their performances meant there was no sting in retirement for me. We did not fail: but we were stopped one pace short of the semi-finals, which would have been happily acknowledged by everyone as success, because we lacked a quality which always separates the winners from the rest at this level. We lacked someone who could provide a flash of brilliance, a player who could suddenly do better than his best and find within himself a moment of rare inspiration or invention. We did not have a killer.

Italy found this quality in Paulo Rossi just when it mattered. He did not score against Poland, Peru and Cameroon in the first round but when the flame was turned up he responded magnificently. He scored three goals against Brazil in the most critical test of all, two more against Poland in the semi-finals and then Italy's vital first strike against West Germany in the final.

Brazil should have skated it, of course. I could not see beyond them. I watched them on television when I was in Madrid and loved them for their skill and style, their panache and sheer joy in the game. They had talent in their kneecaps and their eyebrows and they would have done football a great favour if they had won the World Cup, by proving that almost everything is secondary to sheer skill. But in the end, perhaps, there was an even bigger lesson in their defeat by Italy in Barcelona. Brazil indulged their skills, they forgot they were ordinary mortals, and they paid the price.

I would have given anything for a pinch of Brazilian skill in our matches against West Germany and Spain and, who knows, Brazil might have been well served by a little of our organization and application in their game against Italy. We conceded only one goal, remember, in five matches. But success in the World Cup belongs to the opportunists, and therein lay our weakness.

My regrets stop there. I do not think we could have picked a sounder squad or sent out better teams or done more in the way of homework. If preparation was the only key to success England would probably have won the World Cup.

Alan Odell and often Doc Edwards travelled all over Spain with me weighing up the values of hotels and training grounds well before it was confirmed that Bilbao and Madrid were to be our centres. We thumped beds, peered around kitchens, tested facilities, listed amenities, quizzed proprietors, noted distances and checked security. We were ahead of the field.

We also made friends with the Basques, and that was important. We

were due to play France in Paris in late March but once we found ourselves in the same World Cup group the fixture did not seem a clever idea
any more. Instead – with the FA and the League in sweet and helpful
harmony – we broke new ground. We played a testimonial match against
Athletic Bilbao in the very stadium, San Mames, that would stage our
three first-round matches. Saatchi and Saatchi could not have improved
on it as a public relations exercise. A full England team played a Spanish
club side and a forty-thousand crowd watched us draw 1–1. The warmth
of the people overwhelmed us and the straight, clean English lines of the
stadium (known locally as 'The Cathedral') impressed us. A real relationship was struck and when we returned in June, on more urgent business,
the people were on our side.

The day after our game against Athletic Bilbao I flew to Paris to watch
France play Northern Ireland, who had smartly taken over our fixture.
France won 4–0, easing up, and confirmed what I already knew about
them: their talent was great, their methods ambitious but their character
unpredictable.

I watched France three times and Czechoslovakia twice before the
finals and, good professionals that they are, Michel Hidalgo and Josef
Venglos, the manager of Czechoslovakia, missed no opportunity to watch
us. I admire Hidalgo, his ideas are similar to mine, and after one game I
even ran him out to Heathrow Airport. Venglos, a man I'd met on many
courses, is a great student of the English game – and, like Hidalgo, he
does not miss much. We were friends and rivals. I did not see Kuwait
before the finals but I sent John Cartwright to study them in a tournament
and I knew I would be able to see them play both France and Czechoslovakia before we faced them.

We took a lot of trouble to find the right hotel in Bilbao which has a
long, grey waterfront, six hundred thousand people, factories, foundries,
breweries, mills, office-blocks and, over a river I wouldn't care to swim
in, a row of bridges that lead to the older, quainter part of the town. It is
a place of character and honest folk but too busy by half for a World Cup
base. There was a good choice of hotels outside the town, though, and
in the end we picked one that looked and proved to be perfect – Los
Tamarises. It is a small-to-medium-sized hotel, modest outside, quality
inside, which overlooks a sweep of beach about ten miles from Bilbao.

I felt sorry for the place soon after naming it as our base. A photog-
rapher found a dead dog on the beach, which like most beaches was looking
pretty scruffy in mid-winter, and he turned it into a nice profit. That
picture, first in a popular football magazine, then in most of the papers,
was used to portray the area outside our hotel as a sort of Mediterranean

rubbish dump. But by the time we got there the beach had been given its annual wash and brush-up and looked more like its real self – a spot favoured by the locals, who ought to know a thing or two.

Jesus, the proprietor, a knowing and caring man, took us on like a big family and spent a fortune on making the first-class even better. His international restaurant offered everything from Basque cuisine to steak, pork cutlets, fish and omelettes, and his cellar was more than a hideaway for a few bottles of plonk. Jesus called it his 'wine museum', and proved the point by giving each person in our party a wine bottled in the year of his birth (except me, 1921; from his collection of three thousand bottles he offered me a 1923). The hotel had a well-equipped games room, lounges, television, bar and everything else essential to a long, comfortable stay. Security, too, was easy because the building backed on to a cliff. No one – media, fans, hangers-on or people with an eye for a main chance – could get in without official approval. Footballers are international-class moaners, but they liked Los Tamarises.

Yet this was only half our set-up. Thirty minutes away, up in the gentle hills above the town, we took over the Athletic Bilbao training camp. It has half-a-dozen pitches, including one all-weather, goalmouths all over the place, every indoor facility imaginable, a restaurant, rest areas and accommodation. And the credit for this belongs to an Englishman, Ronnie Allen, an old playing foe of mine, who had managed the Bilbao club. He got the whole thing off the ground and, as a member of our party, he proved invaluable. He spoke the language, knew the people and the area and had bags of contacts. He was something more than a favourite in Bilbao: he was a cult figure.

We trained there daily and, to give a twist to routine and get away from everything, we stayed the night there before each game. Then we would go down the winding hill into town, with police escort, and straight to the stadium. There were a few groans to begin with. The English professional is not used to seclusion, unlike the continental, who will happily become a hermit on the Tuesday or Wednesday before a Sunday game. But our players then found they rather liked the arrangement; the unfamiliar had become familiar. I wouldn't mind a little bet that we had the best training set-up of any side in the tournament. Great credit is due to the Bilbao club and the local organizing committee: they were fantastic.

I had a decision to announce now. Ray Clemence and Peter Shilton had been sharing the goalkeeper's job ever since I took over, an unusual but practical solution to the problem, if problem it was, of having two of the best in the world. I also had in mind that day in Mexico in 1970 when Gordon Banks went down with a bug and Peter Bonetti was suddenly pitched into the quarter-final against West Germany. It proved costly because he lacked match-practice and any sort of understanding with the defence in front of him, and I did not want to make the same mistake.

Ray and Peter accepted it immediately when I told them they were going to share the position. They were good mates and it was no problem for them. It was other people who saw it as a problem. But I also told them that if and when we got to the World Cup finals I would make a choice.

For a long time I could not separate them. I defy anybody to say which was the best. Both were magnificent. There was an early stage when I felt Peter lacked Ray's complete control of his area. Ray was like a third back, even a sweeper, with the speed and understanding to go straight to the source of any trouble. During his Liverpool days he had the total confidence of the men in front of him and I could understand why. But then Peter broadened his game in this way, especially after he moved to Nottingham Forest, and he acquired massive authority anywhere near his goal.

It was possible to look at them and be hyper-critical. Peter, for example, could be a little weak on the back post: he did not always extend his arms to their full length. Ray, for his part, would sometimes worry when he saw Peter working mightily to improve his game. Ray was more of a natural and was far more interested in scoring goals at outside-right in five-a-sides, but when he saw Peter slaving away, covered in mud, he felt his friend and rival might get the nod because of his attitude. But this never bothered me. A player must be true to himself.

There were other differences, too. Peter shouted more than Ray. It was the way he got involved. He liked making a noise, which is not a bad thing because it reassures the defenders that there is someone behind them. But above all they both commanded. I never worried for a moment about either. Then we reached the World Cup finals and a choice had to be made. I decided Peter was my man, but I will also say that Ray was unlucky.

Ray had moved from Liverpool to Tottenham at the start of the previous season and, with a new defence in front of him, he had a sticky start. He had to reassess a lot of things and his form suffered. Every time I saw him in his early games for Tottenham he'd say 'What, you here again?'. West Ham beat them 4-0 at White Hart Lane and, coming off the pitch, he spotted me in the stand and just shook his head. Then, at the end of the season, Ray missed one or two internationals because Spurs and Queen's Park Rangers took their FA Cup final to a replay. Peter established himself in a side that was bedding down at a critical point of our build-up and so, in a sense, my choice was made a little easier. Ray was not too happy when I told him: I wouldn't have been delighted myself. But I had been very fair to both, a decision had had to be made, and inevitably one had to be disappointed.

Choosing the other ten players to face France did not give me a headache either, although it was now obvious that Keegan and Brooking were unlikely to be of any use in the first round. Keegan was complaining of back trouble and Brooking had a groin injury, but they were central figures in my plans and as long as there was any chance of them playing I wanted them available.

I felt it was vital to get off to a good start and the team I named for England's first match at this level for twelve years was designed to take the game to France. Mills, a man I could depend on to eternity, captained the side from right-back with Sansom on the left. Thompson and Butcher, six-foot four tall and still growing in authority, were the central defenders. Coppell on the right, Wilkins and Robson, three Manchester United men, gave us variety and unity in the middle with Rix floating wide on the other flank. In front there was Francis with his threatening pace and Mariner who was on song – he had scored four goals in his last three internationals. It was a side that could play football from the back and there was a lot of quick, positive support for the strikers. It had balance and shape.

The French are interesting to play. They always have two or three players of the highest quality up their sleeves and their ability to improvize constantly presents the unexpected. Their football over the years has passed from day into night and then back again but when Hidalgo took over in 1975 they acquired more character and a consistent line of thought.

I felt Francis's speed would give us some joy against Christian Lopez and Marius Tresor, their sweeper, and that Coppell was the man to have a go at Max Bossis whom I'd seen turned inside out by Northern Ireland's Noel Brotherston in Paris. But I also suspected that if Michel Platini and Alain Giresse got a grip in midfield they would stretch us dangerously. Platini was the artist, a lovely player, but Giresse was the man who made things tick, an influential little chap who wandered and supported and was full of bright ideas. He reminded me of Johnny Giles and, indeed, proved to be one of the tournament's more obvious successes.

The weather during our early days in Bilbao was typically British. Perhaps a few rain-clouds travelled out in our big articulated lorry . . . along with a hundred and twenty training kits, eight playing kits, thirty footballs, a lifetime's supply of breakfast cereal and brown sauce and Lord knows what else. But on the day of the match there was a sudden change: it was oven-hot. The temperature kept on rising and by the time we arrived at the San Mames, with its tall stands, it must have been at least one hundred degrees down on the pitch.

I could sense the mood was just right, though. Everyone was geeing up everyone else in the dressing-room, though I'm not sure how much listening was done. Don Howe and I just moved around calmly, having a quiet word here and another there, because the period immediately before a game is no time for speeches. The hard work has already been done.

There was one possible variation which occurred to me, however. We'd had a chat together in the morning during which Don ran through some of our set-piece drills, and one of these was Sansom's long throw from the left to Butcher at the near post with Rix providing an alternative and Robson moving up late. 'Let's do it on the right as well' I said in the dressing-room. 'Steve reckons he can make the distance but we don't seem to use him. So let's have Terry at the near post for him as well. Exactly the same.'

The game had hardly begun when Wilkins played the ball out to the right to Coppell, who forced a throw-in and prepared to take it himself. Butcher got up quickly to the near post and, as the ball looped over, a good throw, tall Terry nudged it back. Robson was there, right on cue, and I could barely believe the amount of room he had. The ball bounced up and for a moment it looked as if he'd missed it, but then he dropped until his shoulder was almost on the ground and, his timing just right, he volleyed it in. That is how the fastest goal in World Cup final history was scored. It was timed at twenty-seven seconds and it won Robson a handsome gold watch. Next day I read it was 'a well-rehearsed set-piece'.

The French came straight back at us, with Giresse beginning to express himself beautifully, and it became a fascinating game in heat and humidity that made every step a challenge. Gerard Soler got an equaliser after twenty-five minutes, well made and well taken, and for a while the French took control, especially in midfield.

Half-time is when managers earn their keep and I didn't want to waste a second when the interval came. The lads complained of feeling faint or dizzy, so shirts were hauled off, cold towels draped over their backs and hot tea and salt tablets were downed. But there was also an important adjustment to be made. 'We're getting lopsided and they're getting to us along our left' I said. 'Graham is floating, Bryan is pushing forward and this is where the hole is. So Graham, come back, square us off on the left and give us four across the middle. It'll give us numbers – and Bryan, you'll be able to get up without any worries.'

The adjustment was just what was needed. Now we had width and a solid springboard, Rix was happier in his new role and Robson's late runs began to look more and more telling. I felt certain it would pay off and, mid-way through the second half, Robson got up for a centre by Francis and Jean Luc Ettori, the small but agile French goalkeeper, was well beaten. Platini and his team seemed to lose their appetite for the battle after that, Coppell and Wilkins opened the way for Paul Mariner to knock in our third and we were there.

The heat had punished us, of course. Weight loss was inevitable and Mariner somehow shed eleven pounds. Coppell and Rix were named for the routine urine test for drugs and it took them nearly two hours to produce. I can think of better ways of losing weight and better advertisements for summer football.

The problem for the next day or two was in striking a balance between confidence and a proper respect for our next opponents, Czechoslovakia, though West Germany's defeat by Algeria was a timely reminder about the danger of taking things for granted. Everything seemed to be dropping into place. The Falklands War was over, something which had never been out of our hearts and minds, and on all sorts of more personal levels the news was good. Bryan Robson's wife, Denise, gave birth to their second daughter the day after he'd scored twice against France and, a few days before the game, we'd heard news of Kevin Keegan's OBE. The room he shared with Trevor Brooking MBE promptly became the 'Royal Room'.

Our two 'Royals', alas, were still a long way from being fit to play and I had the rare pleasure of naming an unchanged side for the game against Czechoslovakia. Don and I had been down to Vallodolid, a round trip of seven hours, to see Czechoslovakia draw with Kuwait and they'd looked technically sound but short of imagination and not too committed. They were the same against us on a cold and grey day. It was an ordinary game, a tight, cat-and-mouse affair which they presented to us. Their goalkeeper, Seman, dropped the ball to let in Francis for our first goal and one of their defenders, Barmos, turned the ball into his own net for the second. The win meant we were certain of a place in the second round but I was not too happy about our performance. The edge wasn't there and Robson could have had a hat-trick before his groin started playing up and I replaced him with Hoddle. But no team can hit the bull's-eye every time; and we were alive and well and making good progress.

We were not just letting things ride with Keegan and Brooking. Brian Roper, the West Ham specialist, was flown out to give Trevor an injection in his groin. It was a tricky one, which had to be given in exactly the right spot, and I felt all the trouble and expense would be worthwhile if his chances of playing improved by even a few per cent. It was done quietly and without publicity.

Kevin went into a nursing home for twenty-four hours so that John Gonzalez, a specialist in Bilbao who was interested in football, could look at his back. All kinds of tests were made and X-rays taken but nothing could be identified or seen. Kevin was getting depressed and he put his fears into words when we met in the hotel one night at about half-past eleven. He had gone to bed early and then got up for a stroll while I was just on my way upstairs. The events of the next hour or so were astonishing.

Kevin said: 'I'm letting everyone down. D'you think it would be better if I went home?' He was very uptight. 'Would I be best out of the place?' he repeated.

He knew about Trevor's injection because he shared a room with him, and the fact that we'd gone to the trouble of flying out Brian Roper just to make one injection had put an idea into his mind.

'I've got this specialist in Hamburg' he told me. 'D'you think I could go and see him?'

'What . . . in Hamburg?' I asked.

'Yeah' Kevin went on. 'I'm sure if he could have a look at me he'd get it right.'

I agreed it was pointless for him to stay in Spain if he felt he had no chance of playing – and this started Kevin off once more.

'I'm really frustrated. I feel bloody useless. And if I don't go to Hamburg I might as well go home. I know I could get to Hamburg.'

'How?' I asked. It was getting on for midnight.

'Well, I could get down to Madrid and catch a plane from there.'

'All right, let's go and see the receptionist.' I felt anything was worth a shot.

The receptionist at Los Tamarises, lovely and helpful girl though she was, immediately said there was no chance of getting a taxi to take Kevin to Madrid at that time of night. 'But if it's really important', she suddenly added, 'I've got this little car he can have'.

I looked at Kevin. 'Yeah. Okay. I'll drive', he said.

The girl said her car was down in the hotel garage and she showed us the way. Sure enough, there was a toy-sized, two-seater car there, surrounded and blocked in by dustbins of every shape and size. Some were as tall as we were and all were full to the brim with rubbish. There was no chance of getting the car out. 'They come and collect the stuff at one o'clock each night', said our receptionist, 'so by the time I finish in the morning it's all gone'.

'I'll wait to one o'clock' said Kevin. 'And don't worry, Boss. I'll see to everything. I've got to do something. Otherwise I'm wasting everybody's time.'

The receptionist said there was an all-night garage just outside Bilbao, so I gave Kevin a pile of pesetas and asked the girl to let him know when the dustbins had been emptied and moved. I wished him luck and went to bed. And an hour later Kevin, in his little car, headed out into the Spanish night towards Madrid, two hundred and fifty awkward, hilly, twisting miles away.

I did not sleep. I just lay there thinking of England's most celebrated footballer pushing on through the darkness towards the Spanish capital. I would not have let anyone else make the journey but Kevin was such a man of the world that I knew he would be all right. I imagined how other players might react if I told them: 'Drive yourself down to Madrid in the middle of the night, jump onto a plane for Hamburg and handle everything by yourself.' They would have thought me stark, raving mad. But not Kevin Keegan. He was different.

Kevin's absence was noticed in the morning, of course, and I simply said he had gone to see a specialist again. After training there was a press conference at the camp: our table was down on the indoor pitch, the press were above in the balcony, and the questions fell like rain. I again said Kevin had gone to see a specialist and was as vague with the details as I could be – the inference being that I didn't want anyone to know where he was. I felt sure, in any case, that someone would soon spot him. He had one of the best-known sporting faces in Europe.

Then, four days later, Kevin suddenly turned up. He had reached Madrid without a hitch, taken the first flight to Hamburg, been treated by his specialist, flown back, picked up the little car which he'd left at Madrid airport and driven back up to Bilbao again. 'I feel a lot better, Boss. Definitely. I can do some training' he said. I announced that Kevin was back, revealed that he had been to Hamburg and said the trip had paid off. It was hardly a story I could have told in full at the time. I let Kevin go because I had as much faith in him off the field as on, but wasn't I glad to see that smiling face of his again.

Joe Corrigan also had a problem, a strained knee ligament, and we felt we owed it to Manchester City to send him home. But once there the trouble eased after a specialist had seen him and big Joe, a tremendous professional, was able to rejoin us. It was a sensible precaution, although while he was away Ray Clemence was injured in training and we faced, briefly, the nasty dilemma of having only one goalkeeper.

Life was anything but dull. We had an 'open day' for the media at Los Tamarises, so that they could see the sort of comfort and facilities we were enjoying, and it was a pleasant, relaxed occasion adorned by the girls of the 'London Ballet'. Their relationship with Covent Garden, though, was distant to say the least. Glen Kirton had received a call asking if the 'London Ballet' could join us at the party. This seemed all right to me. What is wrong with culture? But without knowing what ballet dancers are supposed to look like, I realized something was wrong as soon as I saw them. They were nice, good-looking English lasses; but ballet dancers they were not. The build was different.

They turned out to be go-go dancers belonging to a group called the 'Playmodel London Ballet' who were appearing at a local night-spot and, once the facts were established, they joined in and enjoyed themselves. The lads weren't too keen on posing with them because the pictures might not have been appreciated at home, but they were all gone in half an hour and no harm was done. It wasn't a bad story for the papers and after reading all about it next morning my secretary at Lancaster Gate, Jill Clarke, a super girl, sent me a telegram which read: 'Hope you are inspired by Swan Lake for next game'.

There was another misunderstanding which was more embarrassing. A rather grand reception was laid on at the Town Hall in Bilbao, complete with entertainment, and later I was told the invitation was for everybody. The players were expected to be there. But there was some hitch in communication and we arranged a training session at the same time. Most of our officials were at the reception as were the press, and I missed the training to go but, understandably, the local dignitaries were not too pleased. It was reported in the papers that we had 'snubbed' everybody but I would not have dreamed of doing this. We owed too much to Bilbao.

This sort of story was usually handled by newsmen who were there to cover events outside the game itself. They were looking for the 'hard' line in everything and I got to know most of them quite well. They admitted in the end that we'd made life difficult for them because there was so little in the way of trouble on or off the field. We were a team with few problems and even the fans largely behaved themselves. I thought this did credit to us.

At this point, with four points from two games, it looked as if I was in a position to manipulate events to get us, in theory, easier opposition in Madrid. To do this we would have had to lose to Kuwait in our final match at the San Mames in much the same way that, back in 1954 in Switzerland, West Germany threw their match with Hungary. The result of that game, unbelievably, was Hungary 8, West Germany 3 – and West Germany, craftily managed by Sepp Herberger, went on to win the cup.

But it is not in my character to lose any game deliberately and I did not seriously consider the idea even for a moment. In any case France and Czechoslovakia drew the day before we played Kuwait which left France second with three points and confirmed us as the group winners.

I made one or two changes for the Kuwait game. I kept Hoddle in for the injured Robson and gave a first cap to Steve Foster of Brighton, a big, uncompromising chap who took the place of Butcher. The Ipswich defender had been booked in our game against Czechoslovakia and another caution would have meant automatic suspension. I did not want to take any chances with the second round just ahead of us.

The pressure was off us for the Kuwait game and I hoped we would turn on a really convincing performance to say goodbye to Bilbao in style. So much for good intentions. It was easily the worst of our three displays, a poor game against a side whose brightest idea was the off-side trap – and it was no credit to us that we fell into it more than twenty times. I thought we lacked application and this showed in the quality of our movement and finishing. We might have had four or five but in the end we took the game with a single, first-half goal from Francis, a good one after a penetrating run. But Mariner was booked and that was a worry. I wasn't very happy about our performance and said so, emphatically, but I also reflected that if we had to have a bad game, then we had picked the right day and the right opposition.

Shilton had an easy game and that was odd in a way. I said to him before the match: 'How would you feel if I gave Ray a game against Kuwait, just to keep him sharp?' But Peter replied: 'Really I haven't had a lot to do myself so far and I'd like to keep myself on the mark by playing in this one.' I decided I had to go along with his wishes, so Clemence lost the chance to play his first and only game in the World Cup finals.

Brazil were the only other nation to win all three of their first-round matches, however, and we moved down to Madrid feeling almost nothing was beyond us. Our headquarters were in Navacerrada, a beautiful area up in the mountains about an hour to the north-west of the city. The hotel was run by a couple of brothers, marvellous people, and again we had the place to ourselves. Our training ground was at the back in the direction of a village below. It was another ideal set-up and again it was the reward for sound groundwork. Of the visiting nations only the West Germans and ourselves had settled on headquarters in Madrid in anticipation of reaching the second round, and they chose a big, modern hotel near the airport. The Spanish, obviously, had first choice: no one blamed the hosts for that.

But now we faced West Germany in the Bernabeu – and all the

memories of Wembley in 1966 and Leon in 1970 came rolling back. We knew the Germans well, of course, but they knew more than a bit about us. And we both knew that this was the real start of the competition.

The West Germans were the European champions and hadn't lost to another European country since Jupp Derwall took over from Helmut Schoen after the 1978 World Cup. It was a wonderful record; but in Spain there seemed to be a crack or two in their make-up. They had lost to Algeria, because they made the unforgivable mistake of not taking them seriously, and they had beaten Austria by a goal to nil in a game so empty of intent that even their own supporters were outraged. There were stories of unrest in their camp, that players were not happy with team selection and playing methods, and I must confess I was surprised when Derwall named his side. There was no place at the start for big Horst Hrubesch, an old striking partner of Keegan's at Hamburg, or the two Cologne forwards, Klaus Fischer and Pierre Littbarski. The German team was clearly designed to contain and protect. Littbarski's omission was the most significant. I had seen him play against Czechoslovakia a couple of months before and his pace and variety were impressive. Bobby Robson followed West Germany in Spain and he confirmed that the Cologne winger was the man we would have to watch. Bobby said Littbarski was really on song; and Tony Woodcock, a Cologne player himself, of course, told me the little German was a potential match-winner. But Littbarski was on the bench. I hesitate to say the European champions were frightened of us but the make-up of their side did suggest excessive respect. I know we had won all our first-round games while they had struggled but Derwall's side was clearly not picked to win – and this was proved by their performance.

I sent out the side that beat France and Czechoslovakia and felt the Germans were there to be taken. But they closed down on us systematic-ally, we didn't find a solution to their man-to-man marking, and I admit that was our fault. Everybody worked to the tightest of margins and I had the feeling for most of the game that one goal would win it. The Germans didn't cause us any problems at the back and I can only recall them making one shot in each half, with the second, by Karl-Heinz Rummenigge, almost winning them the match. Five minutes from the end, in a single moment of aggression, he thumped the ball against our cross-bar from twenty-five yards. By then Derwall had sent on both Littbarski and Fischer and I had called in Francis and given Woodcock a chance to see if his experience of their tight marking could find a chink somewhere. But we couldn't get them to come at us and although we created more chances than they did it was a game that went sour on us.

The result was a goalless draw, and if Derwall felt that was his best bet against us then I suppose he was well pleased. He said to me after the game: 'If we're not going to go through we hope you do and wish you well.' But it was not my sort of football. I took no pleasure from it. I had hoped we would play to the ceiling of our ability, and we did work desperately hard, but we lacked a moment of inspiration.

There was a lot of whistling and jeering at the end of the match, which I could understand, because Madrid had been waiting for the World Cup for a long time and the seventy-five thousand people there expected something more than a rigid stalemate. The Bernabeu Stadium is a marvellous old place with incredible atmosphere and, from where I sat, the terraces seemed to tower up to the sky. It was a theatre which deserved a grander production. But the draw meant everything hung on the two final matches of the round, Spain's games against West Germany and England, with most things in the host nation's favour. Our own chances were just as good as they were before the game against West Germany; and with the Germans playing first we would know exactly what we had to do when our turn came to face Spain.

We had a full week before our game with Spain, a valuable week because Keegan and Brooking were now almost ready. They were not a hundred per cent match-fit but both were training and Keegan was playing a lot of tennis, a useful extra test for his back, and he was clearly feeling stronger every day.

I decided it would be better if the players watched the game between Spain and West Germany on television at the hotel. I did not want them to get caught up in the hustling pressure of an occasion like this and, in any case, players are not always the best judges. They tend to see everything as 'brilliant' or 'useless' when mostly it is neither.

Don Howe and Geoff Hurst came with me to the game. This time West Germany's team included Littbarski and Fischer. Their priorities were different, for they knew they had to win. They did, too, by 2–1 in front of a crowd of ninety-eight thousand, with all the goals coming in a frantic second half – and their scorers were Littbarski and Fischer! Spain again looked just a moderate side. In the first round they had beaten Yugoslavia with the help of a penalty, drawn with Honduras with yet another penalty, and lost to Northern Ireland who had to play with ten men for most of the second half after Mal Donaghy had been sent off. Now Spain had lost again and I saw nothing to fear in them.

We had to beat Spain by two goals to reach the semi-finals and I did not think this was beyond us. But we also assumed that if we beat Spain 2–1 we would still go through because FIFA regulations clearly stated that, where two teams finished the second round with the same number of points and goals, 'the team having had a better classification in its group at the end of the matches of the first round will be qualified'. We had won all three of our matches while West Germany had won two and lost one. I firmly believed we had a 'better' classification. But FIFA read it differently. They insisted that 'classification' meant just position – and West Germany had also won their first-round group.

We got very heated up about this. Professor Sir Harold Thompson, a FIFA man himself, said it was 'a bad day' for the World Cup and we protested formally; but an appeals board met for an hour and decided we'd got it wrong. I do think the rule was ambiguous – and an ambiguous rule is a bad rule. If group 'position' was intended to be the deciding factor why not use the word 'position'? There was nothing we could do about it, however, and we were informed that if we beat Spain 2–1 we would have to draw lots with West Germany, a 'lucky dip' affair involving a bag and a few balls.

But the main ball was still in our court. Victory by a couple of goals would put an end to the nonsense. I had to make one change, Woodcock for the injured Coppell, but on the bench there were a couple of important new faces – Brooking and Keegan. I told them they were two trumps I was going to keep up my sleeve. 'If things are not going well I'll send you on' I said. 'I'll try to get the moment just right and then you'll set them fresh problems when it matters.'

I was not sure what the Spanish attitude would be because they were out of the World Cup and I didn't know how strongly their disappointed crowd would get behind them. But it soon became obvious that the players and fans of Spain were bent on restoring their pride. It was a night for honour if not victory. Spain bristled with defiance and made things difficult for us in every corner of the pitch.

Yet once again the match was ours for the taking. I thought we played some of our best football of the tournament: our effort, determination, movement and reading of the game were always good. We failed only in the one area that mattered. We created chances, and then we missed them. An old tune, I know, but this time we were just a step away from the semi-finals of the World Cup. The misses mattered and hurt more than ever.

I decided to play my two trumps. I signalled to Keegan and Brooking that I wanted them on, and with twenty-seven minutes left they stepped into football's biggest event, the World Cup finals, for the first time in their long careers. It was a marvellous moment for them – and for me, too.

Those wise people who always know better asked later why I didn't play Keegan and Brooking from the start, but the fact is neither were perfectly fit. They wouldn't have lasted the full game so how would I have handled my substitutes if someone else had got injured? Brooking, in fact, did not play after this match until the following March. It was a risk sending him on at all, but at this point risks were worth taking. And this one nearly paid off.

Both could have scored. Robson set up Keegan's chance brilliantly, a cross from the left that put the ball onto Kevin's forehead in front of an empty net. But he placed it wide, and to this day he can't explain how or why. Brooking, who immediately injected a new level of skill into the game, made his own opening in a way I'd seen dozens of times since I first knew him as a boy. It was a great chance but somehow Arconada, the Spanish captain and goalkeeper, managed to get in the way. 'Normally you just screw that sort of chance in' I said to Trevor afterwards. 'I was going to', he replied, 'but the ball ran away from me at the last moment and I had to poke the ball instead of wrapping my foot around it'.

Spain nil, England nil. It was over. I went straight to our dressing-room. Heads were on chests and I spotted the odd tear but I told them all how terribly proud I was of them. 'None of you have let your country down' I said. 'You have done your best – and your best was very good. Things just didn't go for you.'

Things went, instead, for West Germany. They lost to Algeria, clawed a goalless draw out of us and, at one point in their semi-final in Seville, were 3–1 down to France. They got the score back to 3–3 by the end of extra time, a wicked foul by their goalkeeper Harald Schumacher on Patrick Battiston having disrupted the French, and then took the match on penalties. We were unbeaten and had bettered France with style; but West Germany were in the final. Jupp Derwall's side got it right when it mattered. That is the knack. And afterwards, having lost the final, they had a big inquest into their 'failure'. That is thoroughness.

It wasn't a classic tournament but among the bonuses was the success of Northern Ireland. They headed their first round group over Spain, Yugoslavia and Honduras, drew with Austria in the second and only met their match against France. Everything smiled on them and, in return, they brought a smile to many faces themselves. Billy Bingham and his team had a real go and the World Cup was better off for them. It was a triumph for collective effort and bags of pride. I also thought Scotland did well: they adapted intelligently and credit is due to Jock Stein. But they were their own worst enemies because they conceded two goals against New Zealand. Scotland won 5–2, but those two mistakes in an easy game cost them their place in the second round.

A film was made of the World Cup, called *Golé*, and in its way I thought it faithfully reflected the 1982 tournament. It delighted in the spectacle of Gentile kicking Maradona in the air about ten times a minute. But it should have relished skill for its own sake. Who matters most, the Gentiles of this world, or players such as Zico, Falcao, Socrates, Giresse, Platini, Rummenigge, Littbarski, Conti, Rossi, Scirea and the Polish pair, Boniek and Lato?

I took pleasure from the brave promise of Honduras, Cameroon and Algeria, and although the new, king-size tournament with twenty-four teams created some problems, it worked out better than I had expected. But I still feel the best formula of all would be a final competition for just eight countries, the cream of the cream, short, manageable and dramatic. This might not make financial sense, however, so I believe the best practical number is the old one of sixteen. The new format is a monster. Fifty games over a month spreads the jam thinly and unevenly. The flavour is poor.

6

There are Easier Jobs

The earth will be flat and the moon made of cheese before England's manager is given all he needs to do his job properly. We are talking about the impossible.

A handy package of improvements would include a complete reconstruction of the Football League, a ban on all 'foreigners' including the Scots, Welsh and Irish, a broadly uniform method of playing throughout the twenty-two clubs of the First Division, a firm acceptance that England's needs take priority over those of the clubs and a commitment to new ideas, enlightened coaching and serious study on the continent by all our managers.

Every man who takes on the England job starts with optimistic thoughts along these lines but then comes reality and with it the problems . . . self-interest, insularity, an inherited suspicion of change, financial expediency, muddled priorities, a confusion of styles and, above all, a lack of time. In the end we settle for doing the best we can.

I am not seriously suggesting that the likes of Kenny Dalglish, Ian Rush and Pat Jennings should be kicked out of the Football League. That could not and should not happen because they contribute so much and, in any case, I would not want to make life any tougher for the managers of Scotland, Wales and the two Irelands. But as Enzo Bearzot once said to me: 'The trouble with your football is that you've got too many foreigners.' He meant the Celts – 'foreigners' with British or Irish passports – who fill about half the places in all the top sides in the League. Once the England manager also discounts those who have the right birth certificates but who are too young, too old or simply not good enough, he finds himself with options that look uncomfortably limited. I have not forgotten I was able to include six Liverpool players in the first England side I sent out, but seven of the Anfield team which won the championship in my last season were outside my net.

The ninety-two clubs of the League employ around eighteen hundred full-time professionals, but only about fifty are of immediate interest to the England manager. Just fifty players, drawn largely from a First Division of twenty-two teams and twenty-two different playing styles.

95

Such is the raw material of his job. He is allowed to borrow the best of them once a month, at most, and in the space of three days he is then expected to weld them into a fighting unit capable of beating every other country in the world with style and efficiency. The managers of other countries have problems as well, of course, but I am only looking through England's window. Winners in international football take care of themselves.

I agree that the wide range of playing methods used by our clubs gives the Football League its strong, highly individual flavour. Some teams play it short and some long. Some are patient and some race around at a hundred miles an hour. Some play it through the middle and some look for corner flags. Some employ wingers and some fill centre-circles. Some play football from the back and some don't play football at all. From Liverpool through to Watford, by way of Manchester United, West Ham, Nottingham Forest and Arsenal, there is such a variety of styles and priorities that every game on every Saturday is different. But while this is fine for the spectators it is not so good for England's manager, who is expected to make up a complicated jigsaw puzzle with pieces from a lot of different boxes. Variety may be the spice of life but it does not produce players who can step quickly and easily into international football.

There is no guarantee, either, that any player is going to be at his best – no matter how hard he tries. Footballers have all the worries that bother and distract other folk, plus a few more of their own. All sorts of things happen to players in the months between internationals; and loss of form, inactivity because of injury, marital troubles, money worries, business difficulties, gambling debts, bad publicity, changes of manager and transfer requests can all affect a player's game.

Yet a team has to be picked. Quality, form, experience, character, balance and fitness have to be related to the style and strengths of the opposition. It requires a lot of thought, and sometimes second thoughts, but every team I sent out was my choice and mine alone. Each was my responsibility and I held onto that with both hands. I was certainly damned annoyed when one or two papers claimed that the side which played Scotland at Wembley in 1981 was picked by the players themselves. The stories said the players had told me they didn't want Peter Barnes in the team. They called it 'player power'. I called it press rubbish.

Picking England teams is everybody's favourite game, of course, and the cry is always for new players, different players, any players other than those actually selected. I would have liked to oblige everybody but someone, somewhere would have objected to me sending out sides containing twenty or thirty players. I listened only to people who picked teams at a quarter-to-three, not at a quarter-to-five. Selection with hindsight is just a parlour game.

Great players are no problem: they pick themselves. But an England manager is rarely over-burdened with such beings and he has to make do with one or two who are outstanding, and two or three who are very good. These are the backbone of his side and around them he does the very best he can. I had a promisingly solid base at one point with Keegan, Brooking and Clemence or Shilton providing a thread of gold from front to back. Coppell, Wilkins and Watson were also there, impressively, and I knew I could always count on men like Mills, Neal, Thompson and Hughes. People said I didn't know what my best side was; but I did, exactly. For while it is vital to hold the basic framework of a side together, there must be room for movement and experiment. Experience cannot be poured out of a bottle and the only way to prove a player is to pitch him in at the highest level. There must always be a shirt ready for a Bryan Robson – and enough leeway to play an occasional hunch.

The England manager has one constant enemy, however. Time is always against him. He seems to have so much of the stuff but the truth is he has very little of the right kind.

I spent less time at home when I was England's manager than when I was with West Ham. I saw more games, travelled more and even talked and listened more. I wanted to be aware of everything that was going on. But the time that mattered most – time with my players – was always chronically short. For a mid-week game at Wembley it would be 'Hello' on a Sunday evening, training and talk on Monday and Tuesday and match action on Wednesday. Clubs were so keen to get their players back afterwards that we would lay on cars to whisk them straight home. Time was even scarcer for a game abroad. Out on Monday, back early on Thursday at the latest. And then no more contact for a month or two.

Some countries do put their national team before their clubs. Others manage to balance the two interests. Argentina got their players together more than two months before their defence of the World Cup in 1982. Brazil, as usual, had a month in happy harmony and then a busy tour. Iron Curtain countries have regular get-togethers, in addition to matches, while other nations make good use of the mid-winter breaks forced on them by their weather. But in England the clubs rule. The fattest and oldest professional League in the world, the FA Cup, the Milk Cup and European tournaments fill a ten-month season to its limits. There is no time to draw breath and no room for rest. Matches mean money. The turnstiles must keep clicking and well-reasoned arguments in favour of a smaller, better balanced and more selective League are strangled at birth or neatly shelved. Even in the precious week England's players had together before the World Cup in Spain I was asked by several clubs to release their players for lucrative little trips to the continent. They were unlucky but, as a former club manager myself, I understood why they had asked.

Once in a blue moon, before an international of over-riding importance, a weekend has been cleared of top League games. Don Revie managed that twice, and in my time it was a luxury we enjoyed before our decisive World Cup qualifying game with Hungary at Wembley in November, 1981. It spared me the usual Saturday-into-Sunday wait for news of injuries. A club call to West Lodge Park after a full Saturday programme was usually bad news but even a silent 'phone meant nothing. Some managers with a doubtful England player just forgot to ring.

A few countries have actually stopped having free weekends before internationals because a lot of their leading players are scattered all over Europe but many others, including Hungary and Portugal, still believe in the idea, and I agree with them. I would like to see major Football League games postponed before every competitive England international. This would give the England manager five clear days with his players – which is something every League club manager in the country, from the top of the First Division to the bottom of the Fourth, takes for granted. It is not asking for much.

Most countries find it easier to make time than England because their professional football developed after ours. They have learned from our mistakes and have smaller leagues. They do not have traditions that go back a hundred years. Change, in England, is always seen as breaking faith with the past. Tradition here is a support but a ball-and-chain too.

The age has long gone when it could grandly be assumed that all the world's best players were British. The Hungarians confirmed this rather effectively in 1953. But I still hear it claimed with great certainty that the English League is the finest of all. I agree it has tremendous depth, none more so, but in quality it is no better than many others. Yet our insularity still persuades us that, ultimately, our way is the best way. Alas, this can't be so. International results prove otherwise.

What we do have are certain characteristics that can be put to excellent use. They are not enough in themselves but, given all the other things that go into the making of successful teams, they are precious assets. We are a nation of fighters and stayers and these qualities show on the pitch. They are admired by other countries and we should be proud of them.

Such assets were evident in the football which Liverpool, Nottingham Forest and Aston Villa played to win the European Cup six years in succession. Each club had a winner's attitude and because each also had good players, intelligent organization and the sort of team understanding which only comes with time and practice, they were able to overcome the best of the rest of Europe.

It is this understanding which is the essential difference between England's successful club sides and England's not-so-successful national side. And unless England's players do get more time together they will never do themselves justice. It is as simple as that. The manager of England realizes very quickly that his job is to make the best of things. He knows what he would like but he is stuck with what he has got.

I attempted to make the best of things in two ways. I changed my squad as little as possible and I tried to introduce a simple, uniform way of playing that everybody could understand. The first was easier than the second.

The stability of the squad did help to build a relationship between the players. A balanced side and good cover were always there. There were problems, of course. I stuck with Ray Wilkins when he was going through a bad patch with Chelsea, I kept faith with Dave Watson when things were not going well for him at Southampton, and when West Ham were relegated I assured Trevor Brooking that it would not affect his future with England. Such men worked well for me and I was always glad to see them in the side. Their experience could not be replaced and they gave us a chance. They also believed in each other, which was important. Their attitude to the game and to England was just right, and I knew they would not willingly let me down.

The importance of 'a basic method of play was stressed at a meeting in Naples with all my coaches after the end of the 1980 European Championship finals. Eddie Baily, John Cartwright, Howard Wilkinson, Bobby Robson, Dave Sexton, Don Howe, Terry Venables, Bill Taylor and Geoff Hurst were all there to watch and learn and be my eyes and ears. We agreed the tournament had not been a patch on the 1976 finals when Czechoslovakia, West Germany, Holland and the host country, Yugoslavia, had been full of lovely, bold invention. The football in Italy was short of quality and fire but it emphasized the way the game was going and provided pointers concerning methods and individuals that would come in useful. We talked about our own international game and, interestingly, it was felt we should settle on a style of play that could run through all our various sides from youth to full level, a simple and flexible general strategy which players could understand and slot into easily. Balance and width would be necessary and one winger, preferably two, would be used.

I had tried this with Barnes and Coppell in my first month or two as

England's manager, but when Barnes lost his touch no strong replacement came through until Rix. Then, adapting the format to meet the immediate needs of the 1982 World Cup finals, we had settled on a loose but balanced 4–4–2 structure. The principle of a uniform style of play is a sound one but its detail always depends on the players available. There was never a big choice of left-wingers but Coppell was a stable and important influence on the right.

Continuity on and off the field and time for preparation are the two factors vital to an England manager if he is to make a fist of the job. The odds at the moment, alas, are heavily against him: one major reason is that, deep down, we care more about our clubs than our national team. The point is often made that success at the highest level influences our football right down to its grass roots, but our attitude to the international game is curious. We care about it for two or three days before a big night and for forty-eight hours afterwards but then Saturday arrives, everybody gets back to watching their Uniteds and Rovers and the needs of England are promptly forgotten for a month or two – except, of course, by the England manager. He lives with one result for months at a time.

That is one of the reasons why it is important that the England manager should also be the Football Association's Director of Coaching. Walter Winterbottom held both posts and Bobby Robson has the dual responsibility now but, in between, Alf Ramsey and Don Revie confined themselves strictly to our international sides. I would have loved the two jobs but when my time came I felt I was getting on a bit. A man with this wide, overall responsibility can establish important guidelines at all levels. He can look at the game as a whole and exercise real influence.

The English manager is as much concerned with a total concept of the game as he is with winning and losing. He has to set and maintain standards, and is judged as much for standard of performance as on results. I accepted this happily because I have always believed, passionately, that there is more to football than just a score-line. I even thought my general philosophy would be better suited to managing England than West Ham, but the opportunities for influencing players at national level are so few that fundamental change is difficult.

I am very sure, however, that international football improves a player. It gives his experience a new dimension, opens his eyes to new ideas, tests him against opponents on a higher plane and lends him fresh status as a performer. There are some club managers, inevitably, who refuse to accept any of this. They talk about their players picking up bad habits, getting ideas above their station, becoming fidgety after hearing what other players earn, or even being tapped. I think a few of these managers are simply frightened they won't be able to handle their players once they become internationals.

Any manager who makes it difficult for a player to turn out for England at any level is not doing the player, his club, or ultimately himself, any favours. I once let Johnny Sissons and Alan Stephenson play for Alf Ramsey in an England Under-21 game on the same night as a League Cup tie between West Ham and Coventry. And we lost! I got some stick from supporters saying I shouldn't have released them but I was proud when my players represented their country. I believed in the importance of international football.

The influence of club managers, for good or bad, cannot be over-estimated. It is club managers who make players what they are, although, in the end, it is players who make a manager. A player whose club manager knows his job is full of good habits and is able to improvize and obey instructions. Club managers have an indirect but important influence on the England team. They should share all the credit and the criticism. When they snipe at the England manager they are, in a sense, having a go at themselves.

After all, the England manager can only pick the best of what the clubs produce. He has no magic wand and an international shirt does not suddenly give a player international quality, though it is difficult to define exactly what this quality is. Broadly, I suppose, a good international is an outstanding player who can relate easily to strangers, thrive in an unfamiliar system and respond well to unusual pressures. This is where many players fail. They may have first-class ability but they only blossom inside their familiar club pattern and alongside team-mates they know well. Ray Kennedy, for example, played better for Liverpool than he ever did for England. He was not a bad international but he only really flourished in the red shirt of Anfield. He did not easily adapt to unusual conditions.

Players miss out at the top level for all manner of reasons. Some do not like travelling and being away from home; and airports and strange hotel rooms are all part of international life. Other men are just born at the wrong time. They are brilliant players but they find themselves up against someone in their position who is so outstanding that they do not get a look in. Billy Wright, Bobby Charlton and Bobby Moore all won a hundred caps for England, but if they had been brain surgeons or astronauts instead of footballers I wonder how many other players would have shared all those caps.

Billy Bonds of West Ham was a player any manager would have loved.

He had first-class ability, a high level of consistency and a heart as big as a football. I fully intended to play him in one game against Brazil but he suffered an injury, the door shut and stayed shut. Luck was dead against him but although I think he would have done well I am not sure he was a natural international. He was, on his own admission, a club man at heart. He loved familiar faces around him and didn't like being away from home. He would have hated going on a long tour, especially if he was a reserve who did not get a game. That was his personality. But many poorer players than Billy have won a pile of caps.

Character is as important in a footballer as technique and this is particularly true on big, one-off occasions like cup or international matches. Some players will always be at their best when 'life and death' has to be decided in ninety minutes. They give good week-by-week performances in the League but they move into over-drive when the going becomes tougher. Bobby Moore never let me down in any match but I knew that when the bugle sounded he would always find another twenty per cent. The bigger the game the better his performance – he would grow to meet the challenge. That is what being a top international player is all about.

Character is a central factor in other ways in international football. National character is an important influence and I have already said the British are fighters and stayers. Equally, though, other countries portray themselves in the way they play. I can only generalize but the Italians are stylish, macho and stubborn in a negative way, the Germans are hard-working, painstaking and always see themselves as winners, the Spanish have talent but lack unity and motivation, the Russians believe organization is the answer to everything but lack the spark of life, the Dutch are receptive and open and the French creative but variable in their moods. It is all there in their football.

Another kind of character is also important at this level – the character of the national team manager. Sometimes his character can be out of step with the natural character of his country's football. Enzo Bearzot, for example, had to fight long and hard to persuade his players to allow their talent free rein. The late Claudio Countinho wanted to inject European qualities into the Brazilian game, a conviction which originally sprang from the battering Pelé and company received during the World Cup in England back in 1966.

National managers as a group are interesting, diverse and talented men; but no two are alike. They all have different attitudes, expectations and resources – and they all have different strengths. Jupp Derwall of West Germany inherited a strong system and is continuing to develop it strictly according to the quality of his players. Michel Hidalgo has a lovely attitude to the game. Football must flow for him and France responded to his call. Guy Thys got the Belgians to play well for him because he is a crafty old foz with a fatherly attitude! he understands his players. Joseph Vengloss of Czechoslovakia was a very good player who went on acquiring knowledge all over the world, including in Australia. He is one of the game's academics. Yugoslavia's Miljan Miljanic brought a rounded, intelligent approach to his job but I always knew he would do well. Every year, in his younger days, he would come to West Ham or Tottenham with an empty notebook and an inquiring mind. To this day he calls me 'Professor'. Some are still going, some have moved on, some have finished now: national football management is a short-term job which gives pleasure and pain in equal measure. But I am a better person for having known all these men.

If I had been given the choice of managing any team in Europe, apart from England, I would have plumped for Yugoslavia. They are the biggest challenge. They have produced so many fine players, from Dzajic through to Petrovic and Susic, and when one of their club sides like Red Star have got their act together they have been absolutely brilliant. I admire their skill, their technical strengths, their ability to learn and improvize, their style and their intelligence. But the national team has never done itself full justice and I think this is because the Yugoslavs lack belief in themselves. Perhaps, again, this stems from their character. They are a mixed race and sometimes it shows. They have more imagination than the Germans, but the Germans have achieved more because of their superb organization. It is in this area that I would have liked the chance to do something for Yugoslavia. There is something in their game which convinces me they could be a major force in world football. I would also add that I would have taken great pride in managing Holland at their peak. They played beautiful football and it gave me enormous pleasure to watch them. They did so much for the game.

In some ways I was very lucky. No one pretends money is not useful and the attitude of some nations' players has made the job of their managers very difficult. But I can honestly say that in my five years as England manager my players did not give me a moment's trouble in this respect. Their attitude was first-class and their priorities were always right. They just wanted to play for England – and they would have played for nothing.

Before we went to Spain for the World Cup finals the players did not even ask me what they were going to be paid. They left it to me to talk to the Football Association and I did not give them any figures until just before our first game in Bilbao. They accepted the terms immediately, and I wonder how many of the other twenty-three managers in Spain could say that? Our bonuses improved according to progress. The sums involved were generous but hardly enough to set anyone up in cosy street.

No extra money was made in Spain: all the players accepted that they were there to play and train. But before we left there were the usual and acceptable opportunities to make a few pounds extra. Harry Swales, Kevin Keegan's agent, a shrewd and experienced man who does things properly, was the players' commercial representative. Others were in the running but he was the players' choice. Kevin himself, Mick Mills, Trevor Brooking and Ray Wilkins were a committee of senior men who controlled the commitments. Millsie kept a big chart that was a work of art. It showed everything, including the income and the time involved, and everybody knew exactly where they were. The players put a lot of time and effort into public appearances and so on, but they always let me know exactly what was happening. I had no worries on that score.

Everybody in the squad was given a fair and proper slice of the cake which meant, for example, that Joe Corrigan who was our third goal-keeper did as well as Peter Shilton who was to play in all our games in Spain. Every player and every member of the staff had a share – and that included me.

I was very lucky in at least one other way. The England staff were a wonderful group of men who backed me to the hilt. We had two doctors in my time, first Peter Burrows, then Vernon Edwards. Tragically, Peter died after a jog and – in the same way that the death of Bill Taylor affected us – we felt we had lost a member of the family. Doc Burrows was a lovely chap who was totally involved and I used to say to him 'Doc, you want to do everything, how about picking the side?' He was replaced by Vernon Edwards who simply moved up from the Under-21s. Like Peter Burrows, he too became much more than a medical officer. Doc Edwards is a man with a twinkle in his eye and again we found ourselves with a sort of father figure, a man who could talk and listen sympatheti-cally and be very good for morale. The England doctor must be a chap who understands young men – and I was very lucky with both Peter and Vernon.

Fred Street, our physiotherapist, was another first-class chap, gifted, enormously experienced and a real football man. I inherited him from Don Revie, Bobby Robson has inherited him from me and, with more than a hundred internationals behind him, I believe he intends to go on for ever. Fred's judgement of injuries always seems right and the confidence everybody has in him is enormous. He knows the right things to say and he sets his own standards. Fred and Norman Medhurst, our assistant physiotherapist, would always have the dressing-room looking like a showpiece, kit, medical supplies, everything immaculately set out, hours before the players arrived. This would set the mood, so that everyone felt they were in business as soon as they walked in. It was a thoroughly professional set-up and a lot of other physios have adopted their standards.

A special word, too, about Don Howe, who took over from Bill Taylor. Don was quiet to begin with but then he began to express himself, showing what an outstanding technician he is. He is a hard worker and a formidable driver, he makes training an interesting challenge and because he has always kept up with the game abroad he is full of ideas and variations. He is a student of football, never satisfied, always learning.

It was said that Don's influence gave England's game a defensive bias but that is being very unfair to him. He loves to see a football team going forward and his whole attitude to the game is balanced and progressive. But, in any case, the overall shape of our game was always my responsibility and never, not once, did we take the field with defence in mind. England in my five years, home or away, were always sent out to win.

7

Beginnings

Worsthorne, the village in which I was born, is at the heart of the game, two and three-quarter miles of honest Lancashire above the town of Burnley; and that was the road I first took to League football. I was five years old and my father, Sam, used to carry me down the hill to Turf Moor, perch me on a barrier, and let me get on with my hero-worship.

Burnley were a First Division club in the twenties, the champions in 1921, and they had a side of such character that more than half a century later I still remember many of the names with great affection. There was George Beel, a strong, tearaway centre-forward, who scored a lot of goals, and Jack Mantle, who was another exciting forward. The full-backs were Andy McCluggage, a tough, indestructible Irishman, and George Waterfield, a more cultured defender. Jerry Dawson was in goal, a celebrated figure, but I could never get his name quite right. To me he was always 'Jelly' Dawson. It was downhill from our house to Turf Moor and downhill all the way back if we won; but if we lost it was like trudging up the face of a mountain.

I was born on 11 November, 1921. The nice thing about making an entrance on Armistice Day was that there was no excuse for forgetting my birthday. I was lucky, too, that Worsthorne was my village. It was a quiet, pretty, rather rural place in those days, with a church and a school, a big obelisk in the centre, a little row of shops and a post-office across the road. It had a couple of mills, one big, one small – the economic pillars of our community. Between shifts the men of the village spent their time in the Reading Room, which was really a men's club, a refuge in which they solved the world's problems and played snooker and billiards.

Worsthorne was a friendly place above all. Everyone knew everyone else and they all knew me. Troubles were shared, doors were always open, work mattered and principles counted for something. Life was hard but also enjoyable. There was peace and satisfaction. We did not realize how fortunate we were. My debt to Worsthorne is a big one.

Our house – 18, Ormrod Street – was at the end of a terrace. It was just a cottage with a couple of bedrooms; it had rugs and linoleum on all the floors, but how that little place shone. To this day, the smell of polish takes me straight back to my childhood. The centre-piece of the cottage, the source of all heat, food and comfort, was a big cooking range in the living room. My mother, Margaret, spent hours blacking it up and it really was a picture. We used to have our baths in front of it, and if cleanliness is next to godliness then our home was the place to be.

My father was a stocky fellow, about five foot eight, a painter and decorator and a useful footballer. He was a kind and sympathetic man who did not anger easily. He never pushed or gushed but his helping hand was always there. He enjoyed life but did not have any illusions about it. His feet were always firmly on the ground and, at the height of the depression in the 1930s, he moved ahead of us to London to establish a new home, a new life. That left my mother, a loving but independent person, to run our home at Worsthorne and she worked, almost literally, round the clock. She had a job at the big mill, where she ran six looms, an enormous task, and would be out of the house by half-past six in the morning. She would come back in time to get my sister Ivy and myself off to school and then return to work. She was also a fine cook who could make something out of nothing. My background was solid and stable and caring.

It did not seem to matter that money was short, although we could certainly have done with more when Ivy had a nasty accident and had to spend nearly four years in hospital, much of that time in Liverpool. Travelling to see her regularly was an expensive business. We were always well-scrubbed and decently clothed and, above all, we were brought up properly. I was in the local choir, which meant church three days a week as well as Sunday School, and these were the only occasions on which I wore shoes. For the rest of the week I wore clogs with leather tops and wooden soles which I wore out so quickly playing football that my mother had a standing order at the cobblers. Most people in the village wore clogs, and when I woke up in the morning I'd hear the villagers clumping along the street on their way to work. These were the days of gaslight and the 'knocker-up' who went from house to house tapping on windows with a long stick.

A lot of people in the village used to lend a hand on the local farms. There was one just down the road from us, and collecting the cows, haymaking and helping the milkman were all part of my life. We used to clatter down Brunshaw Hill into Burnley, the churns rattling on the cart behind the old horse. Our delivery area was near Turf Moor, and I would fill a can from a churn, knock on a door and walk straight in. Inside a jug would be waiting on the table. Lovely, innocent days.

Football was always at the centre of life but, on reflection, that is not really surprising. This part of Lancashire is the home of the professional game and its importance was never questioned. Places like Burnley, Nelson, Darwen, Preston, Bury, Rochdale and Accrington are some of the old cornerstones of the game and I am proud to have my roots there. Despite all the time I have spent in other parts of the country, and despite all my travelling round the world, I am still what this corner of Lancashire made me.

As boys, we used to play football until it got dark on the local recreation ground at the top of the village. We did not always have a proper ball, coats acted as goalposts and the weather never mattered. Tens of thousands of other small boys played the same kind of football and there is no doubt it produced many fine players. It was self-education and, above all, it developed a relationship with the ball. Kids' football has more to do with the real spirit of the game, perhaps, than any other kind.

Football, even then, was an obsession with me. Well-meaning teachers would tell me that if I devoted half as much time and energy to my lessons as I did to football I'd go a long way. Their argument fell on deaf ears. Classes were just unwelcome interludes between games of football.

I got my first job in the game at the age of six. The village had two major sides, church teams but deadly rivals, who played in the Burnley Sunday League. One was Wesleyan, the other Church of England, and I was appointed official ball-boy to both. They did not have nets and, usually at the bottom end where there was most open ground, I was simply a retriever; but it was a job I did with enormous pride and all the dash I could muster. Oddly, although they called it a Sunday League, the two teams always played on a Saturday – probably because they were church teams.

Most of the players worked at the big mill, and the only time they really got on together was when they played for the mill's own side. It was a good team and, in fact, they won the Burnley Hospitals' Cup – the knock-out tournament which mattered locally – with the final played at Turf Moor itself. I was appointed mascot and, at the age of seven, I suppose that was my first job on a League ground.

It was at this time that I first set eyes on the FA Cup itself. One of our opponents on the way to the Hospitals' Cup Final was Cornholme, another mill side, and Blackburn (who had beaten Huddersfield at Wembley the previous May) sent the trophy along. I could hardly take my eyes off it, and certainly never imagined that one day I would sleep with it under my bed! I had actually been to Wembley itself, though. An uncle of mine managed a decorating firm, with bases in Bingley and London, and we used to visit him in his big house at Shepherds Bush, just

a short distance from Queen's Park Rangers and not so far from Wembley·
I was taken there in 1925 to see the British Empire Exhibition: I was
three years old, Wembley just two. We have acquired our wrinkles
together.

I went to the local school, the only school, at Worsthorne and by the
time I was eight I was playing with fourteen-year-olds in the first eleven.
My first game, alas, was not exactly a triumph. The day was bitterly cold,
the pitch was a mixture of mud and water, and I was flattened so often
by opponents who towered over me that in the closing stages I ran out
of everything. I just stopped functioning. I couldn't move. My team-
mates picked me up, carried me back to school and left me in front of
the caretaker's furnace to thaw out.

We followed my father to London when I was ten – to Alperton, a
mile or so from Wembley. Our house had a real luxury, a bathroom!
At Alperton Secondary Modern School I discovered something else new:
I had what was known as a Lancashire accent. Every time I read aloud,
which seemed increasingly often, the rest of the class fell about with
laughter.

Football, though, was a common language. I joined in the games in
the playground and it wasn't long before a chap called Doug Wiggins,
who later became a schoolboy international centre-forward, started
speaking to me. That was my breakthrough, socially as well as in sporting
terms, and soon afterwards I was the youngest and smallest member of
another first eleven. I played at left-half and went on to captain the school
and Wembley Boys at under-13 and under-14 levels. I was also picked
for a trial with Middlesex Boys but, with a rotten sense of timing, I broke
an arm and that was that.

There were frequent visits back to Worsthorne during the holidays,
but I always made the journey on my own. Mother would put me on the
bus at Victoria, while relatives met me at the other end. A young chap
called Tommy Lawton was also there once on holiday: he was then a
sixteen-year-old with Burnley, and courting a girl in the village. We
managed a glimpse or two of him through the window . . . peeping Toms
all of us, and happy to admit it.

I tried my first flutter in the transfer market at this time. A talented
Welsh lad called George Greaves was playing for the District side and I
moved heaven and earth to get him transferred from East Lane School
to ours, which was much nearer his home. Alas, it was his last year at
school and the transfer was blocked.

I left school at the age of fourteen. My father used his connections
in the decorating business to get me a job with a firm of sign and glass

writers run by a Mr Westby, a Preston man and an honest-to-goodness
Lancastrian. In return for £30, a princely sum in those days, he launched
me on a five-year apprenticeship at five bob a week. It was a friendly,
well-run firm and they taught me the job properly. Simple little signs to
begin with but, once I had learnt my trade, the work was often very
delicate, especially when glass was involved which meant working from
the back in reverse. Sometimes, too, I worked in gold which needed
painstaking accuracy. I discovered the value of patience.

My employers were the contracted sign-writers at Wembley, Olym-
pia and, later on, Earls Court, which meant I enjoyed a free seat for much
of the best sport and entertainment in Britain. I liked working at Wembley
most of all, in the stadium itself and in the Empire Pool. I watched ice-
hockey, speedway, rugby league and big boxing matches . . . men like
Len Harvey, Maurice Strickland and Walter Neusel seemed to become
part of my life. Great men and great moments almost queued up for me
but, oddly perhaps, I enjoyed the six-day cycle race more than anything.
It is a marvellous event that is all about stamina, determination, skill and
tactics, and I always did my best to be around when it was on. I was there
for the very first six-day race with the track newly laid, the curves perfect
and the wooden surface impeccably prepared and sanded. It was a major
feat of construction and, once it was ready, our somewhat simpler task
was to write all the signs.

We always seemed to be fighting against time in our job, mainly
because we could not start until everything else was finished, but on this
occasion there was the added problem of erecting scaffolding on the
steep bends. I was a bit like Michael Crawford's Frank Spencer in those
days: if an accident happened I was sure to be involved. A large advertisement had to be painted in red above one of the bends and I was right on
top of the scaffolding, a big pot in my hand, when the whole structure
gave way. I crashed down onto the track, poles and red paint flying all
over the place. There was a heck of a mess. Then I heard my governor,
in that broad Lancashire accent of his, saying 'Ee, bloody 'ell, Ron, look
at that track.' I might well have broken most of the bones in my body,
much of the red paint could have been blood, but the only thing that
bothered my boss was the mess!

Another of our jobs, in those days before big electrical scoreboards,
was writing out the team changes for the various cup finals. They had to
be written quickly and legibly, and they were then wheeled around the
stadium on a sort of mobile sandwich board. Fred White, our foreman,
always did the writing for finals and nobody envied him more than me.
This was the job of all jobs although, just occasionally, there were no

changes and therefore no work to be done. Eventually I made it: I was given a rugby league final – no one else seemed to want it – and my first task was to wait outside the dressing-rooms which were then at the office end of the stadium. (The present dressing-rooms, at the other end, were built for the Olympic Games in 1948.) The teams arrived, carrying their boots wrapped in newspaper, and I scurried around, with mounting anxiety, in search of somebody from each club who could give me the team news. I was lucky: no changes.

Sometimes I worked at Wembley for months on end. I did the signs for the dressing-rooms, and later – after the war – I did much of the work for the Olympic Games. My father eventually became maintenance manager on the painting side at Wembley, while I was so involved with the stadium that I was part of the scenery.

Then, at last, I got the big one. I was deemed good enough to handle the Cup Final itself. It was the famous Preston–Huddersfield final of 1938 and, as I saw it at the age of sixteen, I was going to be tested – for skill, speed and character under pressure – in much the same way that the players would be. I was ready; the right man for the job. But, once again, there were no changes . . . though there was a complication. I was due to play in the Middlesex Youth final that same evening, kick-off 6.30, and time was going to be short. I watched the Wembley final from just below the old Tote scoreboard, a long, long way above the ground, and I knew I would not be able to get away until the crowd thinned out.

The game itself was a bit of history, of course, with Joe Hulme, once of Arsenal but then of Huddersfield and right at the end of his career, playing in his fifth final, and Billy Shankly at the heart of the Preston team. The match went into extra time and by then I was beginning to panic. FA Cup Finals were one thing, but what about my Middlesex Youth final?

The climax directly below me came in the last minute of extra time with the celebrated and controversial Mutch penalty. The silence was uncanny; the drama tremendous; my view perfect. But I was begrudging the seconds as the ball flashed past Bob Hesford in the Huddersfield goal, struck the bar and went into the net. The whistle went, I climbed down from my lofty perch as quickly as I could, ran the three miles to my home with something approaching desperation, picked up my gear and tore onto the ground. I was in time . . . and we won the cup.

I was turning out for a variety of sides, among them Ealing Road Methodists, a very successful side who played at King Edward's Park, a stone's throw from Wembley, and Alperton Old Boys, of which I was a founder member. It was around this time that one or two League clubs decided they might make something of me. I was picked to play for a representative side, the Wembley Juvenile Organization Committee League (happily shortened to Wembley JOC) and the goalkeeper in that team, Harry Brown, told me he was going for a trial with Queen's Park Rangers. 'Why not go with me?' he asked. It seemed a good idea but when we got there we found an army of lads just kicking a ball about between themselves. There did not seem much organization, but we joined in and I started hitting the ball pretty cleanly with my left foot.

Eventually a dear old chap called Alec Farmer approached me and asked:

'Where do you play?'

'Centre-half' I replied.

'Right' he said 'you're in the next game'.

They gave me a shirt and I must have done reasonably well because afterwards they invited me to sign for them.

I had also heard, however, that Chelsea were coming to Alperton in a London Minor Cup semi-final and so, with youthful confidence, I told Rangers I wanted to wait a little while before making a decision. Remarkably Chelsea invited nine of our side for a trial and again, despite a few nerves, I played well enough to catch their eye. Billy Birrell was Chelsea's manager but it was Norman Smith, their trainer, who invited me to sign. 'Yes, thank you, I'd be very happy to' I said. It was all very brief and formal.

Chelsea's traditions and style appealed to me and I knew that because of the war they were forming an under-19 side, instead of the usual reserve-team mixture, to play in the London Combination. That was the start of the famous Chelsea youth scheme, and I was one of its first products.

8

Better than Work

One of the big milestones in every player's career is his first senior game of football. It is a game that winds up mind and body like a clock-spring, a game to worry about, a game in which to do better than best, a game to relish and remember. My own was an unexpected bonus.

Just after Christmas in 1940 I was at Fulham with Chelsea's reserves when the message reached me that the first team were a man short for their home game with Aldershot, and that I was wanted to fill the hole. Getting a full team together was a nightmare during the war years because players were always being held up or moved on for 'national' reasons.

I scampered out of Craven Cottage, jumped into a taxi and shortly after reaching Stamford Bridge I was stepping out onto the pitch. I remember feeling fairly nervous as I walked out and then becoming very nervous when I realized the quality of the opposition.

Aldershot is the home of the British Army and, with so many sporting stars in uniform, in those days their side was one of the strongest. Their half-back line that afternoon consisted of Joe Mercer, Stan Cullis and Cliff Britton – a marvellous blend of experience, character, skill and craftsmanship. Not that Chelsea had a bad side: players such as George Mills, Dick Foss, George Barber and Vic Woodley, who made goal-keeping look a simple business, were gifted enough for most company. They were good to know, too. Dear Dick Spence came over to me immediately and said: 'If you get into trouble, son, just find me on the right wing and I'll take over.' I won't claim I had an outstanding game, but I survived. The papers were very kind to me – and to Chelsea. We beat Aldershot 6-0.

Chelsea's manager was Billy Birrell, a Scot and a university man who had been a quality inside-forward before learning the business of management with Bournemouth and Queen's Park Rangers. He was solidly built, always neatly dressed and a quiet chap who thought before he spoke. He had an easy, natural authority and most people respected him. He was an astute businessman, setting the club squarely on its feet at a difficult time, but he also knew his football. He became one of the first major influences on my career because he taught me that football at its best is a thinking game as well as a physical one.

Birrell believed that a quick mind is as important as quick feet and that football is as much about skill and improvization as strength and pace. He always wanted players to use their natural gifts rather than attempt things outside their range. He encouraged them to be true to their own God-given ability. It was a philosophy I agreed with then; and I still do, fervently. First beliefs are often lasting ones.

The Scot always had time for youngsters and – an immodest little story – he said to a group of us once: 'Among you here there's a boy with the best football brain I've ever come across.' I glanced around and I could see everyone was thinking 'That's me'. Such is the way seventeen-year-olds look at life! Smart psychology on Birrell's part, I thought. It was not until a good fifteen years later that my father let it drop – accidentally, because he rarely praised or flattered anyone – that the 'football brain' in question had been me. He had met Birrell shortly after that team-talk all those years before and the Chelsea manager had told him about his comment and the lad he had in mind. It was a great compliment and I have never forgotten it. Everyone likes to hear that sort of thing, true or not.

During those early days of the war I met Lucy, the girl I was to marry. My father was a warden and, one black night, a bomb failed to explode after hitting a house just up the way from us in Sunleigh Road, Alperton. It was the home of Lucy's family who had moved there about six months before. My father decided they would have to spend the night elsewhere but he did not like the idea of them sleeping in one of the local air-raid shelters which had never been used and were damp, unfriendly places full of cobwebs. So, at two o'clock in the morning, he brought Lucy's whole family round to our place. It was not exactly love at first sight. She referred to me as 'that stuck-up boy Greenwood', and a few days later, when my name cropped up, another boy said to her: 'You don't want to worry about him. All he cares about is football.' That was not quite true. Lucy and I were married in 1941, the best match of my life.

We were married, in fact, during my first leave after I had joined the RAF and been posted to Northern Ireland as part of a mobile radio unit. I was stationed in an old vicarage in Maghera, a lovely little town in the north, and on hearing of my Chelsea connections, short and modest though they were, a local publican put me in touch with Belfast Celtic. This was one of the most famous of all Irish clubs and for years, before the club was closed down in the late 1940s, it was managed by Elisha Scott, the old Liverpool and Northern Ireland goalkeeper who was something of a legend on Merseyside.

I played my first game for Belfast Celtic at Larne on the coast, and in that same side was a sixteen-year-old with no meat on him but more than his share of ability. His name was Charlie Tully and he, of course, became a darling of that other Celtic over in Glasgow. I turned out for Belfast Celtic regularly, rewarding days in talented company, and to ensure I was free every Saturday I made myself semi-proficient at cooking and got all the meals for the rest of the week. I was a humble LAC and privileges had to be earned, but it was worth the trouble.

There were a lot of gifted players about and I felt I was learning something new every time I took the field. By now, for example, I had played in front of three international goalkeepers – Vic Woodley of England and Johnny Jackson of Scotland, both with Chelsea, and Tommy Breen of Northern Ireland, with Belfast Celtic. Centre-half, I had also decided, was my best position. As a boy I fancied myself as an inside-forward, mainly because I was too small to play anywhere else, but then I grew a few inches, my options increased and the central defensive job seemed to suit my kind of ability and temperament. I enjoyed the responsibility and the view of the game it gave me.

I had one or two other short-term postings, including one on Goodwood racecourse, but eventually I found myself back in London and signed as a professional for Chelsea. I even renewed my old friendship with Wembley because in 1944 Chelsea reached the War Cup Final (League South), and our Alperton paper made much of the fact that I could become 'the first local footballer to play on the Wembley pitch in a first-class final game'. The truth is I did not play in any of the cup games on the way to the final and was only reserve for the big match itself – and 'reserve' in those days did not mean 'substitute'. I was merely a stand-in should anyone drop out; and no one did.

The Chelsea team was full of clever, experienced players such as Charlie Mitten, Joe Payne, who wrote himself an indelible line in the record books by once scoring ten goals in a League match, George Hardwick and John Harris. The occasion gave me a sniff of the big-time and I liked it.

The war took me to France with the Task Force but that was some weeks after the main landing, and as a member of a radar unit I was never at the heart of the real action. I played a few games for RAF Command – it takes more than a world war to stop football – but then I went down with acute appendicitis and was sent home. Our first child, Carole, had arrived by now and with the doodlebug bombs making a mess of London, Lucy and the babe moved north to stay with relatives in Bradford. I applied for a posting up there and was moved to Lissett, near Hull.

Immediately several clubs invited me to play for them. Bradford Park Avenue were among them, and for family as well as footballing reasons it seemed just the club I needed. The choice proved to be a good one.

Park Avenue's centre-half was Alan Brown who was later to have a great influence on me. He was in the police at the time and shortly afterwards he was moved to another area which meant the club were without a number five. They turned to me and I guested for them until the end of the war.

The war bit deeply into the careers of many players. Some lost five good years and were past their best when peace came, but others lost so much more, their lives or their health, and I was just grateful that it was over. I had made a lot of good friends and, above all, the war taught me how precious life is. I was twenty-three when it ended which meant I was starting the serious part of my playing career later than most, but I did not feel resentful. Some things are a great deal more important than football.

I dutifully returned to Chelsea, because I was still registered with them, but John Harris had established himself at centre-half and I could not see a place for me in their first team. I was able to tell Billy Birrell, however, that Bradford Park Avenue were keen to sign me, that my family was there and that I liked the club and the area. Mr Birrell immediately agreed to let me go and accepted the Yorkshire club's offer of £3,500 – the most they had ever paid for a player.

Football and cricket lived in happy harmony at Park Avenue. They shared a stand and big-hitters often managed to lift a drive over the top and onto the football pitch. I watched a lot of cricket and was lucky enough to see Don Bradman and his great Australian side of 1948 in action. Poor Bradford PA were to lose their place in the League in 1970, a loss which deeply saddened me, but in those years after the war they were a useful Second Division club, full of life and hope. The people of Bradford loved their sport, too. Many would watch football one week, Park Avenue or Bradford City, and then rugby league, Bradford Northern, the next. They liked to see the ball being whacked towards a corner-flag, no matter what code they were watching!

Fred Emery, an honest soul, was the manager at Park Avenue but he was hardly a 'manager' in the modern sense. He was also the club's secretary and only used to see us just before the kick-off on Saturdays. He left things to his trainer, first Harold Taylor and then Allan Ure, who prepared Jack London for his title fight with Freddie Mills in 1944. No one talked tactics: we worked things out as the game went along.

I played in several different positions to begin with, right-half, left-half and right-back as well as centre-half, and I did not really mind. I believed then, and still do, that experience in more than one role gives a player a greater appreciation of all that is happening around him. He knows more about the problems and responsibilities of others and how best he can help. The picture in his mind is a bigger one.

Park Avenue's centre-half when I joined them was Bob Danskin: he was also their skipper and a permanent fixture, a hard man who was always in over-drive. He had joined the club from Leeds in 1932 and a Bradford PA side without him was unthinkable. He bossed everybody on the field. It was 'Go there Ronnie' or 'Come here Ronnie' and, without doubt, his orders were a valuable part of my apprenticeship. Young players learnt their trade on the pitch from old hands like Bob. He was a bit of an ogre yet, oddly, he had skin like a baby: there was hardly a hair on it. He looked like a red lobster when he got out of the bath.

Len Shackleton was also a key member of the side, a player with lovely, almost unbelievable skills and tremendous confidence in himself. There was no one quite like our Len. He was a showman, a crowd-pleaser, a character who was larger than life. Some of the things he did had nothing to do with the winning and losing of a game, but the crowds loved him. He could even cut his foot under the ball so sharply that it would spin towards an opponent and then come back to him as if on a piece of string. Len also had an instinct for being in the right place at the right time, something which was often illustrated in practice when he liked to keep goal. He would stand between the posts and use everything except his hands to stop the ball. He would use a heel or thigh, his head or chest, a shoulder or his backside to stop shots, just to prove he was different. During a game this same instinct told him exactly the right moment to stick a leg out to intercept the ball. I used to play right-half behind him in the early days and he always liked to have me behind him for support; but when I was defending and under the whip I never got much help from Len. 'How about lending a hand?' I used to shout.

Shack lived in a little village up in the hills outside Bradford, but in 1946 he moved to Newcastle for a record fee of £13,000. As one of his neighbours, a little old lady, said to him when she heard news of the transfer: 'Ee, Leonard, you aren't half a lucky lad getting all that money for yourself.' Some players give their team all they have all the time, and they demand everything in return. Len Shackleton was always just himself.

I had the good luck to play with many other fine footballers during my three years at Park Avenue. Johnny Downie was a thinking inside-forward with a canny positional sense who eventually went to Manchester

United; Billy Elliott was a clever winger who later played for Burnley, Sunderland and England; while Jimmy Stephen, who like Shackleton had been a Bevin Boy in the mines, was a Scottish international full-back who made his name by blocking out Stanley Matthews during a war-time international. Tom 'Chick' Farr was our goalkeeper, a nice chap but an iron professional who had been with the club for more than ten years. When a goal was put past him everybody on our side 'disappeared'. His nearest team-mate got all the blame.

A lot of our goals were scored by Jack Gibbons, an England amateur international, who later moved to Brentford and became their manager. He chose me as his first signing. Later on our attack was led by George Ainsley who first awakened my ideas about coaching. The boot of his car was always full of footballs and when I asked him why he replied: 'I go coaching at the schools . . . and I take my own footballs because they don't have many.' He coached almost every afternoon and was even allowed to miss training to do so. Coaching then, remember, was a new science.

Bradford Park Avenue held their own in the Second Division during my time there, without ever setting it alight, but we were always a handful in Cup competition. One of our best moments came in the fourth round of the FA Cup in 1945–46. Each round in that first season after the war was played on a two-leg basis and Manchester City beat us 3-1 in the first leg at Park Avenue. Our cause seemed hopeless and, to rub things in, our coach ran into a blizzard right on top of the Pennines on our way to Maine Road for the second leg. The wind howled, the snow swirled, our coach struggled. Len Shackleton said to me: 'Let's turn back . . . we don't stand a chance anyway.' That seemed a fair assessment, but we pushed on and eventually got to the ground with less than twenty minutes to spare. Our trouble proved worthwhile. We won by eight goals to two on a pitch covered with pools of water – and Jack Gibbons scored six. The sight of the great Frank Swift picking the ball out of his net eight times is something I shall never forget. Everything went right for us. It was one of those days.

Our finest hour and a half, though, was in the 1947–48 season. Arsenal won the League championship by a clear seven points. They headed the First Division from start to finish, but in the third round of the Cup at Highbury we beat them by a goal to nil. I was Bradford PA's captain and, without any shadow of doubt, it was one of the most marvellous after-noons of my career. Our win was so unexpected but so honestly deserved that even now it seems unreal.

The occasion had all the proper trappings. We went into 'special' training before the game, which meant a slap-up lunch at a big local hotel and a glass or two of egg and sherry. I used to say to the club: 'If this is so good for us why don't we do it all year round and not just for Cup-ties?' But nobody was in the mood to listen to sane little questions like that. Cup fever is a form of insanity.

It was the first time most of us had played at Arsenal, and as our train slipped past Finsbury Park on its way into King's Cross we got a glimpse of the Highbury stands. The stadium looked even more impressive as we walked through the main doors into the famous marbled entrance hall. The place has style but, more than that, the lay-out is just about perfect. The administrative offices are all on one side, the well-equipped players' area on the other and the board-room, guest-rooms and bars are all upstairs. It is simple, functional and forever modern. To this day it is still a model football ground.

I think most of us felt that just playing at Highbury was an achievement. Victory was there, in our minds, but the thought of defeat did not frighten us. It would not be a disgrace to be beaten by the best side in the country, a side with players of the calibre of Joe Mercer, Archie Macaulay, Jimmy Logie, Leslie Compton and Reg Lewis. It would be an afternoon to relish whatever the result. My own family were there in strength, so were many of my friends from Alperton and so were fifteen hundred Bradford fans singing *On Ilkley Moor Bar Tat* at the top of their voices. Our simple intention was to play the game of our lives; and if it was necessary to lay down our lives, well, the cause was a good one. And that was why we won with a first half goal by Billy Elliott.

Victories like this cannot always be properly analysed because, basically, we had a go and it came off. Arsenal had a wonderful side but they did not really get up off the floor. They could play but we did not let them. We had several narrow escapes but if we had a bit of luck I think we deserved it. Perhaps there was a difference in attitude. Perhaps, in their hearts, Arsenal expected to win and took it for granted – but who can say? How can commitment be measured?

Results like this are part of the beauty of the FA Cup and I think at the end of the day – this one particular day – we were entitled to think we had won because we were the better side. I was happy with my own contribution and, with unforgivable immodesty, I quote from a morning-after report by Alan Hoby:

'Towering like a giant over the whole fantastic and fanatical game was the figure of Bradford's centre-half Greenwood. Every Bradford footballer was a hero. But Greenwood was the greatest of them all.'

How could I not cherish that?

Afterwards I sought out Joe Mercer because I had a message for him. George Stabb, a member of the Park Avenue staff, a former player with the club, had been in the army with Joe and asked me to pass on his regards. So, an opportunity for a last word between the captains, I went up to Joe and said: 'Mr Mercer' – I was formal because I had a lot of respect for players of his era – 'George Stabb sends his regards.' Joe, to put it mildly, was a bit curt and although I could understand why he wasn't in the best of moods I did not like his attitude. Years later I reminded Joe about the incident and he remembered it immediately. 'Yes', he said, 'I wasn't very pleased with myself about that. I was rude.' And to this day Joe apologizes almost every time I see him; which is good. That is what respect between professionals is all about.

We were given a tremendous reception when we got back to Bradford. The town gloried in our win, its folk shared our pride; and when, on the Monday, we were drawn to play away against a non-League side, Colchester, I think there were even dreams of Wembley. We had won at Arsenal, hadn't we? Victory at Colchester would surely be a formality despite the fact that they had also beaten a First Division club, Huddersfield, in the third round.

Colchester's player-manager was Ted Fenton who, years later, was to precede me as manager of West Ham. He was making his name and obviously enjoying playing the publicity game. Oysters, we read, were part of their magic formula – but that did not worry us, because we had our own little plan. Again we downed raw eggs and sherry, again we had a posh lunch. This time we were joined by Bruce Woodcock, the British heavyweight champion, who lived at Doncaster.

We seemed right on course again. I won't say we were cocky but I don't remember thinking about defeat. Lose we did, however, by 3-2, and we lost for exactly the reason Arsenal lost to us. Arsenal had been our big opponents, while we looked big to Colchester. We lifted our game at Highbury and Colchester raised theirs against us. We did not play badly but they had the edge. I realized afterwards how Joe Mercer had felt! The bubble had burst: but life went on.

Self-analysis is never easy for a player but, if pressed, I would say I saw myself as a centre-half in the mould of Stan Cullis and Neil Franklin. I am not pretending I was as good as that marvellous pair but I related to them because they were 'thinking' men. I was not a battling centre-half although I was always ready to tackle hard: the ability to mix it is often essential. Basically, though, I avoided contact just for the sake of it. I was convinced there was more than one way of winning possession and was only hard when there was no alternative. I was more concerned with the ball than with my opponents. I tried to read the game intelligently, holding back to mark space rather than a man and to win the ball by thinking first and moving first. My game was all about anticipation, whether the ball was on the ground or in the air. I was very single-minded and drove myself hard. I knew what I wanted and gave everything.

This is why I thought so highly of Cullis and Franklin. Billy Birrell once sent me just to watch Cullis play. 'You'll never be as good as Stan so don't attempt to do what he does', he said. 'But look at his game as a whole and learn from him. Don't watch him as a spectator but as a student.' Cullis's grasp of the game was superb yet he always seemed to be learning and improving. It was the same with Franklin, who in my opinion was everything a centre-half should be: quick, firm, perceptive, constructive and full of authority. I once made a special journey from Bradford to Goodison Park to see Franklin play for England against Ireland . . . for the full ninety minutes I watched him and him alone. Neil went to Bogota in Columbia for a while, enticed by easy unofficial money, and when he returned he was suspended; but then he joined Hull and he has told me of the problems he faced there. 'Every time I put my foot on the ball in our penalty area the whole row of Hull directors wet themselves' he said. His coolness in critical areas was something they could not understand. It frightened them. But he had his own standards and never compromised. This is why I admired him so much and why I chose to play the same sort of game.

I cannot pretend life was always perfect at Bradford. It was always a bit of a battle at Park Avenue. Very few people there tried to lift their colleagues' spirit or confidence and it was a case of 'if you don't do it you're out'. In my early days there I used to go home and say to Lucy: 'I'll show them. I'll become captain of this club.' I managed that, and we had moments of success and some good times, but when the chance came to join Brentford and return to London just before the transfer deadline in March 1949 I took it gladly. Jack Gibbons, who had moved from Bradford to Brentford as a player eighteen months before, was now the West London club's manager and I was his first signing, as I have mentioned. He knew I was not very happy at Park Avenue and he signed me to replace Jack Chisholm who had gone to Sheffield United. The fee was around £9,000.

Brentford were good for me; and I like to think I did my bit in return. I had three wonderful years at Griffin Park and to this day I have a great affection for the club. I enjoyed the atmosphere of the ground, the players and their approach to the game, and their crowd, with whom I always got on well. I was particularly lucky in meeting Malcolm

McDonald, the club's player-coach, a Glaswegian who had learnt the game with Celtic during the 1930s. He had played in just about every position for them and when, later, we went north to play Celtic in a friendly every last man in a crowd of thirty thousand remembered him and gave him a presidential reception. He was that sort of person.

Malcy thought a great deal about football, in much the way Billy Birrell did, and he quickly began to restore some of the confidence I had lost in my latter days at Bradford. He had a lot of ability and self-belief himself and more than once I saw him put his foot on the ball on his own goal-line. Malcy would say to me: 'Look Ronnie, if you want to do something and you've got the confidence, then do it. If you haven't, dôn't! It's your judgement that matters.' I could feel myself responding.

I settled down to play some consistent football in a better than average Second Division side and, before long, I was made captain. Into the team at that point came young Jimmy Hill, a forceful wing-half who had spent a short time with Reading after leaving the army. Brentford were not afraid to give youth a fling. They had brought on a lot of good youngsters and Jimmy was given an early chance which he snapped up. He established himself in the side in front of one or two seniors. I immediately found another job for him as well. 'You're an intelligent lad' I said to him. 'You can be the Players' Union representative and collect the subs. Nobody else wants the job!' It is now a matter of history, of course, that Jimmy became chairman of the union – later the Professional Footballers' Association – and successfully led the campaign for the abolition of the maximum wage and the old retain-and-transfer system.

There seemed to be great quality in almost every side we faced. Peter Doherty, that great Irishman, was player-manager of Doncaster, a man who led by example, full of fire and energy, demanding a lot from his players but giving even more himself. He was never out of tempo with a game because he always set the tempo himself. Raich Carter was player-manager of Hull, again a great inside-forward who was coming to the end of his playing days. He led his side commandingly but with stealth, and the quality I remember most about silver-haired Raich was his anticipation. Whenever I went up for the ball I was always aware he was trying to decide where I was going to put it. He seemed to guess correctly about nine times out of ten and as I went for every ball I had to think: 'Where is the ------ now?' Raich came to Brentford once when the pitch was in a terrible mess and the coin, when we spun it before the start, stuck edgeways in the mud. We tried again and this time it fell flat. 'That's how I'm going to be in a couple of minutes' he said. We had a wing-half, Tony Harper, who was a celebrated hard man.

The pitch at Griffin Park was a notorious mud-heap, and there were times when the only visible grass was on the wings and along the goal-lines. But some players could play in any conditions, or at least make the best of them, and Tom Finney of Preston was one of them. Tom had everything, he was a brilliant individualist but also an intelligent and adaptable team-man who could play on either wing or in the middle. He had a full deck of cards and on one occasion at boggy Brentford he used the lot. At the end of the game twenty-one players were covered in mud. The exception was Tom Finney, who looked spotless. He never left our little fringe of grass – and he murdered us!

An important day for me, for reasons that had nothing to do with football, was 9 February 1951. I left the ground with Johnny Paton after training and in the minutes between changing buses at Ealing Broadway I 'phoned the Perivale Maternity Hospital at Greenford. Yes . . . congratulations . . . a son. Neil had arrived. Named after Neil Franklin.

My third and last full season at Brentford was 1951–52. We hit such consistent form from the start that coming up to Christmas we were in the frame at the top of Division Two with one of the best defensive records in the League. I was playing like a modern sweeper and the system, which we had worked out for ourselves, suited us perfectly. But at Christmas we lost 2-1 to Southampton, our first home defeat, and after the game Jack Gibbons came storming into the dressing-room and – immortal phrase – 'blew his top'. Everything we were doing was suddenly wrong, and that included the way our defence played.

'Hang on a minute' I said. 'We've been playing this way all season and I can't remember anyone complaining before. We've lost one game. All right! But one defeat doesn't make it a bad system or us a bad side.'

A blistering row developed and in the heat of the moment some damaging things were said on both sides. I lost my temper and started charging about, and I even shouted: 'That's it . . . I'm going to ask for a transfer.'

The criticism mattered to me deeply because I believed in what we were doing. I suppose I was a bit idealistic, perhaps I was even the sort some managers might call a trouble-maker, but I cared about our side and what we were achieving. It was a pity that by this time Malcolm McDonald had left us to become manager of Kilmarnock because I am sure he would have sorted things out. But it seemed ludicrous to me that we should have to take such a broadside for one defeat after so much success.

The story leaked out – that I had said the manager's attitude was 'bloody ridiculous' and that I'd asked for a transfer – but all the players seemed with me. 'We're behind you, Ron, don't worry' they said.

A board meeting was called and I was invited to attend and say my piece, along with any of the other players who wanted to support me. But when the moment came only one man stood up to be counted. Only one member of the entire Brentford staff walked beside me into the boardroom. That man was Jimmy Hill. It was the start of a close and enduring friendship. Jimmy has always known that if he is in trouble he can call on me. I will not have a bad word said about him. He has a streak of independence which means he will always be his own man. It is one of the reasons he has achieved so much. He can be counted upon when it matters.

I understood well enough why the other Brentford players did not support me. There were a lot of footballers around in those days who would have been only too willing to take their places. They had their living to earn and they were looking after themselves. That is perfectly fair. I simply felt that if principles mattered at all, then I had to follow mine all the way. I could have been wrong, but my belief in my case was absolute. Life frequently teaches lessons the hard way but often you don't realize at the time time that you are being taught something.

The boardroom at Brentford in those days was not very big but it was panelled and rather dignified. As Jimmy and I entered, we found the directors sitting solemnly round a table. I had my say, in detail, and so did Jimmy, more briefly, but it was an argument we were never going to win. The board obviously had to back their manager. Our transfer requests were granted.

Jimmy went to town with the press: he couldn't resist it. I think it was then that he started learning about the media and the way stories are handled. I was eventually asked to stay but my immediate answer was a question: 'What about Jim?' 'He's gone overboard in the press', said Jack Gibbons. 'We insist he goes.' Jimmy told me that he was still keen to leave anyway, and shortly afterwards he was transferred to Fulham. I think they were right for each other. It was a good marriage.

Several clubs, among them Wolverhampton Wanderers, were reported to be interested in me but I agreed to settle my differences with Brentford because I cared about the club. I believed it had a good future and yet, ironically, there are still Brentford supporters about who insist that from then onwards things started going wrong at Griffin Park. Two seasons later Brentford were relegated. I cannot believe a couple of transfer requests influenced destiny to that degree; but, if it is true, it is a cross I must bear.

During this uneasy period Tommy Lawton joined Brentford, a

signing which gave the club a tremendous lift. Here was one of the great men of football, a centre-forward who had devastated defences and delighted crowds with England, Burnley, Everton, Chelsea and Notts County. He was in his early thirties then, but still a marvellous player, and I admit with pride that I was instrumental in getting him to Griffin Park.

Brentford were playing Notts County at Meadow Lane one day and Tommy, an old friend, said to me quite casually: 'I'm a bit fed up here. They might be putting me on the list.' I pricked up my ears and after the game reported what he'd said to Jack Gibbons. His reply, though, was unenthusiastic: 'I don't think we're interested.' But soon after I mentioned Lawton's words to a Brentford director, just in conversation, and his response was very different. The board decided to go for Lawton. The negotiations were lengthy but in the end everybody met at a hotel, shut the door and got down to business. Brentford paid more than they had anticipated but the move, when it happened, received tremendous publicity. Lawton was always big news.

Tom was just Tom, flamboyant, wonderfully talented, a honey-pot for the media. He was everybody's idea of what a centre-forward should be. He looked good and he was good. Billy Birrell told me that one of the first things he noticed about Lawton was that when the ball was played to him there was always a buzz of expectancy from the crowd. He was full of confidence; in his early days, indeed, he was almost too cocky. I like the pre-war story of how he bounced into the Everton dressing-room just after he had been picked for England for the first time. 'Hey, isn't anyone going to congratulate me?' he asked. Ted Sagar, the Everton goalkeeper, said quietly: 'Look son, just stand over there by that wall.' Sagar then turned to the rest of the Everton team. 'Stand up lads', he said, 'and tell us how many caps you've got'. One by one they stepped forward: Joe Mercer of England (who joined Arsenal after the war), T. G. Jones of Wales, Alex Stevenson of Ireland, Torry Gillick of Scotland, Wally Boyes of England . . . the total of caps mounted like a cricket score. They finished and Sagar turned back to Lawton. 'And you've got bloody *one*?' he asked.

Tommy was a beautiful striker of the ball, always hard and flat, and a man who would lay the ball off sweetly, then turn away, big and powerful, and go at the defence shouting for the return. But it was in the air that he was unbeatable – he seemed to climb and then hover. An illustration: he was playing for Brentford against Blackburn once when the ball was played up to him in the air. His left-winger moved into position but, as Tommy jumped, he saw Ron Suart, the Blackburn right-back who later became manager of Blackpool, nipping across to intercept. And with the ball still on its way Tommy seemed to hang, adjust, allow the ball to go on just a little bit further – and then nod it *inside* Suart for our winger to move onto. Tommy had made his decision and the corresponding adjustment after he had jumped!

I know from hard experience that Tommy was a difficult man to pin down. It was a hopeless exercise trying to beat him in the air so I always attempted to stay goalside of him, never more than a yard or two away, and do my best to intercept. But I found him a delight to play with because he had such a clever football brain and took up such intelligent positions. He was always easy to find. Tommy happily accepted that I was captain but a season later, after I had moved on to Chelsea, he became Brentford's player-manager before finishing his League career with one more tilt at the big-time with Arsenal. What wouldn't England give now for another Tommy Lawton!

I gained a spot of international recognition myself in my last full season with Brentford. The Bogota affair had ended Neil Franklin's career at the top and the England centre-half spot was there to be won. Several papers said I had a good chance of getting the job and, in fact, Walter Winterbottom, the England manager, came to watch me at Brentford. The trouble was he saw us beaten by Sheffield Wednesday for whom big Derek Dooley scored a hat-trick. The ball went into the net off his knees, even his backside – anything rather than his head or feet. I had already played for various FA representative sides but, in the end, my major honour was to be selected as England's captain for a 'B' international against Holland in the Olympic Stadium in Amsterdam.

Holland put out their best side against us because in those days, in the early 1950s, they were not considered strong enough to warrant a full international. Their game was in a transitional stage, they were just moving towards professionalism, and no one imagined that only twenty years later Holland would be sending out some of the best sides in the world both at international and club level. They were full of ideas even then, however, and their national side often played English clubs to help their development. Brentford played them twice and this was my introduction to continental football. I liked what I saw. They had some fine players and their style of play was thoughtful and progressive.

That international honour in Amsterdam in the spring of 1952 meant a great deal to me. Pulling on a white England shirt for the first time was something I will never forget. It was a moment of deep fulfilment. We won the game squarely by a goal to nil, with little Tommy Harmer of Tottenham full of bright ideas, but as Bernard Joy, the old Arsenal defender and a respected reporter for the London *Evening Standard*, said to me afterwards: 'It was a good performance but the reports won't be much because it was such a cold, miserable day!'

I think I would have given anything to win a full cap for England, but it was not to be. I do believe I came very near it, though, which to me is an achievement in itself. In later years I used to say to Walter Winterbottom: 'You didn't give me a cap . . . but I earned this' – and I would point to my FA coaching badge.

It was while I was at Brentford, in fact, that my interest in coaching became a passion. We travelled everywhere by train at the time and there would always be two quite separate groups of players, each in a different compartment. In one they played cards and in the other they talked football. Jimmy Hill and I were always in the latter, and we listened to Ted Gaskell, our goalkeeper, and Jackie Goodwin, our outside-right, talking with tremendous enthusiasm about the courses they had attended. They said coaches like Walter Winterbottom, George Smith, Alan Brown, Syd Cann and, an old colleague, George Ainsley, had opened their eyes. One or two of us became sold on the idea and we applied to attend the summer coaching course at Lilleshall, the first to be held in that splendid, rambling old mansion in Shropshire. What an exciting, enlightening week it was.

Walter and his coaches – Walter above all – gripped us with their ideas. They taught us how to teach but, more than that, they seemed to take us right inside the game. There were new subtleties to think about, new dimensions to work on, new experiments to be tried. Theory and practice were always nicely balanced and everything was geared to getting the best out of individuals and teams.

I was very nervous to begin with and when I was called out to take my first session George Ainsley halted me after a few minutes. 'Would you stop saying "please" all the time' he said. Players with big international reputations sometimes froze when their moment came to confront the class. How times change! In those days everyone could play but couldn't talk . . . now they can all talk but can't play. That is unfair to many, I know, but it contains a grain of truth.

Jimmy Hill, Johnny Paton and myself, the three Brentford players on the course, came to be known as 'The Three Musketeers'. We wore smart blue tracksuits, by kind permission of our club, and we shared a room on the first floor at the top of the baronial staircase. We would stay awake until three o'clock in the morning, taking imaginary coaching sessions, and more than once there was a loud bang on the door followed by a blunt suggestion from one of the staff that we got some sleep. Our enthusiasm was endless, the touch-paper had been well and truly lit, and at the end of the week I remember wishing the course could go on for ever.

My wife, Lucy, spotted something different in me the moment I got home. 'You've changed', she said. 'You've come alight!'

9

The Bridge and the Cottage

I was thirty years old before I played First Division football but the challenge when it came was irresistible. My old club, Chelsea, gave me the chance, in October, 1952, and in a way it seemed my past, present and future had suddenly all come together.

Ted Drake was Chelsea's new manager. He had moved from Reading to take over from Billy Birrell, who had retired by choice – and not many managers finish in that happy way. Drake, a former England centre-forward and an Arsenal hero in the 1930s, a strong, fearless sort of chap, arrived at the Bridge like a breath of fresh air. The time was right for change.

Drake moved straight into the market place. His first signing was Johnny McNichol, the Brighton inside-forward, and I was his second. They paid Brentford the equivalent of £16,000 for me – a part-exchange deal involving Seamus 'Jimmy' D'Arcy – which was a lot of money for someone my age. The transaction pleased both clubs and it certainly delighted me, because in a sense I felt I was coming home. Chelsea was where my career had begun and now, after a little re-routing caused by the war, I had a chance to show what I could do at the highest level.

I went straight into the League side and really relished the whole experience. Playing at Stamford Bridge had always given me a lift as a lad and I found it still did. The pitch was a good one with quite a crown on it, the atmosphere was intoxicating when the crowd was big (it usually was in those days) and I felt king of all I surveyed. The Chelsea fans accepted me immediately and after one interception, a hook down followed by a push out of defence, a paper reported I got the 'longest ovation' ever given to a player at Chelsea. I also found that First Division football posed no unexpected problems; if anything, I felt it gave me more time to do things.

There was, however, no sort of social scene at the club. Players turned up, trained or played, and that was that. They were left very much to themselves although, oddly, I made a lot of friends among the fans. Our home was at Northolt, overlooking the old racecourse, and I travelled to Stamford Bridge by train; and while I was travelling I got to know many supporters. Players were ordinary members of the community then and were known as individuals. The fans identified with them because they felt they belonged to the same world. There was a lot of banter and the friendships struck were easy and unforced. This is one of today's problems. The modern player drives to the ground in his expensive car, does his job and then drives away to his expensive home. He has little in common with the chap on the terrace.

There was a gap of another kind at Stamford Bridge. The offices and the players' quarters seemed divorced. The distance between them made them separate branches of the same club. And, while I liked the stadium, I was always conscious of the greyhound track around the pitch. Sometimes in mid-week footballers and greyhounds would find themselves practising together – and we would have to stop because we were distracting the dogs! I never watched a greyhound meeting in all the time I was there.

Nothing in football can be taken for granted and things went wrong for me for a while after a game against West Bromwich Albion. It started with a single incident. The ball came down the right side of our half and Ronnie Allen, a super player, very talented, very mobile, moved towards it. I stuck close to him and as Ronnie went for the ball I moved to go in front of him. My game was all about interception and I thought my timing was right. But Ronnie felt me alongside him, eased me round with his backside, let the ball run and was gone. His shot went near to scoring and at half-time Ted Drake asked me what I'd been doing.

'I was trying to intercept' I replied.

'You can't do that', said Ted.

To this I replied: 'It's what I've been doing all my life and I presumed that's what you'd bought me for.'

'I say you can't do that', Ted went on.

'Oh yes I can', I answered, 'but what I know now is that I can't do it against Ronnie Allen. But it'll work against others.'

Eventually I was to learn that those precious ten minutes of the half-time interval should never be wasted by arguing. Argue . . . and they're gone. Every second should be used, everything said should be constructive or uplifting.

The outcome of this disagreement with Ted was that I was left out of the side for the next game. Results were indifferent and things looked ominous for me. I was brought back for the odd game or two but I wasn't a regular, and when Plymouth Argyle made an offer for me early the following season I felt it might be best for all concerned if I left. Lucy and I went down to Plymouth and had a long chat with their manager, an engaging chap called Jimmy Rae. We liked what we saw but one of the things which bothered me was the future of my coaching interests. I was chief coach for Middlesex FA, I was coaching Oxford University and I had even got all the Chelsea players to go on courses. I asked what the coaching situation was like in Plymouth and was told: 'It hasn't really taken off down here, but if someone like you came down you could get it all organized.' Plymouth made me a very good offer and I said I would think about it.

I went straight back to Stamford Bridge to have a word with Ted Drake, but the only person around was Mrs Metcalfe who had been Billy Birrell's secretary in my early days at the club. She was a dear old soul, a real stalwart of the club, and she asked if she could help.

'Well, I've got this offer from Plymouth', I said, 'but I know Jack Saunders is injured and I'm wondering who'll be at centre-half this weekend.'

'I don't know about that', said Mrs Metcalfe.

'I've got a feeling that if I stay here I'll be in' I went on. 'So could you ring Plymouth, thank them very much for their interest and tell them I've decided against joining them. I'm going to take a chance.'

My hunch was right. I was picked for the following Saturday's match against Burnley and I have never been more determined in my life to do well. I did have a good game, too, but at a cost. Burnley's centre-forward was big Bill Holden and during the game he whacked my mouth so hard with his elbow that one of my teeth was virtually removed. It just hung onto my gum and there was blood all over the place. But I was so determined that I carried on playing, and although I had to go to hospital immediately afterwards I had made my point. I kept my place in the side and the next three centre-forwards I faced – Nat Lofthouse of Bolton, Charlie Wayman of Preston and Jackie Milburn of Newcastle, a formidable trio – scored only one goal between them. I played for the rest of the season despite managing a spectacular 'own goal' that got us knocked out of the FA Cup, by West Bromwich of all teams.

It was a third-round tie, at the Hawthorns, and we played so well we should have won easing up. But the goals would not come and, with six or seven minutes left, a long ball was pumped towards our goal – once again it was Ron Greenwood versus Ronnie Allen. It was a high, difficult ball and I knew I had to get it. I did, too, a long way above Allen and almost on the edge of the penalty area, but the ball hit the top left side of my forehead and spun like a bullet onto the underside of the bar and then into the net. I sunk to my knees and beat the ground with my fists; in the dressing-room afterwards I felt heartbroken. I actually shed a tear or two, silly I know, but they were tears of self-reproach rather than self-pity. It was a game we should have won but a fluke had beaten us. We were out of the Cup.

Ted Drake called us together on the Monday and I must admit I was apprehensive. But Ted simply smiled and said he was sorry about the result. 'I thought you all played well and it's no disgrace to be beaten by a side like Albion, especially by a goal that was just one of those things. No problems . . .' He then announced that for the weekend of the fourth round we would be going to Switzerland to play in Zürich and Berne, and that we had been selected to play a series of exhibition matches in America and Canada at the end of the season. That was good management.

West Bromwich went on to win the Cup under Vic Buckingham and, in the years since, I've often said to Ronnie Allen and the rest of his team that they only made it with my help. The trouble is they agree! Albion came near to completing the League and Cup double that season, finishing second to Wolves in the League, and Chelsea, no doubt, were one of the reasons they didn't make it. Albion came to Stamford Bridge late in the season and we beat them five-nil. We had a score to settle and for ninety minutes there was only one side in it.

Chelsea finished eighth, the club's highest spot for nearly twenty years. We went unbeaten for fourteen games at one stage and we were the most successful of all the London clubs. Ted Drake had a lot to do with it. He was an honest, sincere man who was good at lifting morale. He was hard and aggressive, he set his sights high and he demanded the best: that sort of attitude is contagious.

So ended a curious season for me – a season of early promise, followed by disappointment and frustration, and finally a good deal of satisfaction. I won a place in England's party of forty for the 1954 World Cup in Switzerland, but in the end I missed the finals as well as the warm-up games in Yugoslavia and Hungary. Hungary had beaten England by 6-3 at Wembley the previous November – a historic game I shall return to with relish in a later chapter – and in Budapest they looked even better: Hungary 7, England 1.

It mattered a great deal to me to be included in England's forty. It was important to my self-respect, and I felt it was an achievement. Although I was eventually one of those left behind I was in good company. Among the others who did not quite make it were the young Duncan Edwards, Allenby Chilton and my Chelsea team-mate, Roy Bentley. I was disappointed but not surprised. I always remembered my own feelings as a player when, as England's team manager many years later, I had to tell someone he was being left out of a team or a squad.

The following season, 1954–55, was the best in Chelsea's history. The club won the championship in its Golden Jubilee year and the fact that fifty-two points were enough is neither here nor there. There was no outstanding side in the First Division and Chelsea finished in front because they kept their heads, played to their strengths and – well shaken and stirred by Ted Drake – were simply more consistent than any other team. By now he had signed a couple of young players, Stan Wicks from Reading and Peter Sillett from Southampton, both defenders of obvious promise, and John Harris and I knew only too well that we were the players threatened. We accepted this because we were in our early thirties and change is then inevitable. But not yet, we decided, and not without a fight.

It was a good side, no question. Roy Bentley, a centre-forward with a delicate touch but also a remarkably consistent goal-scorer, led the front line well. Johnny McNichol was a splendid inside-forward, a typical ball-playing Scot and the first man I saw really curve shots and passes with the outside of his foot. He was a player who made things happen and was famous for his 'Bovril ball' – a long pass hit towards a Bovril advertisement in one of the corners. Eric Parsons, fleet of foot on the wing, always used to chase it: we called him 'Rabbit' because he showed the soles of his boots as he ran. Ken Armstrong, at right-half, was a wonderful club man, a player you could count on, and so, of course, was John Harris at full-back. John was dedicated to football, thoughtful and intelligent but made of steel.

We had some tremendous games but none better than our home match with Manchester United – the pre-Munich United. The result: Chelsea 5, Manchester United 6. The match was breathtaking to play in: it must have been sensational to watch. At one stage we were 2-5 down. Eight goals were scored in half-an-hour, and I remember one above all, the one scored by Tommy Taylor, a centre-forward in a million and a friend of mine from our early days in Yorkshire. Johnny Berry took a corner for United and, as it came across, Tommy just soared into the air with me somewhere beneath him. As I started to fall I could see him heading the ball into the net like a cannonball; and, as I hit the ground, almost before I made contact, I remember looking up at him and saying: 'Tommy, what a great goal'. It was so good you just had to admire it!

Ted Drake was waiting as we got back to the dressing-room. 'What are you doing?' he asked me.

'Well . . .' I began.

'Don't give me that', said Ted. 'Stand on his toes so he can't get off the ground.'

After the game Ted went into his office and took a telephone call from his chief scout, Jimmy Thompson, who had been watching a junior game. Ted, bubbling with excitement, said: 'Jim, you've just missed the greatest game of all time.'

'Blow the game', replied Jimmy. 'I've just been watching the greatest player you'll ever see in your life. A little chap called Jimmy Greaves.' Jimmy Thompson, a marvellous scout, had made his biggest find.

Everything went right for me in the first half of the season, but then we went to play Arsenal at Highbury on Christmas morning and they beat us 1–0 with a goal by Tommy Lawton who by now had left Brentford and was enjoying his last fling in the First Division. It was a simple, classic goal: a centre by Wally Barnes and a touch-in at the near post from Lawton. I knew Chelsea had been waiting for a chance to bring Stan Wicks into the side and I said to Tommy afterwards: 'I don't think I'll be seeing you for the return on Boxing Day. I think I'll be out.' Tommy smiled and said: 'I'll tell you what. If Stan Wicks plays I'll murder him. Don't worry, I'll get you back in.' What happened, in fact, was that Wicks hardly gave Lawton a kick, the result was a 1–1 draw, young Stan kept his place and Chelsea went on to win the championship.

I had played twenty-one League games, however, and I got my championship medal. But a month or so after Wicks replaced me Fulham made an offer for me and Ted Drake, always honest, advised me to accept. 'Obviously your future's not here now' he said. I was thirty-three and I realized this was my last major chance. Chelsea did not need me any more: Fulham wanted me. They were convincing reasons for a change. I was sorry to leave Chelsea because they had always looked after me and, at the end of the season, they invited me to all the championship celebrations, something I appreciated enormously.

I was very enthusiastic about my move to Fulham and the fact that I was dropping into the Second Division did not concern me. They made me captain immediately and I looked forward to playing with a talented bunch of chaps. The forward line, for example, was Arthur Stevens, Bobby Robson, Bedford Jezzard, Johnny Haynes and Charlie Mitten. That was a line with class and, with my old friend Jimmy Hill also in the side, the only future I could see was a bright one.

How could I have been so wrong? I am sorry to have to say this but the two years I spent with Fulham were among the most distressing and traumatic of my whole career. 'Oh Lord', I remember thinking later, 'I'm not going to end up like this, am I?' There was no discipline at all at Craven Cottage. The players were excellent but the set-up was abysmal. Everything was horribly lax and sloppy.

Fulham deserved much better because, basically, it was a smashing little club. It was friendly and homely and full of good humour. The cottage sat snugly in one corner of the ground and the tips of white sails on the Thames peaked over the back. Frank Osborne, the old Spurs centre-forward, was joint manager and secretary and a nicer chap you could not meet. He had been there years and loved nothing more than a few jokes and a game of billiards with the lads. But he did not have any real control over the team, over its training and tactics, and I often wondered who actually picked the side. Frank rarely watched a game because of some superstition he had. He would shut himself up in his office and listen to the crowd.

Frank Osborne was a character all right. Jimmy Hill tells the story of a Christmas Fulham spent down at the Mumbles before a game with Swansea. They were hoping for some peace and quiet but there was a a noisy party down below which seemed to go on for ages; and even when it finished the staff made a clatter putting away the tables and chairs. Frank stormed downstairs and started picking up chairs and throwing them all over the place. 'If you're going to make a noise, then make a noise', he shouted at them.

Being a lovely chap, however, is not high among the qualities needed to run a professional football club. I went in one morning and found the training schedule for the day read like this: 'Five laps . . . four laps . . . three laps . . . two laps . . . one lap . . . five-a-side.' It was ridiculous.

Even the lapping was often a farce. We did all our training at the ground itself and because the outside track was a bit hard we used to run around the edge of the pitch. We did our best to save the grass by running outside the corner flags and behind the goals, and the front pack, which I led, always ran the full distance. But the majority of the players behind would take bigger and bigger short cuts until eventually they were just running around the centre-circle! I was captain but I was not in charge of training. I was furious because it indicated so clearly everyone's attitude of mind.

It became increasingly obvious that something would have to be done and eventually they decided to appoint a team manager. Frank Osborne called me into his office and with him was Mr Deans, the club chairman. Frank said: 'We're looking for a manager and they tell me you've got ambitions.'

I was surprised; the idea was right out of the blue. 'Yes, I'd be interested', I said, but made an instant decision I have never regretted. 'I'd take the job on one condition', I continued. 'And that is that you sack the staff.'

Frank asked: 'Can I stay?'

And I laughingly replied: 'Yes, you can stay . . . you're okay.'

Frank and Mr Deans looked at each other. They ummed and aaahed. Then, together, they said: 'All right . . .' I meant nothing, of course, and that was the end of the conversation.

I walked out into the corridor and there was Vic Buckingham, the manager of West Bromwich Albion, who had come down to sign Bobby Robson. 'Hello son, how are you?' he asked. 'Fine' I answered. He then went into Frank Osborne's office and shut the door. I knew the walls of the office were paper-thin and I could not resist pausing a moment. 'That cheeky bugger who has just left', I heard Frank say, 'he wants to manage us – on conditions'. And then I heard Vic say: 'Well, why don't you give him a chance? Let him have a go.'

But nothing more was said to me and not so long afterwards we heard our new manager was to be Dugald Livingstone who had been in charge of the Belgian national team. He was a dry old stick who did not say a lot but he was as honest as the day is long. He managed Belgium when they held England to a 4-4 draw in the World Cup in Basle, after being 2-1 down at half-time, and – always after knowledge – I asked him what he had said to his players during the interval. 'Well, Ronnie lad' he said, 'I went down to the dressing-room but they were all jabbering away and I couldn't understand a blessed thing they were saying. So I just went into a corner and had a cup of tea.'

I have never regretted my decision about the Fulham job, because if I had taken it without making conditions I believe I may never have progressed or achieved anything. So much was against the manager at Fulham in those days. Beddy Jezzard had a go but eventually went to run a pub, Johnny Haynes tried but then went to South Africa, and even Bobby Robson took his turn. I don't think he regards it as one of the high spots of his career, but he learnt from it and went on to much more distinguished things with Ipswich and England. I do not think Fulham were really knocked into shape until Alec Stock went there in the 1970s.

It is surprising that Fulham achieved anything on the field but they did because of the quality of their players. They were capable of beating almost anyone on their day. We scored five against Barnsley early in my first full season there, for example, and all we did was let them come at us, pick off the ball and give it to Haynes who set things up for Jezzard, Robson and Mitten. It was almost too simple. But there were days when Fulham could only blame themselves for being beaten. They might have achieved so much.

Johnny Haynes was a brilliant player, an inside-forward of the old school, an expert passer of the ball. I played behind him regularly but I was constantly surprised by his vision. Sometimes I would not spot his target until the ball found its man. Nothing would seem on but he would turn sharply on the ball and slant one of those long passes of his through a gap and into space for a colleague to run on to. But there was a touch of inflexibility about him and, come what may, the angled ball inside the full-back was never far from his mind. Opponents who read him right could cut his effectiveness by fifty per cent.

Johnny was an enigma, a strange lad. I once said to our long-serving full-back, Joe Bacuzzi: 'Johnny's a problem because he's always had his own way. You old pros should have got him into shape when he was younger.' But Joe told me: 'We weren't allowed near him. He was protected.' Haynes had been a prodigy who made his own rules as he went along. He was always at the centre of everything. Others had to adapt to him and he tended to murder team-mates who liked the ball at their feet. Charlie Mitten was a winger of this type and he and Johnny never got on. Johnny *always* put the ball into space, which was why he liked Tosh Chamberlain outside him. Tosh, a delicious character, would run for ever. Tosh came into the side during my latter days at Fulham and struck up a rapport not only with Haynes but with Tommy Trinder, one of the country's top comedians who was to be chairman of the club for many years. They would carry on a running argument, Tosh on the pitch, Tommy in the stand.

Haynes was the ring-master, however, and no one set higher standards. That meant he was difficult to live with. A referee even came marching up to me in a game at Lincoln and warned me that if I did not stop Haynes swearing at him he would be sent off. 'Ref', I said, 'he's not swearing at you. He's not even swearing at the opposition. He's swearing at his own team-mates!' It was an attitude that helped Haynes become captain of England.

Beddy Jezzard was a first-class centre-forward, quick of mind and very sharp in the box, and in fact he was described by some papers as England's 'secret weapon' for the game against Hungary in Budapest in 1954. But as Hungary scored seven he did not have a chance to do himself justice. Charlie Mitten had given his best days to Manchester United but, although his pace had lost its edge, his ability and experience were always a threat.

Bobby Robson was just a youngster then, very talented and very single-minded, an orthodox inside-forward who usually left his mark on a game. Neither of us had the remotest idea we would both manage England one day but as I've said to him since: 'Don't forget I played with you. I'm not that old!' Jimmy Hill was another of Fulham's up-and-coming players, an angular, thrustful player who had some fine moments. He covered a lot of ground, especially after he scored a goal! No one could catch him: no one could even get near him.

Jimmy Langley, our left-back, a hard, dependable man-to-man marker, was also to play for England, while just coming onto the scene were George Cohen, who was to play at right-back in the England side that won the World Cup in 1966, and Alan Mullery, who played in the World Cup finals in Mexico four years later. George, a schoolboy then, would run round the track at lunchtimes, and Alan would travel up with me on the trolley-bus from Hammersmith.

Tom Wilson, an irregular at full-back and a good friend of mine, became chairman of a big London firm of chartered surveyors. I was able to tell him in later years that his name was 'hated' at West Ham. The reason, simply, is that while I was manager at Upton Park I always held him up as an example of what a professional footballer could achieve if he used his time and money wisely.

Other Fulham players of the time had other kinds of success. Roy Dwight helped Nottingham Forest win the FA Cup in 1959, scoring a goal but then breaking a leg, and Tony Barton, another winger, managed Aston Villa to European Cup success in 1982.

It is impossible to say why so many ultimately successful men wore the white shirt of Fulham, or why the club produced so many colourful characters or earned itself so much affection. Perhaps the answer is in its happy spot beside the Thames or in the old history of the place. But if the club was exhilarating in one sense, it was endlessly frustrating in another. I could see the club was not going anywhere, and this is not merely hindsight – I felt it very strongly at the time. I vowed that many of the things which went on at Fulham would not happen if ever I got hold of a club.

In any case I was now beginning to feel my useful playing days were over. I had kept my sign-writing business going and there were moments when only this outside interest kept me sane. It gave me an extra purpose as well as extra income, and it occupied my mind. I had no particular regrets about hanging up my boots because my innings had been a good one. I had played regularly for Bradford, Brentford, Chelsea and Fulham, won a championship medal, gained some international recognition and learnt a bit about the game. I did not have any money problems and, indeed, I did not draw money week by week from the FA for all the coaching I did. I drew it out in one lump sum and spent it on holiday.

I captained every club I played for, with the exception of Chelsea, and made an army of friends in the game although I did not often mix with the other players socially. I kept a wedge between my work and my family and when people asked me why I did not take Lucy to games I would reply: 'Do you take your wife to work?'

The friendship, the humour and the shop-talk of football were important to me. I was certainly never a loner. But I was independent and my private life was not something I shared lightly. As it was, Lucy would sometimes say I was never at home, especially after I started regular coaching. 'If I'm going to cement my future I've got to start working now', I would tell her.

I would dearly have loved a full international cap but, that apart, I have no abiding regrets about my playing career. And I take great pride in the fact that for years I could go back to any of the clubs I played for and there would still be a groundsman or gateman who would remember me and say 'Hello'.

10

Revelation

I sometimes think I have a little insight into how Paul felt on the road to Damascus. My own moment came at Wembley on a misty November day in 1953, when Hungary beat England by six goals to three – and proved to me beyond all doubt that football can be a game of beauty and intelligence, a lovely art as well as a muscular science.

In the back of my mind there had always been a vision of the way I felt the game should be played. I had seen generous hints of it in the Spurs' push-and-run side when they won the championship in 1951 under Arthur Rowe; and Arthur, remember, had coached in Hungary. West Bromwich Albion, too, played a rather similar game under Vic Buckingham, a thinker, a man receptive to new ideas, who had been with Arthur Rowe at Tottenham in their early days. Their game was simple, quick, intelligent and adaptable; it was an exercise in wit. The ball was used with respect but it was made to do most of the work. I felt this was the way football would have to go, how it would develop naturally, but somehow the 'British' way persisted.

Perhaps without realizing it, I was waiting for someone to show me the way. My ideas on the game were firm; but proof – undeniable, public proof – was needed that football had more to offer than the average League club's performance on a Saturday afternoon. When the proof came, on 25 November in Coronation Year, it was as if someone had removed scales from my eyes. All my basic ideas on the game suddenly came together. Hungary's victory was written up like a national disaster (after all, it was the first time a continental side had won at Wembley) but for me it was a new start.

The Hungarians had been given a big build-up before they arrived. Their record spoke for itself: they were Olympic champions, they were strongly fancied to win the World Cup in 1954, and they had not been beaten for nearly three years. They were clearly very special but it was Walter Winterbottom's enthusiasm that made me promise myself to watch the game. He had seen the Hungarians himself and he was always talking about their talent and methods.

I got to Stamford Bridge at my usual time that morning, around 9.30, and fifteen minutes later we were 'training' – the obligatory laps around the pitch. I had a bath and it was then confirmed that the club had laid on transport and tickets for those who wanted to watch the international. About half the Chelsea team decided to go. We discovered our position was a pretty good one – it was in the stand opposite the Royal Box, up in the right-hand corner and level with the goal.

There was an unmistakeable sense of expectancy in the air although I was far from sure what I was going to see. The Hungarians did not look anything special when they came out in their cherry-red shirts but then Ferenc Puskas, their captain, a surprisingly ample-looking chap, went to the centre spot to spin a coin with England's Billy Wright, and I noticed him fiddling with the ball. 'What's happening here?' I wondered. All Puskas did, in fact, was flick the ball up a couple of times, catch it with his instep and return it to the spot. A million kids now do the same in their back-yards, but nobody then had seen it done in the centre circle at Wembley. We all sat up and took notice.

Not many people thought England would actually be beaten. Indeed, a long time later, I learnt that Dave Sexton, Malcolm Allison and Jimmy Andrews (who were going to become outstanding coaches) had gone to watch the Hungarians warming up before the match in the old grey-hound area outside the stadium. The visitors had been told they could not use the pitch so they found this bit of grass at the back, and Jimmy Andrews happily tells the story of how he pointed at one of the Hungarian players and said to Malcolm Allison: 'Look at that fat little chap there . . . we'll murder this lot.' The fat chap was Puskas.

The confidence of the English was understandable. No overseas side had ever won at Wembley and the England team that day was a good one by any standard. It was experienced and gifted. Players like Billy Wright, Alf Ramsey, Jimmy Dickinson and Bill Eckersley had been regulars for years, while Stan Matthews, Stan Mortensen, Ernie Taylor and Harry Johnston were there from Blackpool only a few months after they had won the FA Cup on the same pitch. I'd had a slim hope of being picked myself, because I was playing well and there had been doubts about the centre-half position, but Johnston got the nod again. In fact I thought the side was the strongest available.

Here then was England's best, a side containing several outstanding footballers, one or two of them really great. They scored three goals and might have had more . . . and yet they were humiliated. That was the measure of the Hungarians. Just think! Puskas and his players were away from home, at Wembley of all places, and they got six. They gave goals away, but what did that matter? I had the distinct impression that no matter how many England had scored the Hungarians would always have managed two or three more. They had so much under their bonnet. It struck me shortly after the start that I was watching something very precious. The game was so near to what I'd always had in mind that I almost purred. It was exactly what I wanted to see and, for a few minutes, I wondered if others were seeing it in the same way. But I remember less and less of what happened around me because I just shut everything else out and concentrated on the play. I have always been able to do that, but it was never easier than on that particular day. I was entranced.

The Hungarians simply played football differently. They used another language in more senses than one. Their game was based on the short pass although they were always ready with a long one when the moment was right; they were never predictable. They kept the ball on the ground and they fizzed it about. Their pace was tremendous but it was the ball that did the hardest work. Their players moved with cunning and intelligence. They understood the value of space, how to make it and how to use it, and they had that special kind of understanding which only comes with familiarity. They were outstanding individuals with the sort of relationship with each other that is normally found only in the best club sides; and, of course, this was not just a happy accident. The Hungarians made a point of playing ordinary little work sides, in countries like France, and beating them by anything up to 25-0. That took a lot of dedication but, in the long run, the dividend was a big one. They were like a well-drilled platoon, and they were all on the same wavelength.

The one quality of the Hungarians' game which impressed me most of all was their movement. It gave their technique its edge and variety and made the most of their marvellous talent. The man with the ball always had good, simple alternatives, and one reason for this was the fact that they were not hide-bound by numbers. Their players were free agents. They ran all over the place and it was this above all which confused England.

English football was very much concerned with numbers in those days. A player was given one to wear, and a particular job went with it: five marked nine, two marked eleven, three marked seven. England's defenders were so used to playing this way that they found it impossible to change for even one game. They were simply caught out. Harry Johnston, for example, found he had no one to mark because Nandor Hidegkuti, the Hungarian number nine, played all over the park. One moment Hidegkuti would be picking up the ball just in front of his own penalty area, the next drifting wide, the next coming into a movement for a second or even third time – but always, lethally, he was ready to become the extra man in the opposition's box. He did not go near Johnston; and he did not let Johnston approach him. Harry wanted someone to latch onto, but all he saw was space. Hidegkuti scored three goals and England were in total disarray.

The point was to be made later that Hungary played in triangles, little clusters of three and sometimes four players giving each other options. So they did, and many tried to copy them, but what most imitators used were static triangles. Players waited for the ball, which not only reduced the pace of the build-up but meant that their intentions could be read. It was negative.

The Hungarian way was different. They used *moving* triangles. Much more difficult, of course, but infinitely more effective. Their players were always on the move so the size, angles and direction of their triangles were constantly changing. Their style was all about understanding, rhythm and intuition; and, linked together by the lovely skills of the Hungarian players, the effect was devastating.

It did not stop there. The Hungarian game was full of other little refinements. They were happy to play the ball to a marked man, to give him the choice of pushing the ball back or trying to turn his opponent, something else we had not seen in those days. Laszlo Budai, on the right, would clip the ball one side of a defender tight on his touchline and then run out of play himself to get past before cutting in. They used space wherever it was. And where they were also very different from the other continental sides we had seen was in the quality of their finishing. It matched all the other riches of their game.

The best goal of Hungary's six, the one that everybody remembers, was the first of the two scored by Puskas. I was right in line with it and his check, drag-back, turn and shot were beautiful. Billy Wright charged into empty air. But I do not think that even then, even after watching this piece of virtuosity, the crowd thought England would be beaten. They were demanding that England should get 'stuck in' and I have a notion they thought it was only a matter of time before we nailed the Hungarians.

Puskas was a roly-poly little fellow who looked as if he did most of his training in restaurants. In fact, he was a natural, a grand master of the game. He was entirely left-footed but, no matter how the ball came, that old left foot went up and his control was instant and precise. It was as if he had glue on the toe of his boot. The pace of his passes was perfect, he shielded so well with his round body that it was difficult even to see the ball, he could beat a man with a nod of the head and a twist of the shoulders and his shooting was wicked. His qualities, however, went beyond these. There was an aura, a presence, about him. He seemed to glide rather than run and, a sure sign of a strong personality, he dictated the shape and pace of the game around him. It was always said he was a major in the Hungarian army, but in a footballing sense he was a general – and no one was in any doubt about it.

I saw Puskas play for Real Madrid, after the uprising, and he was still a player who filled the eye; and then, many years later, in 1981, when I was manager of England and we played Hungary in a World Cup game in Budapest, he took part in a nostalgic exhibition match. It was the first time he had been back to Hungary since the revolution but the magic was still there. Lord knows how old he was, and he was fatter than ever, a real Michelin man, but he just ambled about in his usual arrogant way, dominating everyone, and scored a quite remarkable hat-trick. He had lost everything except his skill – but that still glowed like a beacon. Puskas was one of the all-time greats.

Hidegkuti was a stylist. He was tall and slim and everything he did looked good. He had a delicate touch, perfect balance and a rare ability to see everything going on around him. He liked to go at his opponents and he had a killer shot but he also brought his team-mates into the game. He was stealthy, perceptive, cunning and very difficult to pin down, because he rarely did the obvious.

I was able to confirm all this at first hand because the following year Chelsea played Red Banner at Stamford Bridge, and Hidegkuti was in their side. As it happened I had a reasonably good game against him because I played in my usual way, slightly behind the rest of our defenders, and made no attempt to mark him tightly. I only made contact when he pushed forward himself and, more often than not, I was able to pick off the ball. But I could never take anything for granted because his mind was so quick.

Untypically, Hidegkuti committed a rather nasty foul on me. We both hit the ground hard but I was more annoyed and perplexed than hurt because he meant something special to me. I got up first and I remember standing over him, wagging my finger and saying: 'A player like you doesn't need to do that sort of thing.' I have no idea whether he understood me, but he seemed to get the general message.

Kocsis, the Hungarians' elegant inside-right, was brilliant in the air, mostly at the far post, and a man who was very difficult to pick up. He was a runner who did not get too involved in build-ups but was always in at the end of a movement. He ran straight and hard from deep positions and his timing was so good that he was constantly getting behind the opposition's defences, the extra man, the uninvited guest. He later went to Barcelona and made a big impression there.

Bozsik was a major influence in mid-field, usually in combination with Puskas and Hidegkuti, and together they formed the most telling triangle of all. They imposed themselves on a game, creating space, using it and promising to make the ball their personal possession. Once their rhythm was established it was almost impossible to break them down. There was something almost unreal about their understanding.

Not much is ever said about the Hungarian defence, partly I suppose because they conceded three goals at Wembley, but I thought it was a good, tough unit. Players such as Lorant and Lantos were muck-and-nettle types who did not take many prisoners. They bit hard in the tackle, covered effectively and, once the ball was theirs, they did not waste it.

The Hungarians were all supposed to be amateurs, of course, but I have never seen a more professional team in my life. They trained and practised like professionals, they kept together like professionals, their eye for detail was professional and their attitude was professional. They may have been Olympic champions but their understanding of amateurism was very different from mine. There was nothing remotely amateur about them.

After Wembley, Puskas and his team immediately became rather a cult, a movement which gathered even more pace when they beat England 7-1 in Budapest early the following summer. A lot of tub-thumping went on. There were inquests and inquiries, demands for reform and dozens of articles calling for 'something' to be done. Everyone thought we should play the Hungarian way and everyone seemed to have a different notion about what that meant.

Walter Winterbottom called a meeting of managers just a few weeks afterwards and invited constructive comment. Not much was forthcoming although a lot was said. One manager even got up and said: 'What can we expect? All our bloody players care about is combing their hair before they go out.' Very constructive! Ted Drake came back to Stamford Bridge after the meeting, summoned all his players together and told us how new the future was going to be. Then we went out and did twenty laps straight off!

For some time afterwards no big coaching course seemed complete unless a Hungarian was there. Gustav Sebes, the Hungarian manager, attended one himself at Lilleshall, by which time I had finished playing and become a staff coach. I took every opportunity I could to chat with him and the most valuable thing he said to me – and it is true to this day – was simply this: 'The English player always stops the ball. He never lets it run.' That is something I have preached ever since. A ball which is allowed to run, especially if it is shielded, will very often catch a defender on the hop; but such a ploy requires intelligence, balance and selection. The secret is in knowing *when* to use it. In later years, Trevor Brooking developed the technique very effectively for West Ham. He did it as it should be done.

Many people who were impressed by the Hungarian way in 1953 said: 'Ah yes, it's very good – but it's not for us.' I could never understand that attitude because the Hungarians based their methods on such simple principles – first principles and best principles. Their talent was prodigious but it was the flexibility of their game which made that talent so effective. They appreciated that space in a football sense is simply a gap between two players, and that once a player moves into a space it is no longer a space. Intentions are signalled; markers can follow. A player should move into a gap to meet the ball and the Hungarians' timing in this respect was brilliant. They changed their positions, altered their angles and left things until the last split part of a second. Their ideas were timeless and impossible to improve on.

Even today those Hungarian methods would improve most competent teams provided three or four players were involved whose technique was good and who understood the point of them. There would need to be trial and error and mistakes would certainly be made; but hard work, common sense and intelligent coaching would achieve a style not so remote from the Hungarian way. It would, of course, be the job of the coach to make sure his ideas were within the range of his players. Systems are for players . . . not players for systems.

It is always, or at least *nearly* always, possible to learn from an outstanding team. The one exception is Brazilian football because at the root of their game is a kind of skill, physical suppleness and sheer exuberance which only they have. No European side, English, German, Hungarian, Dutch or Italian, could play the way the Brazilians did in, say, the 1982 World Cup. Their casualness is partly their strength, partly their weakness, and in the end they committed suicide in Spain. But overall, no quibbling, they were magnificent. Their kind of football is in the blood. Tactically they can be ordinary and even inflexible. I remember asking Vicente Feola, Brazil's coach during the 1966 World Cup, why he did not change his tactics at half-time in a game that was going all wrong for them. He replied: 'We never change our plan.' Plans, surely, have to justify themselves.

Only one team has enthralled me as much as the 1953 Hungarians, and that was the great Real Madrid side which dominated the European Cup in its early days. Most of all I relish their 7-3 victory over Eintracht Frankfurt in the 1960 final at Hampden Park. It is doubtful whether there has ever been a better team although in the real sense this was hardly a 'club' side. It was full of the world's best players, including Puskas, Di Stefano, Kopa, Gento and Del Sol, a perfect mixture, a side with everything. They delighted and educated. They took my breath away.

Puskas got four goals in that game while Alfredo Di Stefano scored the other three; and Di Stefano was in the same class – a class apart – as Puskas. Di Stefano was broad-chested, strong and fast, a formidable sight in action, a supreme craftsman. There was an explosive quality about his game, and his finishing was deadly. When he was off the ball his head and eyes always seemed to be moving as if he was taking mental pictures and, once again, he always seemed to know where to go – and, equally importantly, when to go. He had great powers of individual expression, but I would say that in a broad sense he was an inspiration rather than a general. Even in that Real Madrid side Puskas was the boss.

I was overwhelmed by the sheer magic of that Real Madrid side, and I can never see enough of the Brazilians, but my first love has always been the 1953 Hungarians. The way they played shaped my thinking, and this is why the best moments of my career have had some kind of Hungarian connection. I was immensely proud, for example, when in later years Hungarian coaches came to Upton Park to study our methods. I was also proud when British coaches said to me: 'I'd never thought of that' or 'I've never seen it that way'.

Whenever I am asked, however, to pick my best moments of all I always quote two: winning the European Cup Winners' Cup with West Ham in 1965 and England's World Cup victory over Hungary in the Nep Stadium in Budapest in 1981.

I was just a player when I saw the 1953 Hungarians, and I never imagined for a moment that one day I would see a side of my own applying so many of the same principles. But when West Ham beat Munich 1860 in that Cup Winners' Cup Final they played in a way very different from the standard English game. They moved on and off the ball in a way similar to the Hungarians – not exactly, of course, because our overall methods were adapted to the players we had – but the basics were the same. That West Ham side proved a point for me.

England's victory in Budapest was equally important, although in a different way. Puskas played in a warm-up game to remind us of the past and then we took hold of the present to win by 3-1. We also beat Hungary twice at Wembley, in 1978 and later on in 1981 (which confirmed our place in the 1982 World Cup finals), and I remember saying to Walter Winterbottom, England's manager in 1953: 'Perhaps we've helped a little to put the record straight.'

11

Apprenticeship

My apprenticeship as a coach and manager was long, varied, eventful, often frustrating and sometimes maddening, but in the long run it was immensely rewarding. It involved England's Youth and Under-23 sides, Ealing Grammar School, Eastbourne United, Oxford University, Walthamstow Avenue and Arsenal. I learnt the trade trick by trick and, inevitably, mistake by mistake. No experience is a waste of time.

The blue touch-paper was lit for me during my first course at Lilleshall; Walter Winterbottom was the man who struck the match. He convinced me coaching had a big future at a time when the majority of professionals looked on it in the same way witch-doctors once regarded traditional medicine. Coaching was new and therefore to be viewed with suspicion. English football had done all right without it in the past, ran the argument, so what was the point? Hadn't players learnt the game well enough on the field? Weren't players born rather than made? Wouldn't all players be the same?

Walter, though, was a visionary. He told me new methods of training were being investigated and that new ways of teaching were coming to the fore. Training was being related to technique as well as stamina; all over Europe the game was evolving fast. He said we might have given the game to the world but now we were in danger of being overtaken. This was revolutionary stuff and many were not only wary but downright hostile. Walter convinced me, however, and I decided that here was my future. I was still a Chelsea player at the time with no immediate thought of retiring, but I knew my sign-writing business was no longer so important.

My first coaching engagement soon followed – six sessions at Ealing Grammar School. I told the school I wanted to take the under-14 side rather than the senior boys because this would give some continuity over a season or two. Each session was supposed to last an hour and a half but the first lasted nearly three hours simply because it was so enjoyable. It was a short course but it gave me tremendous hope and confidence. I learnt as much as the boys did. They were receptive and keen and one in particular, Paddy Walsh, their skipper, was a very good player who later captained Oxford University and played for Pegasus.

The Football Association then told me that Oxford University had picked me from a short list of three to be their coach. This prospect filled me with a new kind of doubt. 'Oh dear', I thought. 'Oxford University – and me just a secondary-modern lad.' In fact, my three years with Oxford were a wonderful experience.

'You've asked me to coach you', I told them at our first get-together, 'but it's all pretty new to me. I've just got my badge and I'm very proud of it, but I'm not sure yet what it's supposed to mean. I know it says I'm a coach, but I haven't done much coaching. So I'll tell you what. I'll try to help you – and you try to help me. Let's muck in together and we might make something of it.'

That is when I really started. Good coaching is a two-way business.

The response was tremendous and many of the lads became long-standing friends – among them Stan Heritage, the captain, Gordon McKinna, who was secretary, and Bob Lunn. Oxford's attitude was excellent and some players were very talented. McKinna at centre-half and Lunn, their left-winger, could easily have made a living as semi-professionals. They were a pleasure to work with.

I also received one early bit of advice. 'Don't let Tommy dominate you', they said. 'Tommy' was Professor Harold Thompson, who had inspired Pegasus, the famous combined University side, and who was later to be knighted. He was also to become chairman of the Football Association and to invite me to become manager of England.

The reason for the advice was that the previous coach had apparently been rather hounded by Tommy; and shortly after the little warning I was standing in the old pavilion watching the team practise when he came up and asked: 'What are they playing at?' I could have said they were practising the art of pushing the ball up to a man who then had to knock it off quickly to someone in support. Instead I said: 'Mr Thompson. I'm the coach. They're doing what I've asked them to do.' I wasn't rude. He had not asked the question aggressively: my reply was not aggressive. But from then on we were friends with a great respect for each other. The formation of Pegasus was just one outstanding facet of his brilliant career.

For a while it continued to worry me that someone who had left school at fourteen should be instructing young men who were studying for degrees in such subjects as philosophy and economics, but I discovered this did not matter at all. We had a common interest and a similar aim – to improve at football. They wanted to be better players and I wanted to be a better coach. Football crosses all boundaries and right from the start they made me welcome. There were cups of tea, scones and long chats in the tea-shop and the whole scene was one I much enjoyed.

An academic brain is not the same as a football brain, of course, but if a player has an academic bent, and with it the ability to assimilate and assess, it is an advantage. A footballer cannot have too much intelligence, of any type. But a good player must have, in the first place, a mind that can grasp the special complexities of football, a mind that can intuitively relate to everything happening around him. It is possible to assess an academic brain by examination, but an instinct for football is impossible to measure. A player does not exist in a vacuum: he has to do things for others. Some of the great old players could hardly read or write, but put them on a football field and they would spot openings, read situations, change tactics and recognize weaknesses. They were 'honours' men in that context.

My Chelsea commitments meant I did not see Oxford play as often as I would have liked, but an injury enabled me to watch them play Cambridge just after the University match had moved to Wembley. One of the first people I bumped into was Bill Nicholson. 'Hello', we said together, 'what are you doing here?' Bill, a good friend, was coaching Cambridge.

Roger Bannister, Chris Chataway and Chris Brasher were preparing at this time for their successful attack on the four-minute mile; and while we practised football on the pitch at Iffley Road those celebrated athletes were getting ready to make history on the track around us. I did not see the famous run itself because on that particular Thursday afternoon in May, 1954, I was with Chelsea somewhere over the Atlantic at the start of an American tour. We got into a taxi outside the airport in New York and the driver said immediately: 'Jeez, fellers . . . you English . . . this Bannister must be some guy.' News of the achievement travelled round the world in a matter of hours, a tremendous boost for British prestige. Just a few days later Bannister was with us at a British Embassy reception in the Empire State Building. He had accepted an invitation from the Foreign Office to visit America, partly for publicity, partly goodwill.

My time at Oxford was a perfect introduction to the art of coaching. It taught me a great deal about handling people. But three years was the normal span and Jimmy Hill then took over from me. By now, however, I was also coaching Walthamstow Avenue and I had two invaluable years with them. They were in the Isthmian League, they were one of the country's leading amateur clubs and the previous year, under Freddy Cox, they had drawn with Manchester United at Old Trafford in the FA Cup before going down in a replay at Highbury. That particular

Walthamstow side broke up before I joined the club with two of the players, Jim Lewis and Derek Saunders, going to Chelsea. Jim was an outstanding centre-forward and his father, Jim senior, who had played for Walthamstow for nearly twenty years and was also an amateur international, was the club secretary.

There were still a lot of good players at Walthamstow, though, including Stan Gerula, a Polish amateur international goalkeeper who was also the club's groundsman, their only full-time employee; Dickie Lucas, their captain and a great character; Ted Harper, a schoolteacher; Johnny Bee, a bricklayer and a forward who would have made a first-class professional; Bunny Groves, brother of Vic, who played for Walthamstow before going on to Orient and Arsenal; big Lou Brahan, a centre-half who later went to Orient; and Len Julians, then just a lad, at centre-forward, who was to have an interesting career with Orient, Arsenal, Nottingham Forest and Millwall.

Walthamstow won the Isthmian League and the London Senior Cup while I was coaching them; but nothing gave me greater pleasure than an FA Cup win over Queen's Park Rangers of the Third Division South in November 1954, a first round tie which went to three games. I missed the first draw at Loftus Road because I was playing for Chelsea, and I missed the second – again 2-2 – because I was committed to captaining an FA eleven against Cambridge University at Grange Road. That same night the players told me: 'We felt we had to draw again so that next time you could be with us.' They told me exactly what had happened and, with second-hand knowledge, I worked out one or two things for them – and the outcome in the second replay, at Highbury, was astonishing.

We won by four goals to nil, a marvellous performance in which we pulled Rangers' defence all over the place. The League side stuck to a man-to-man marking system but we out-manoeuvred them just by doing the simple things well. Our running and use of space slayed them. Johnny Bee was unbelievable, Len Julians had a fine game and right through the side shone a seam of intelligence and application. Walthamstow had matched and then beaten a League side over three games so there was no argument or talk of luck.

In the next round we were drawn to play Darlington at home. The Walthamstow lads could see only victory and a place in the third round ahead of them. Again I had to miss the game because Chelsea were at home to Aston Villa and – so much for confidence – Darlington won by three goals to nil.

Vic Groves still trained with us a couple of nights a week and he used to say Avenue were going bust because they paid me so much. In fact, I got £3 a session which also covered my long journey from South Harrow by tube and trolley-bus. It was not a fortune but it was useful money. Those were not affluent days. The additional reward for me, once again, was experience. I knew this was the way the Hungarians brought on their coaches, giving them jobs with schools and smaller clubs and then gradually raising the standard. It gave them an insight into all levels of the game and got them used to handling all kinds of people.

In the late spring of 1956 I received an offer, out of the blue, which made me decide to end my playing career. Eastbourne United asked me to be their coach and, at the age of thirty-three and with nearly four hundred League and Cup games behind me, I knew I would have to think very seriously about the offer. Eastbourne were prepared to match the money I was getting at Fulham, £1,000 a year, and everyone I asked had a good word for them. They played in the Metropolitan League, a fair standard, and all first reports suggested a bright, progressive club.

Lucy and I went down to the south coast one Sunday and we liked what we heard and saw. Princes Park was a smart ground with a new stand, new dressing-rooms and new offices; their chairman, Percy Woods, a councillor and a big trade union man, was a go-ahead chap who became a very good friend; they had a lucrative lottery, one of the first football lotteries in the country; and George Smith, their previous manager, had done an excellent job in finding and schooling players. It was George, I learnt, who had recommended me for the job.

Eastbourne wanted me to develop the game in the town itself, to help create a community spirit. This was an idea which interested me. Lucy and I talked it over again and there was no doubt in our minds that here was a worthwhile challenge. It meant my playing days would be over but I cannot say I felt unhappy about that. The time was right for a change in direction, and Eastbourne's offer was attractive in all kinds of ways.

I accepted their offer of a three-year contract without reservations but then, within twenty-four hours, I got a 'phone call from Malcolm McDonald who was returning from Kilmarnock to become manager of Brentford. He wanted me to be his player-coach . . . and I was so torn between Eastbourne and the new offer that it literally hurt.

I owed much to Malcolm. I admired him as a professional and liked him as a man – and here he was offering me a major job at the club where I had been so happy. The thought of getting back into a real footballing set-up was almost irresistible. I would not have played much but the prospect of coaching there was tremendously exciting, and given a straight choice I would undoubtedly have plumped for Brentford. Nothing in football would have pleased me more. As it was there was only one answer I could give Malcolm. 'I'm sorry', I said, 'but only yesterday I promised Eastbourne I'd join them. I gave my word and they're the sort of people I wouldn't like to let down.'

For the second time a principle had influenced my decision about a job. The first involved Fulham; now it was Brentford. I have often wondered how different my career might have been had I accepted either. But perhaps the dear Lord was on my side. I cannot say I made the right decision in either case – but I believe I made my decisions for the right reasons.

The story leaked out, as they always do, that Brentford had offered me a job, and the Eastbourne management was quickly on the 'phone wondering what I was going to do. I said I was going to keep my word. I then explained the situation to Frank Osborne and Fulham, kind club that it is, agreed to release me. My playing career was over, quickly and painlessly laid to rest. Nothing lasts forever in football. There were good years behind me: but a new career lay ahead.

George Smith had built up a very useful first team, using his excellent contacts to bring a few players down from London, and Eastbourne had reached the final of the Sussex Senior Cup. I had rather different ideas. 'You're paying me a lot of money to come here' I told the club. 'The players from London aren't really your future, so let's start from scratch. Let's have all the kids in from the local district and let's do it properly with our own players.'

Suddenly there were new problems to face. I promoted one boy from the juniors and after he had played two or three games for the seniors I was informed he could never again play for the youngsters. I had a few battles trying to change regulations of similar stupidity, but I was only thinking of the game itself. Legislation of this kind is a menace, a barrier to progress. There have to be rules but they must have a basis of common sense.

Sussex County FA made me their chief coach and I spent an enormous amount of time at teacher-training colleges and on education courses all over the county, involving kids, improving techniques, suggesting new ideas and generally spreading the gospel. It was very hard work but extremely worthwhile: I learnt humility, and I discovered the value of the game at this basic level. I also had the privilege of working with a lot of decent people whose interest in the game, and concern for it, was as great as Matt Busby's or Bill Nicholson's; and I really mean that. Their standards were different but not their commitment. Their only reward was provided by the game itself.

I had a wonderful nine months at Eastbourne and everyone in the club, from its top officials to the dear old lady who did the washing, were magnificent. We did not win an important trophy in my short time there, but I think I helped build a solid and durable platform. I took on only two youngsters from London – one of them Joe Bacuzzi's son, David, who had started with Fulham. (There was no 'A' team at Craven Cottage so when a player became too old for the juniors he either played for the reserves or did not play at all.)

Soon after joining Eastbourne I was invited to take over England's Youth team, and I am sure one of the reasons the FA picked me was that I was considered 'safe'. All the youth team players in those days were ground-staff boys with League clubs, and Lancaster Gate had a suspicion that if a coach from a professional club took charge of England's Youth team he would soon start enticing the youngsters onto his own staff. I was with Eastbourne, who were not seen as a magnet for the nation's best.

I had already been involved with England's Youth side at Lilleshall where I attended courses as a staff coach, and it was always exciting when the cream of the country's youngsters turned up for pre-season get-togethers. Clubs could recommend as many players as they liked. At one such gathering I remember saying to Walter Winterbottom: 'Just look at them . . . the future of English football is no problem.' There were so many good players: David Cliss, Jimmy Greaves, Barry Bridges, Jimmy Melia. Len Ashurst, Bobby Charlton and Alex Dawson among them. When we ended the course with a game between coaches and players, Bobby Charlton was not even picked. He could not get into the side.

But, of course, players change as they grow older: it is the same in all walks of life. Some develop and some lose their fire or interest. Some have staying power and some do not. Some understand the need for discipline and some resent it. Much depends on a player's club, on the way he is coached, paced and brought on, but much also depends on the individual. Greaves and Charlton, for example, became great players; others became first-class professionals; still others flickered brightly and faded. I can only repeat that nothing is certain in football.

I saw as much youth football as I could and one spring evening I was at Stamford Bridge watching London Grammar Schools play Glasgow Grammar Schools when I noticed a young, blond lad called Bobby Moore playing for the London side at centre-half. He looked a good player and the fact registered. The following season he turned up at Lilleshall for the usual early selection course and I spotted he was playing at left-half.

Afterwards I took him to one side and said: 'I saw you playing for London Grammar last season: correct me if I'm wrong but didn't you play at centre-half?'

'Yeah, but my club West Ham like me at left-half', he replied.

'Well, I though you were brilliant', I said, 'and I'd like you to captain our side at centre-half'.

'That suits me fine' he said simply.

Bobby thus became the cornerstone of an England side that played regularly and won consistently. I was involved in the game at several fascinating levels, with young stars of the future and more ordinary chaps who played largely for fun, and I was learning fast. Lucy was still complaining that she never saw me and I was still replying that I was working for our future. I was so busy I did not have any thoughts about my next move although I was not short of opportunities. In my nine months at Eastbourne I was offered six jobs. Raich Carter wanted me as his youth coach at Leeds, Portsmouth offered me a similar post and, among one or two others, Workington wanted me as manager. None tempted me but then, unexpectedly, something much grander beckoned.

Following a youth international at Hillsborough, in which we had beaten Belgium more easily than a two-nil scoreline suggested, I returned to our hotel to be told there had been a telephone call for me from a Mr Bob Wall of Arsenal. The message said he would ring back, and I did not have long to wait. Bob Wall came straight to the point: he said the Arsenal board wanted me to become the club's coach.

'I'm very interested', I said immediately, 'but obviously there's my contract with Eastbourne to be sorted out'.

'We know all about that and we'll work it out. We'll be in touch' said Bob.

I rang Lucy with some hesitation because we had moved into a new home at Eastbourne only six months before, and now another upheaval seemed on the cards. She backed me all the way, however, and saw the opportunity as I did. It was another offer, another challenge, I could not refuse. I kept quiet until Arsenal made their formal approach and then had a long talk with Percy Woods. 'I've been very happy here and feel I've only just started', I said, 'but I don't think I can turn the chance down'. Percy said he agreed and Eastbourne released me from my contract without any demand for compensation.

There was, though, a special arrangement. It was late November in 1957 and Eastbourne had reached the first round proper of the FA Amateur Cup which was to be played early in the New Year. It was agreed therefore that until Eastbourne found a replacement for me, or were knocked out of the Cup, I should do both jobs. I found myself coaching at Highbury during the day but popping down to Eastbourne on Tuesday and Thursday evenings and also being with them for their Saturday game. I was coaching Arsenal but not watching them play.

It was an almost impossible arrangement which I agreed to only because I wanted to be fair to both clubs. I also knew there was more to my Arsenal job than met the eye. I discovered Arsenal had asked the FA to help them find a coach and the FA, as usual, had produced three names. I was chosen: the first full-time coach Arsenal had appointed but, more than that, the first FA staff coach to be given such a job by any League club. I was not a manager, I was a coach pure and simple. The whole concept of coaching was on trial because the FA felt that if I made a success of it then other clubs would follow. If I failed, the traditional resistance to coaching would harden. The rift between the new and the old would widen.

For a while I found things very difficult. I had two clubs and two sets of players always on my mind. The two jobs meant a lot of travelling, long hours and a great deal of frustration. I simply was not able to get involved with Arsenal as deeply as I wanted or intended to be. How can you coach a professional team without watching them play? Jack Crayston, Arsenal's manager, told me I was like 'a breath of fresh air walking down the corridor' but I knew one or two players resented the whole idea of a coach. They believed they knew it all and I would hear them saying: 'Oh, here comes the coach . . . now we're OK.'

The impossibility of my position was clearly shown when the third round of the FA Cup came round in early January. Arsenal were away to Northampton of the Third Division South and I trained and prepared them but had nothing to do with general tactics. Then I linked up with Eastbourne who were away to Brighton's 'A' team in the Metropolitan League that Saturday. After the game we went for a meal in West Street, down near the front, and one or two of the players got hold of the local football paper. 'Hey Ron', they shouted, '. . . see you got beaten'. Northampton had beaten Arsenal by 3-1. I thought: 'Jeepers, what a start!' I did not really feel responsible because I had only been at Highbury for a few weeks on a part-time basis – but there have been better moments in my life.

The following Saturday Eastbourne played at Finchley in the first round proper of the FA Amateur Cup, and as there was a clash of colours I got Arsenal to lend me a set of their shirts, superbly made in a sort of velour. Eastbourne looked a million dollars; but it did not help and they lost by 2-1. They were out of the Amateur Cup and I was free to start full-time work with Arsenal.

Arsenal, I had discovered by now, were set and stodgy in their playing ways. Cliff Holton and Peter Goring were the wing-halves but they were not supposed to cross the halfway line. Jimmy Bloomfield, at inside-forward, was a runner with the ball and a short-passer; the long pass was not part of his armoury and I doubt if he could have kicked the ball more than thirty yards. But he was expected to hit long, angled balls inside the full-back for one of our wingers to run onto – just as the great Alex James had done before the war. The club's playing methods were unbelievably traditional. The past was always part of the present. I set about changing things, trying to work out what was best for the talent we had. Although I knew one or two knives were out for me I did not feel them. I insulated myself from criticism. I was engrossed in my job. I loved every minute.

I started experimenting straight away. I tried all kinds of things, new little routines, variations on old themes, novel training ideas, and the players were quick to respond. Their attitude became more positive: they liked and understood what I was asking them to do. David Herd told Walter Winterbottom they couldn't wait to get to training because they didn't know what I was going to do! Herd, Bloomfield and Vic Groves, all good players, were especially receptive, and so was Danny Clapton, a lively, elusive winger, who to my mind had not been properly used. He was a player who needed understanding and the improvement he showed was particularly rewarding.

Cliff Holton was often a bit sarcastic but that is the way he was; no harm was done. My job was to convince all the players that there were different ways of doing things – perhaps even better ways. They were set in their outlook and it took me about six months before I felt I had really got my message across. It was not before time. Things had gone rather sour at Highbury and I knew it was up to me to sort matters out. During five-a-side games, for example, the main aim was to see who could make Joe Haverty jump the highest. The others tried to kick lumps out of the little forward and took nasty liberties with him: it was definitely time for some changes.

On the field we had some magnificent games and results. One game in particular was both a classic and an epitaph: Arsenal 4, Manchester United 5 . . . United's last game in England before the Munich aircrash. The date was 1 February, 1958. Duncan Edwards, a real swashbuckler, a brilliant young man, scored for United early on, Bobby Charlton got a second and Tommy Taylor made it 3-0 by half-time. We were being overrun by sheer quality. I went into the dressing-room and said: 'You're so busy worrying about their forwards that you're forgetting their defence can be opened up. Let's be positive, let's take the game to them. We've nothing to lose – let's have a go.'

The team took me at my word and the gamble came off. We threw everything at United; their defence was forced into errors, David Herd thumped one in and then Jimmy Bloomfield stole in for two more: 3-3. But United were a great side. They composed themselves again, started to measure the ball about once more and Dennis Viollet and Tommy Taylor made it 5-3. Still we didn't give in though, and added a fourth through Derek Tapscott. Unfortunately that was the final score – 5-4 in United's favour – but I am not sure anybody lost. A few days later we heard the terrible news from Munich: but all of us who shared in that splendid match at Highbury have evergreen memories of those wonderful young men who perished.

We also drew 4-4 with Tottenham at Highbury. The memory of that game is not so happy because we were winning 4-2 with only minutes to go. Sir Bracewell Smith, Arsenal's chairman, used to leave his seat five minutes before the final whistle to beat the crowd and get on his way to Frinton for the weekend. He did the same at the end of this game, with the score 4-2, and his chauffeur told the story later of how they were away down the Gillespie Road when the results started to come through on the radio. 'Arsenal 4' said the reader. 'Yes, yes, we know that', said Sir Bracewell. '. . . Tottenham 4.' He did his best to go through the roof of the car.

Lucy and I decided to have a holiday abroad at the end of the season, but then Arsenal sacked Jack Crayston, who had been a player, assistant manager and then manager with the club, and we promptly cancelled our trip. We felt we shouldn't be spending money we might need to live on. With Jack Crayston gone, I did not know where that left me. But Bob Wall assured me they wanted me to stay and then, a little while later, he called me in again.

'I've got an idea' he said. 'I'd like to know what you think about it. What would you say if I proposed that I became general manager and you became team manager?'

'I'd like that very much', I replied, 'but one thing would need to be clear. I wouldn't want any interference on the playing side.'

'That's fair enough', said Bob.

I do not know if Bob ever put his idea to the directors but, Arsenal being Arsenal, all sorts of other names were soon being linked with the club. It was a plum job, one of the best, and although the club had finished in mid-table the potential was enormous. Joe Mercer, an old Highbury favourite, then manager of Sheffield United, came down for an interview. Harry Johnston, who had become manager of Reading, and Arthur Rowe were also sounded out. Bob Wall then came to see me and, still without confirming whether he had floated his idea, he told me: 'The board are very impressed with what you are doing, but they feel you're possibly a bit young and inexperienced at the moment to take over as manager.' I think with hindsight they were right. I know now, of course, that Billy Wright became Arsenal's manager very soon after his retirement and he found the job too much for him. He was not a real failure: he simply did not win anything and that is not good enough. I think it was a blessing in disguise I did not get the Arsenal job.

Harry Johnston was offered the post, but the Reading board refused to release him from his contract, and I was put in temporary charge. This was fair enough: the club did not stop just because it was in between managers. There was still a lot of work to be done. There were also summer courses at Lilleshall for me to attend, and it was at one of these that I took Arsenal's first step towards buying Tommy Docherty from Preston North End. Tommy, a strong, influential wing-half, had just been put on the transfer list and I told him: 'I can't commit the Arsenal because I'm not the manager, but I feel we need a player like you. Whoever takes over, I'll recommend strongly to him that we move for you because I think you'd be ideal. I can't promise more because I'm not in a position to.'

I could have changed clubs myself during that summer of 1958. Eric Taylor, the much respected general manager of Sheffield Wednesday, invited me to become team manager at Hillsborough, but although a move back to Yorkshire had its attractions I was not convinced it was right for me. I said to Eric: 'I can't make up my mind at the moment because I don't know what's going to happen here. I'm enjoying life with Arsenal and would like to stay. But that depends on what the new man wants.'

So I stayed with the London club, prepared the schedules, worked hard with the players and got them into excellent shape for the new season. Everything was ready. Then, shortly before the start, Arsenal announced that George Swindin was to be the new manager. I did not know him although I had played against him on that famous day when Bradford beat Arsenal in the Cup. George had been Arsenal's goalkeeper, a position he filled with distinction either side of the war. Now he was returning to Highbury after a spell as Peterborough's manager.

We left immediately for a tour of Holland and while we were in Enschede, on the border with Germany, I got another telephone call from Eric Taylor. 'Are you coming now?' he asked.

'What do you mean?' I replied.

'Well', he went on, 'after what's been said by your new manager I don't reckon you'll be staying at Highbury'.

George Swindin had marked his appointment with some outlandish comments on what was going wrong at Arsenal. He criticized the way we had been playing, our methods and our attitude, and made no reference to the fact that we had set the place alight with our form at the end of the previous season. Everything was wrong, apparently, and he was going to change it all. I'm in right trouble here, I thought.

I told Eric Taylor, however, that I had not had a chance to have a good talk with George and I would rather wait until I had. The chance soon came. 'What's all this criticism about?' I asked George. 'Oh, it didn't have anything to do with you' he replied. I pointed out that as I had been in charge of the team, trained them, prepared them and told them how to play, it seemed to have everything to do with me. He apologized and insisted he had not meant any criticism of me. In any case, he added, his words had looked stronger in print than they really were. I believed him because I do not think he had made his comments nastily. He had sounded off without much thought, perhaps trying to make an impression. 'Fair enough', I said. I felt sure we had the basis of a good relationship. I liked the job and the club and believed we could achieve something together.

George Swindin, I discovered, was a dynamic sort of chap. He was full of personality, a real enthusiast who cared deeply about Arsenal. I am sure that when he cut himself his blood ran Arsenal red and white. He did not involve himself much in training and his part in preparing the team was basically a lengthy team-talk on Friday mornings. His outlook was never deeply tactical but he was a good motivator and dealt with each game in a strong, general sense. But in no way were we working along different lines. I felt strongly that it was my job to know what he wanted and to work to that end with the players. We were on the same wavelength.

I told George about Tommy Docherty and he bought him without delay or argument, an influential player at a fair price, and by November we were at the top of the First Division. Our ideas and players were in harmony and we were getting the best out of what we had. No more can ever be asked. Then Preston beat us at Highbury, the first time we had lost at home, and George sounded off after the match: he really blew his top. He said Preston's goalkeeper, a young lad who had made some miraculous saves, was lucky, and he also upset one or two other people. He made his comments at his usual post-match press conference and, naturally, the reporters loved it. George was good value at these talks and he certainly got the club a lot of publicity.

It may have been just a coincidence but soon after this things started

Roy Swinbourne versus Ron Greenwood. Underneath the arches of Molineux. Wolves 4, Chelsea 5 – and Chelsea are on their way to the 1955 League Championship. *Press Association*.

Bradford Park Avenue, circa 1946, set off to meet Manchester City in the fourth round of the FA Cup. Left to right: Ron Hepworth, Bill Hallard, Len Shackleton, Richard Dix, Ron Greenwood, Harold Taylor (trainer), Johnnie Downie, J. Canning (director), Tom Farr, H. Hudson and J. W. Turner (director) and Bob Danskin. Manchester City 2, Bradford Park Avenue 8.

Left Ron Greenwood leads out England's 'B' team in Amsterdam in March 1952. England beat the full Holland side 1-0. 'Pulling on an England shirt was a moment of fulfilment . . . a physical experience.' *Robert van der Randen*
Right The science of football. Ron Greenwood coaching Arsenal with the help of radio before the start of the 1960-61 season. Sitting: Arsenal director Jimmy Joyce. Standing on right: Arsenal manager George Swindin. *Keystone*

England's demolition by Hungary at Wembley in November 1953 is well under way. Ferenc Puskas (10) has just beaten Billy Wright (third left) to score the third of Hungary's six goals. *Fox Photos*

Walter Winterbottom – 'everybody listened to him' – talking with the England class of '61. Left to right: Jimmy Robson (8), Harold Shepherdson (trainer), Walter Winterbottom, Bobby Robson (kneeling), Johnny Haynes (lying down), Ron Springett, Jimmy Armfield, Mick McNeil and Stan Anderson. *Press Association*

The FA Cup is West Ham's for the first time. Front row (left to right): Jack Burkett, John Sissons, Johnny Byrne and Eddie Bovington. Back row: John Bond, Jim Standen, Bobby Moore, Geoff Hurst, Bill Jenkins, Ron Greenwood, Ken Brown (half hidden), Ronnie Boyce and Peter Brabrook. West Ham 3, Preston 2. *Monte Fresco/Daily Mirror*

Johnny Sissons hurdling with hope during the 1965 European Cup Winners' Cup final between West Ham and Munich 1860. Radenkovic, the Munich goalkeeper, and full-back Wagner have the ball. West Ham 2, Munich 1860 nil. *Press Association*

Martin Peters – 'a connoisseur's dream' – heads past Gordon West of Everton at Upton Park in October 1966. Geoff Hurst, right, provided the centre. *Keystone*

Geoff Hurst, cheeks puffing, fires past John McGovern, Dave Mackay and Roy McFarland of Derby County at Upton Park in November 1969. *Keystone*

Left Johnny Byrne – 'the di Stefano of British football'. *Press Association*

Right Bobby Moore helping England beat the Rest of the World by 2-1 in the FA Centenary match at Wembley in October 1963. Josef Masopust of Czechoslovakia arrives too late. 'When the bugle sounded Moore would always find another 20 per cent.' *Keystone*

John Lyall – West Ham's fifth manager. 'John is a strong character, stable, straight and single-minded . . . I knew I was leaving the old club in very good hands.' *Bob Thomas*

No 10 Downing Street. Kevin Keegan, Mrs Thatcher and Emlyn Hughes before England's departure for the European championships in Italy in 1980. *Keystone*

Buckingham Palace, February 1981. Ron Greenwood CBE with Carole, Lucy and Neil. *Press Association*

Ray Wilkins and Diego Maradona with a common interest. Wembley, May 1980: England 3, Argentina 1. *Keystone*

Left A nearly private moment under the chandeliers at West Lodge Park. The vital World Cup game against Hungary at Wembley in November 1981 is just two days away. *Press Association*

Right Kevin Keegan – 'his value was boundless: he was different'. Scheiwiler of Switzerland keeps him company. Basle, June 1981: Switzerland 2, England 1. *Keystone*

Trevor Brooking versus the Hungarians at Wembley, November 1981. 'The best runner with the ball since Bobby Charlton.' England 1, Hungary 0.
Bob Thomas

Tension on the bench as England are minutes away from beating Hungary in Budapest in June 1981 on the way to the World Cup finals. Left to right: Fred Street, Bill Taylor, Ron Greenwood (who intended to retire after the match), Don Howe and Dr Vernon Edwards. *Bob Thomas*

Press conference . . . English style. Left to right: David Lacey (Guardian), with crossword, Donald Saunders (Daily Telegraph), Bob Driscoll (Star), Steve Curry (Daily Express), Alan Odell, Ron Greenwood, Frank Clough (Sun), Jeff Powell (Daily Mail) and Bryon Butler (BBC Radio). *Bob Thomas*

Press conference . . . World Cup style. Ron Greenwood and helpers at table down on indoor pitch, international press in gallery. 'The questions fell like rain.' Location: Athletic Bilbao training camp. *Bob Thomas*

Ron Greenwood telling Ray Clemence that Peter Shilton would be England's first choice goalkeeper during the 1982 World Cup finals. 'Ray was not too happy. I wouldn't have been delighted myself. But a decision had to be made.' *Bob Thomas*

England's first game in Spain is just 27 seconds old . . . and Bryan Robson scores the fastest goal in World Cup final history. Jean Luc Ettori, the French goalkeeper, raises his hands in horror and Paul Mariner (11) and Jean Francois Larios (13) just watch. June 1982: England 3, France 1. *Bob Thomas*

Basking, Basque-style, in the Bilbao sunshine. Left to right: Trevor Brooking, Terry Butcher, Don Howe, Geoff Hurst (half hidden), Tony Woodcock, Glenn Hoddle, Ron Greenwood, Steve Foster, Kenny Sansom, Graham Rix, Peter Shilton, Viv Anderson. *Bob Thomas*

Bobby Robson, Ron Greenwood and Enzo Bearzot at the Savoy Hotel, January 1983. 'A lovely and memorable night' organised by the Football Writers' Association. *Daily Mail*

to go wrong. We even let in six against Luton at Christmas – the kind of defeat that does nothing for anyone's confidence. Tommy Docherty did not help with some comments about his team-mates: this chap couldn't play, said Tommy, that one was a bad player. Tommy was being Tommy.

We were still in with a chance of the championship towards the end of the season, however, until Jimmy Bloomfield was injured. He was a key player, an inside-forward with touch and vision, and when he played well the team played well. Jimmy had cartilage trouble and, being a good friend of mine, he confided he was not very happy about his knee. 'It should be showing signs of improvement by now' he said. I meant no disrespect to anyone at Highbury, but I suddenly remembered a physiotherapist I had met on courses at Lilleshall. 'Tell you what', I said to Jimmy, 'let me run you down to a clinic at Camden Town for a chat with a chap I know there. He's called Bertie Mee. He's good.'

Bertie Mee examined Jimmy's knee and then said: 'There's something wrong here. It should be better than this.' He gave us some advice, we listened carefully and that seemed to be that. Somehow, though, the news leaked out, and I was carpeted. I was ordered to appear before the directors and Bob Wall asked me for an explanation.

'My only thought was for the good of the club', I said. 'I was worried about Jimmy's knee so I took him to the best man I knew.'

'Well, the surgeon and doctor at this end say it was unethical', Bob Wall continued, 'and they're creating merry hell. Why did you do it?'

I replied that Jimmy's knee clearly wasn't right, and he had been unhappy with the treatment he was getting.

I had to apologize to everybody in the end, which did not please me, but Bob Wall then went into things a little more deeply, taking soundings from everyone, and the eventual result was some important changes. Billy Milne, a long-serving club servant who had been Arsenal's trainer since the managerial days of Tom Whittaker, was retired, and so was the doctor. Alan Bass became the club doctor, and later England's doctor, while Bertie Mee became our physiotherapist. Bertie, of course, later became manager and led Arsenal to their remarkable League and Cup double in 1971. And it all began with a knee . . .

At the end of the 1958–59 season George Swindin made a move for Mel Charles of Swansea. George was also interested in a young Scottish wing-half, Dave Mackay of Hearts, but was told he had 'weak ankles'. He accepted that information at face-value and completed the signing of Charles. Meanwhile Spurs, who had also been interested in the big Welshman, turned instead to Mackay. We finished third in the First Division and the future looked rosy.

The following summer we went on our usual pre-season tour, again to Holland, and in a game against Den Haag we really turned it on. Mel Charles looked particularly good and although he was not in the same class as his brother, John Charles, a prince of a player, he was a good, strong, straightforward competitor whose influence was significant. We had scored about six goals when there was a thunderstorm and the lush pitch became difficult. Mel went into a tackle much harder than he needed to and came out of it, sadly, with knee trouble. He was never quite the same again. By contrast, Mackay, our alternative choice who was now with Spurs, became a remarkable player, one of the best, a wing-half who combined strength with great ability. Weak ankles indeed.

We also had an interesting argument about goalkeeping on that tour. We were having a free-kick session during practice when Jack Kelsey, our Welsh international goalkeeper, a fine performer by any standard, started talking about our defensive line-up for set-pieces. He said: 'I've this system in which we don't line up directly in front of the ball. Our wall stands on one side of the goal and I take the other – so that I've got a clear, direct view of the ball.'

George Swindin said that as an old goalkeeper himself he did not like the idea, but I pointed out that Jack had done this many times and it had worked even in internationals. So we decided to put it to the test and, with a wall of defenders on one side, we started firing in shots of every kind: we tried power, chips, angles, swerves and aimed high and low. But Jack saw them all coming, handled them well and obviously thought he had proved his point. George continued to argue, however, and eventually Jack was so incensed he asked our manager that terrible old question: 'How many caps did you win?'

That did it. I thought George was going to explode. It had always hurt him that he had never won a full cap and Jack Kelsey's question was the last straw. But Jack stuck to his argument – and his plan – and when the season began it worked well for a while. Then we played Leicester. We conceded a free kick just outside our penalty area and Jack organised our defence to his liking: the wall on one side of our goal, himself on the other. Leicester's little winger, Howard Riley, ran over the ball and kept going, Ken Keyworth played the ball in after him and there, suddenly, was Riley with the ball, unmarked, in front of our goalkeeper. The ploy was ridiculously simple and very effective. As it happened Riley wasted his chance. He hurried his shot and Kelsey was able to get a hand to the ball. But the message was clear and afterwards I said to Jack: 'That's the end of that idea. I blame myself for not foreseeing that little trick. Everyone will be on to it now.'

The idea of not having an orthodox wall came up many years later, at a meeting of coaches at Lilleshall soon after the 1978 World Cup in Argentina. We were talking about defensive situations when Malcolm Allison said brightly: 'How about not having a defensive wall at all?' I simply recounted the above story. This is the key to coaching: relating theory and experience.

Nothing is ever achieved without experiment and once – just once – we even used radio to help us with our training. The method was being used in America and a major company, Phillips, asked us to have a go. There was nothing complicated about it. A circuit was established round the pitch, half our players strapped on a little receiver and ear-piece, and I had a microphone on the touchline. All the players on one side could hear everything I said; the rest were on their own.

'This could be murder in the wrong hands', I said before we started, 'so I'll only talk to a player when he's off the ball. Don't forget I won't have the same picture of the game as you . . . and when I say something I want the player concerned to raise his hand to show he's heard.' The trial proved to be good fun and quite useful, and I think I only made one mistake. I told Len Wills, one of our full-backs, to do something, promptly realized I was wrong, apologized, and up went Len's hand: no problem.

At one point I spoke to the team as a whole. 'We're going to concentrate on Danny' I said. (Danny Clapton was a talented winger but sometimes a sleeper; he had to be brought into a game.) 'We're going to make him work, work, work' I went on. 'We're not going to let him have forty winks on the wing. We're going to give him the ball all the time. It's pressure time for Danny.' Again it worked well.

A little while later Jack Kelsey was slow in coming off his line. 'Jack, you could have been sharper on that one', I said, and waited for the signal. Nothing happened, although I saw Jack drop his head to his chest. After the game I asked him if he'd heard me. 'Sure', he said, 'and I answered you back'. He thought our radios were two-way!

The Phillips people asked me for my opinion, and I told them their system could be very useful if handled properly. But in football it could only be used sparingly as a training aid because players must always think for themselves during a game. It is now used for training firemen and other rescue services, and also in industry.

It was now becoming apparent, alas, that George Swindin and I were not a perfect partnership. There was no personal animosity between us and as people we got on reasonably well. But we were two very different personalities. George was a flamboyant character who loved publicity while I was more down to earth about the game. The chemistry was not right. Jimmy Bloomfield once told me: 'Until I read what George has said in the papers every morning I can't enjoy my toast and marmalade.' Any reporter stuck for a line could get one from George, which is not a bad thing, but then he would say to me, 'I didn't say that', and often I would have to reply 'I'm afraid you did'. I learnt quite a lot from George . . . especially about the pitfalls of management.

The difference in our opinions became so marked at one point that I suggested I should concentrate on the reserves. I felt the first team were getting two opposing sets of advice; which was confirmed in later years by Jack Kelsey. He told me that whatever I said, George would say something different. Clearly that couldn't continue so for a while I did concentrate on the reserves. That arrangement came to an abrupt end with a 6-0 defeat at West Ham. The next day George said to me: 'I think you'd better come back with the first team.'

We both wanted the same thing: a successful Arsenal. There was no doubt about that. Our responsibilities were well defined with George motivating, publicizing and handling all general matters, and myself training and coaching. But I was becoming increasingly certain that one of us – or even both of us – would have to go.

I would have loved to manage Arsenal, and to this day I am proud to say I was once a member of the staff. I had great hopes, too, that I would get the job one day, especially as I had been told it was only my in-experience which prevented me succeeding Jack Crayston. Arsenal has always been a club that matters. It is sometimes accused of being too conservative, too staid, but I admire its traditions, its image, its strength and its principles. Highbury Stadium is a model ground and the organiza-tion of the club solid and honest. In short, it is a wonderful set-up.

Sir Bracewell Smith, the chairman when I was there, was a former Lord Mayor of London. He was a hard, down-to-earth man, rather an impersonal figure whom it was difficult to know well. He developed an unfortunate habit of coming into the players' dressing-room before games, and he annoyed them because he never got their names right; but he always meant well. Bob Wall was one of the game's leading adminis-trators, perhaps the best, and a fair and open man. He ran a very tight ship, and he invariably gave his support when things were not going so well on the pitch. I could always talk with Bob and I think he more than anyone understood the differences between George Swindin and myself. Bob was eventually made a director and that was nothing more than his due.

Arsenal's prudence cost us Denis Law. He was then with Hudders-field, where he had developed from a sapling into a match-winner whose reactions were quicker than lightning. Arsenal made an offer for him – money plus David Herd – and George Swindin asked me to pop across to Huddersfield from Sheffield where the England Under-23s had a game. Arsenal were playing at home that same day so George was tied to Highbury. Les McDowall, the manager of Manchester City, was already there when I arrived but Huddersfield told us, quickly, that both our offers had been refused.

The tricky thing about Arsenal's plan was that nobody had told David Herd he was being offered to Huddersfield. So when I rang Highbury and spoke to George at half-time I asked immediately:

'Have you told David yet?'

'No, I'm going to tell him after the game', replied George.

'Well, hold on, because Huddersfield want more money' I said.

The position was explained to Sir Bracewell but he refused to increase our offer, and Manchester City got themselves a great player.

In my three seasons with Arsenal they finished twelfth, third and thirteenth in the First Division. During this time I also became manager of the England Under-23 team, in succession to Bill Nicholson who had joined Spurs. But, as I have said, George Swindin and I ran along on different tracks and, although I wanted to stay, my position was quite untenable. Our partnership had begun well but it became progressively more difficult and I knew that sooner or later the board would be obliged to do something about it. As one door threatened to close, though, another suddenly opened. West Ham asked Arsenal if they could interview me with a view to becoming their manager.

My other job (managing the England Under-23 side) had been going smoothly and I was conscious that my horizons were broadening. I was travelling a lot, studying different styles, picking up a wealth of little tips and meeting many interesting and knowledgeable people to whom I listened carefully. There is no substitute for this kind of experience and I do not think it was a coincidence that my predecessor, Bill Nicholson, was the manager of the first English club to win a European trophy, and I was the second. Travel does broaden the mind; and a knowledge of continental football is not acquired easily or at second hand. I still don't think English managers travel enough or study other countries' methods seriously enough – but in those days that criticism was even more valid.

Right from the start I thought there was a tremendous spirit among the Under-23 players themselves. Maurice Setters, Jimmy Greaves, Peter Dobing, Jimmy Armfield, George Eastham and Bobby Charlton were the sort of youngsters who were in the side then: they thought a lot about the game and I thoroughly enjoyed helping them. We won many more games than we lost although I remember one match particularly for a reason that had nothing to do with football's mechanics. It was against France in Lyons and it was the first time Bobby Charlton had flown since the Munich aircrash. We felt for him but it was a battle he had to win for himself – and he did.

One of the first things which worried me about the England Under-23s was the lack of professional help when they travelled abroad. The manager was not only expected to supervize the kit and travelling but he also had to carry the sponge and attend to injuries. No doctor or trainer travelled with the team and I wasted no time in saying to Walter Winterbottom: 'This is ridiculous. I've no experience of this side of the game. I'm not qualified.' Home games were different: England made use of the local club's doctor and physiotherapist.

'But what happens if anything goes really wrong when we're abroad?' I asked Walter.

'There's no need to worry', he replied. 'Our opponents have always got a doctor!'

The problem came to a head in that same game against France in Lyons. Wilf McGuiness went down heavily and grazed a thigh rather nastily. I did the best I could and wrapped it up, but when he got back to Manchester United they were less than enthusiastic about my efforts; and I understood their point of view. United complained to the FA and this was the one bit of supporting evidence I needed. 'There you are' I said to Walter. 'These players are worth a lot of money and it's too risky to leave them to someone with no knowledge or experience of medical matters. We've had one complaint and we're bound to get more.'

Every mistake recognized is a lesson, and soon afterwards a doctor and physiotherapist were always included in every England squad travelling abroad. Walter Winterbottom was England's first full-time manager and, as such, he was navigator, explorer and innovator. Alf Ramsey benefited greatly from Walter's experiences and discoveries when he took over the job.

We went on a memorable tour in May, 1960, at the end of my last full season as manager of England's Under-23s. We beat East Germany 4-1 in Berlin, then we beat Poland 3-2 in Warsaw and finally we went down to Tel Aviv – the first time an English international team had played there. We were expected to win, even though we were playing Israel's full international side, but it was one of those games in which fate seemed to be against us. Mendi, who had been one of the Hungarian coaches at Wembley in 1953, was in charge of the Israeli side and he kept telling the press how good England were and insisting his own side did not have a chance. Alas, we were travel-weary, the temperature was nearly ninety, we did not have many friends among a crowd of forty thousand and, to make matters worse, Tony Macedo in goal apparently decided it was better to throw the ball into his own net than catch it. We missed a few chances but Israel won by four goals to nil, and Maurice Setters, our captain, who was playing in his last Under-23 game, literally cried in the dressing-room afterwards. The shame of losing to Israel was more than he could take. But Mendi was an instant national hero. He had used the press to build us up and then let his players knock us down. It was a skilful bit of gamesmanship – and another useful lesson for me.

I returned to England to find myself at the heart of an unpleasant incident. George Eastham was having his celebrated dispute with New-castle at the time – a row which eventually led to his historic case in the High Court and the end of the old retain and transfer system. Wilf Taylor, a Newcastle director and a member of the FA Council, had been with us on the tour, and he suddenly and publicly accused me of tapping Eastham on Arsenal's behalf. It is true that George and I were close friends but totally untrue that I made any attempt to persuade him to join my club. It was absolute rubbish. I had no authority from Arsenal to make such an approach, and although Eastham did eventually join Arsenal it was certainly nothing to do with me. I was not involved in any way. It peeved me enormously, however, that Wilf Taylor should have trumped up such a story. I never forgave him for that.

12

West Ham...Part one

I spent sixteen years with West Ham, a very large and rewarding part of my life, and yet I was reluctant to join them. I was loth to leave Arsenal, a club I admired, and doubtful about taking on West Ham, a club I knew little about. On balance, though, I think things worked out rather well.

The first hint that my career was about to take an abrupt change in direction came in March 1961. England were playing West Germany in an Under-23 international at Tottenham on the Tuesday but, the night before, Walter Winterbottom took the senior squad to Upton Park for a practice match. That same evening, by sheer coincidence, Ted Fenton left West Ham, suddenly and without real explanation. All the press were there and next morning the story was given royal treatment. I read the reports but did not feel involved.

Next day we set off for the Under-23 match and Walter, who was sitting next to me in the coach, started talking about the game at Upton Park the previous evening.

'West Ham beat us 1-0' he said 'and if you think Bobby Moore's a player you should see this chap Geoff Hurst. He scored this goal against us, from left-half. It was unbelievable. Almost from the halfway line!' Then, suddenly, he asked: 'Would you be interested in the job at West Ham?'

'I'm happy at Arsenal', I said. 'In any case, if they're going to sack people like they did last night it's obviously not a happy club.' I promptly forgot all about this exchange.

Easter came along and I spent our spare day with an army of school-boys at Highbury. I was on my own because Arsenal were holding a board meeting at the Dorchester Hotel. One of the club's directors lived there and when they wanted total privacy the rest of the board joined him at his lodgings.

The boys' match finished and Bob Wall immediately came across. 'Mr Pratt, the West Ham chairman, has been on', he said, 'and he's wondering if he can approach you with a view to you becoming their manager'. I told him I thought my future was with Arsenal and asked him if George Swindin knew about the offer.

'Well . . . yes' he replied, and then added: 'You know, I think this job may be of interest to you.' He then painted a glowing picture of Mr Pratt and it was obvious he knew him well.

I got the message loud and clear. 'All right' I said. 'I'll pop across and see him.'

I drove across to West Ham on the Tuesday morning and met Reg Pratt and his vice-chairman, Len Cearns, members of two families who *were* West Ham. We talked in a little private room just off the old Upton Park boardroom, and I must confess that when I sat down I did not have any firm notions about the job or the club. They came straight to the point and said they wanted me to be West Ham's manager-coach. I was perfectly frank with them and said I was enjoying my job with Arsenal and the England Under-23 side, and that the decision facing me was a difficult one. 'But if I do take the job', I added, 'I would want full control of all team matters and no interference'.

Mr Pratt and Mr Cearns assured me I would have complete charge. I said I was getting £1,500 a year from Arsenal, and they offered me £2,000. That satisfied me: it was not a fortune but it wasn't bad and, in any case, I was more interested in the possibilities of the job than the money. And as we talked I started thinking about the many promising young West Ham players I had met on courses. It was obviously an area rich in talent and, with the two West Ham directors talking with sense and enthusiasm, I began to warm to the job.

I told them I would let them know after the following weekend, and went home to talk things over with Lucy. We were living at Twickenham at the time, near the rugby ground, and our daughter Carole was taking a secretarial course at a local technical school. Lucy was properly concerned that Carole's studies were not interrupted, but I said we could continue to live at Twickenham and that I would drive over to West Ham every day. Lucy and I had both just learned to drive in our first car, a Morris Minor. I did not realize it would take me two and a half hours, against the traffic, to get to work.

We did not make an instant decision but the following Saturday, before a home game, my reluctance to leave Arsenal was changed by a single comment. Sir Bracewell Smith came into the dressing-room and said to me: 'I hear you might be leaving us.'

'Well, there's a possibility', I replied, 'but I haven't made up my mind yet'.

His answer was not what I'd hoped for. 'Well, never mind', he said. 'If you leave us we might eventually come to you and say we want you back here.'

That was one of the most disappointing things ever said to me, and I was so angry that I muttered under my breath: 'Over my dead body'. I had, in fact, almost made up my mind to join West Ham, but I was furious that Arsenal made no attempt to keep me. On reflection I was being less than realistic, but I was convinced at the time that no one could have done a better job and that Arsenal were close to having a very handy side. I had worked so hard it was even showing physically: my face was drawn and I was thinner than I should have been. I felt, in my innocence, that instead of letting me go the chairman should have talked about the continuing challenge at Highbury. But he didn't – and I told West Ham I would be delighted to be their manager.

I returned briefly to Highbury on the Monday to clear things up and started work at Upton Park the following day. It was as quick and simple as that. One moment I was saying goodbye to a bunch of lads I knew well, the next I was talking to a new squad – all in their tracksuits and sitting on the wall in front of the main stand at Upton Park. First meetings and first impressions are always important so, after introducing myself, I told them how I saw the game in general, what I was hoping for and what I intended to do. They listened intently and I felt their response was warm.

The West Ham players were by no means all strangers to me. I had met some on courses, others when they had played for England at Youth or Under-23 level and still more when Arsenal played West Ham; and within a matter of days I began to realize what a goldmine I had inherited. I felt like someone who had scratched what looked like ordinary metal and found something precious just under the surface. An excellent rapport was established, and in just a few weeks I was thinking: 'This is going to be good.'

I did not have a contract, for two reasons. West Ham said they did not give them . . . and I did not want one. I felt the West Ham directors could be trusted and my confidence in myself made me feel we did not need to be handcuffed together by a few lines of small print. I had signed a contract with Eastbourne and it could have caused complications.

My first game as West Ham's manager was the following Saturday, at home to Manchester City. It was an important match because we were too near the bottom of the First Division for comfort and there were only a few games to go to the end of the season. Between Ted Fenton's undignified departure and my arrival the side had been run by Mr Pratt and Phil Woosnam, the club captain, and I told them we would play the side they had in mind for the Manchester City game. I wanted to watch my new players before making any decision about the best line-up.

The game was drawn, but several things bothered me about West Ham's methods. They were, for example, very man-to-man conscious in defence. On one occasion our right-back, Joe Kirkup, was so intent on marking Dave Wagstaffe, City's outside-left, that when Wagstaffe trotted down the wing Joe followed him all the way – and forgot about the ball. My first impressions about the side as a whole were confirmed, though: it was full of talent.

The following week was important in all sorts of ways. We had a re-arranged game at Burnley on the Tuesday, Phil Woosnam was to play for Wales against Spain in a vital World Cup qualifying game at Ninian Park twenty-four hours later, and the following Saturday we were to play Cardiff there. We decided to stay in Manchester on Tuesday night, travel down to Porthcawl on Wednesday morning, watch the international and then stay on for the weekend game. Everything linked up nicely and I felt that being together for the best part of a week would give me an early chance to get to know the players better.

We trained at Upton Park on the Monday and Bill Jenkins, our physiotherapist, a wonderful chap and a real man's man, told me something which triggered off an interesting sequence of events. 'John Bond won't be fit for the Burnley game', he said. I asked for more details and Bill elaborated. The message I got was that John picked his own matches, and that he did not fancy playing at Turf Moor. John was almost a cult figure at Upton Park, a big chap with a strong personality and a survivor from the older school of Malcolm Allison, Noel Cantwell and company. Bill added that Bond would still like to travel with us and said he would be fit for Saturday. 'Fine, if that's what you think is right . . . who's the reserve left-back?' I asked. Bill said it was John Lyall, so we agreed he should play and that Ronnie Boyce, who had played his first senior game earlier in the season, should take the place of Phil Woosnam.

At our hotel in Manchester, on the corner of Piccadilly, I took the chance to have another long chat with the players. I said I did not like their rigid man-to-man marking and stressed the need for flexibility. I sorted a few other things out, and then talked to them about the Saturday game at Cardiff. It was a talk which, years later, John Lyall said he still remembered.

Burnley, with due respect to my old home town, can be a desperately miserable place when it tries; and on that Tuesday night it excelled itself. The rain poured down, there was a chill wind, the crowd was small and, in next to no time, we found ourselves two goals down. 'Oh dear' I thought. I was not a happy man. Doubts about everything began to hit me. But all of a sudden West Ham began to click. Instead of making the game look complicated it now seemed easy. We pulled a goal back, then managed an equalizer and, in the end, we were unlucky not to win. I could sense the relief. Everyone was bubbling afterwards, really delighted, and the spirit of our party when we left for South Wales was remarkable.

The international proved well worth seeing, although Wales were a trifle unfortunate to lose by 2-1. Phil Woosnam had a fine game and scored an early goal, but Spain had players of the quality of Di Stefano, Del Sol and Suarez. In fact it was Di Stefano himself who scored their winner near the end.

The Spaniards left for home immediately after the game and we moved on to Porthcawl to discover we were taking over the same rooms in the hotel just vacated by Spain. In a drawer in my room I found a dossier left by one of the Spaniards. It contained notes on his immediate opponent in the Welsh side and, although it was in Spanish, I could see it was a very thorough breakdown. That was another little notion I stored away.

We trained hard on a local school pitch for the following two days and although I noticed general discipline was rather slack there were no particular problems. Phil Woosnam rejoined us, delighted with the point we had won at Burnley, and the mood of the party was excellent.

Just before lunch on the Friday Bill Jenkins said to me: 'John Bond is fit . . . he can play.'

'That's good', I said, 'but let's get one thing straight, Bill. It's your job to get 'em fit: it's my job to pick them. John Bond may be fit to play, but he's not in the side.'

Bill Jenkins was a West Ham evergreen, and when he died from a heart attack in 1966 something went out of the club. He looked surprised at my decision, but an important point had been made. No heated words were exchanged but we had clarified the relationship between us. We knew where we stood. I announced the side with John Lyall still at left-back and Phil Woosnam back at inside-forward.

The next person to approach me was Roland Brandon, one of the West Ham directors, a charming chap who took his Rolls Royce with him wherever he went – at home or abroad.

'Why isn't John Bond playing?' he asked.

'I haven't selected him' I replied. 'And it is my understanding with Mr Pratt and Mr Cearns that I've got full control of team matters.' Again there was no argument; but again a point had been made.

Next it was the turn of John Bond himself. 'Why aren't I playing?' he asked aggressively.

'Because I've picked John Lyall. He played well at Burnley and keeps his place', I replied.

'But Phil didn't play at Burnley and he's back and I don't think that's fair', John went on.

'Wait a second' I answered. 'Let's be quite clear who is who in this club. I am the manager and you are a player. I am in charge, I pick the team and that's something you'd better accept for your own good.'

I did not mention his 'injury', or my suspicions about him wanting to pick his games, but I left him in no doubt that I was my own man.

John Bond was known as Muffin – Muffin the Mule – and I was to discover that as well as having a strong kick he could be both stubborn and rude. He was a rebel who did not always see things as they really were. But, once again, an early difference of opinion did no harm and in years to come he was to admit that my firmness helped him. Indeed, I felt those three conversations, with one of the staff, one of the directors and one of the players, had been invaluable. The team knew what was going on and I think everyone got the message. We also drew at Cardiff to complete a profitable week.

Inevitably, as I got to know the club and its players, other problems became apparent. There were too many players on the staff and, in one or two cases, the attitude was wrong. There were undercurrents, personal problems, personality clashes and a few people outside the club whose influence with the players was too strong to be healthy. All these things needed to be resolved – and, to complicate matters, the maximum wage had been removed and I had to work out new contracts. This proved simple enough in the end and was certainly very different from the sort of negotiating that goes on these days: £30 a week was a lot of money then.

West Ham, I discovered, was my sort of club. It belongs to its own patch in East London, a local club in the best sense, with a crowd that is second to none. The West Ham fans identify with the players and there is a genuine relationship between them; they all belong to the same family. No other club in London is quite like it.

The club itself is well equipped and well administered, while Upton Park is compact but not small and has a style and atmosphere all its own. The old Chicken Run has now gone but, in my early days there, this popular area opposite the main stand somehow stood for West Ham. It was low and tatty, its steps were wooden and occasionally I would wander over and marvel that it had never burnt down. There was usually a lot of paper and rubbish underneath, and although we had a regular clear-out there was always a chance that a cigarette or match carelessly thrown away would start a blaze. Sometimes we would find something smouldering, but the Chicken Run survived – and the sight and sound of the crowd in the old place letting rip with *I'm forever blowing bubbles* always delighted me. I suppose the Chicken Run was a bit of an eyesore but it was all part of the West Ham tradition – and tradition is, after all, the foundation of our game.

The club was also lucky to have some excellent local newspapers covering its fortunes, *The Stratford Express*, *The Ilford Recorder* and *The Dagenham Post*. They had a big circulation in the area and they did us proud, contributing to the community feeling.

I discovered I was really an outsider at Upton Park because everyone else went back a long way with the club. Eddie Chapman, the secretary, a good friend and a very able and loyal official, had been a West Ham player – in fact I played against him. It was the same with the rest of the staff. Wally St Pier, our chief scout, was another former West Ham player, a man who knew the game inside out, and then there were stalwarts like Ernie Gregory and Albert Walker. They were worried when I took over in case there were going to be major changes, but I actually involved them even more closely in the club's affairs and they were still there when I left. My secretary was Pauline Moss – I always called her Mrs Moss – and I sometimes felt the whole club was built round her. She had also been Ted Fenton's secretary and was a pillar of our establishment. All these people had one thing in common: West Ham was their life.

My first office was at the end of the old boardroom, where the bar is now, and I thought it a most imposing place. The only thing wrong with it was that it also housed the machine which calculated the number of people coming through the turnstiles on match-days. It ticked away furiously and my office was no place to be just before a game. Not that I spent more time there than I had to. My place was with the players.

I found no immediate difficulty in taking the step from coach to manager. My apprenticeship had been a good one, I knew what was expected of me and the new, broader responsibility was something I shouldered happily. Basically, I believed it was all a matter of common sense – and that included the transfer market, which was something new to me. I kept my eyes and ears open, covered a lot of miles, thought carefully and expected to pay a fair price for the right player.

My first need was a goalkeeper. Brian Rhodes, our man at the back when I took over, was an immensely likeable chap, but I felt we could and should do better, so I took an early chance to see one or two internationals at the end of the season. I went up to Hampden Park to see Scotland play the Republic of Ireland, and although Scotland won easily the Irish goalkeeper had a brilliant game. The trouble was that his name was Noel

Dwyer. He had already been a West Ham player and had left the club under a cloud.

Dwyer seemed to be just the kind of goalkeeper I needed but he was a part of the club's history, not its future, and instead I went for Scotland's goalkeeper, Lawrie Leslie of Airdrie. He was my first signing and he fitted the bill excellently, a good 'keeper and a first-class man. My second buy was another Scot, Ian Crawford of Hearts, an Under-23 international and a left-winger with flair and intelligence.

Some players had to go and one I sold had so much ability we called him 'The White Didi' – after the great Brazilian mid-field player who starred in the 1958 and 1962 World Cups. This was John Cartwright who, many years later, I was to appoint England's Youth team manager. He had everything as a player, an absolutely brilliant prospect, but his attitude was wrong. He had been influenced by fawning outsiders and felt everything should come easily to him. I let him go to Crystal Palace for £7,500 and this early disappointment helped him reassess his career. He eventually became a very good coach indeed, a first-class asset. Another young player who left us was Harry Cripps, a real enthusiast who went on to do a good defensive job for Millwall for many years. Both Harry and John have told me since they wished they could have stayed at Upton Park.

Seven of the side which was to win the FA Cup in 1963 were already at Upton Park when I arrived, although they were not all in the first team then. They were Ken Brown, John Bond and, the new wave, Bobby Moore, Eddie Bovington, Jack Burkett, Ronnie Boyce and Geoff Hurst. The younger ones made their mark in their own way and in their own time, but to begin with I was simply bent on getting together a side that would establish the club in the First Division. I knew a winning side would not develop overnight, and I was grateful for the support of my more experienced players.

If I read the script correctly I think Phil Woosnam hoped to become West Ham's manager himself. He was very close to Jack Turner, his agent, a businessman but a father-figure too. I suspect the two of them hoped Jack would become general manager and concentrate on the commercial side of things, with Phil taking over as team manager. If that is true, then Phil overcame his disappointment very quickly and was a genuine source of strength. He was an excellent skipper and motivator and was full of ideas. We worked well together and talked about the game for hours.

Phil was a creative inside-forward who moved the ball well, held things together with tremendous authority and was always first to spot and exploit opposition weaknesses. But he was to have a problem period caused by some of the very qualities which made him such an asset. He wanted to do everybody's work and would even drop back and take the ball off his own defenders. He smothered the younger players and robbed them of their individuality. He 'helped' them so much they couldn't express themselves. In giving so much himself he took something away from others. Responsibility weighed on him like a ton of coal and, as a result, he lost his fine edge. He did everything with the best intentions, but the result was that the side often lost much of its momentum. It is a trap other strong characters have fallen into, but once I had isolated the trouble we were able to cure it.

Ken Brown was a pillar of the side at centre-half, a stopper who never gave in and a brilliant header of the ball. He had a most wonderful personality – he was a pleasing, friendly man who was always smiling, and I knew I could count on him. His interest in football, however, was confined to playing; he did not involve himself otherwise and I think that was a pity. He won one cap for England but I believe he would have been an even better player if he had had a broader outlook. I judged him as a former centre-half myself, and I felt he could have played more football at the back. His mind and his technique were certainly sharp enough to take on this extra dimension. He and John Bond were at West Ham together for about fourteen years and later, of course, they formed an effective managerial partnership. Ken's interest in the game as a whole has certainly grown!

Malcolm Musgrove was another player I counted myself lucky to have. He was a very useful winger and even when he was not at his best he still gave everything. He was always shouting for the ball and trying to lift the performance of others. He had effective days and modest days but he was the sort of player managers warm to. He was a great help to me when I joined West Ham, and later went on to become an excellent coach and chairman of the Professional Footballers' Association. Johnny Dick was a different sort of character, a tall, angular Scot who had been with the club nearly ten years and scored a lot of vital goals along the way. There was talk that he was finished, but I did not believe this so we worked hard with him, he responded magnificently and we had one more profitable season out of him. We then sold him to Brentford, late in 1962, for about £17,000. It was a move he wanted, and it proved good for him and good for us.

Johnny Dick was the only member of the West Ham side who did not attend a coaching course I laid on at Lilleshall in my first season with West Ham. It was his choice and I did not argue, but he missed one of the most exhilarating courses I can remember. It was just for West Ham and we took Lilleshall over for a whole week – the first time a club had done this. Every day we worked morning, afternoon and evening. My plan was to give everybody a notion of what coaching was all about so that it would be easier for me to transmit my ideas.

The response from all the players was tremendous, and as Phil Woosnam and Malcolm Musgrove were both full coaches we were able to get right inside the game. Then, to round things off, the players sat down on the Friday for an examination – a paper on refereeing which lasted an hour, and then a two-hour theory paper. Brian Lee, now warden at Bisham Abbey, was then second-in-command at Lilleshall and took the examination. The results were tremendously encouraging: Ron Tindall, who had joined us from Chelsea, got his full badge and many others passed the preliminary.

The same afternoon I took the first team down to a hotel just outside Bedford, where Johnny Dick joined us, and the reserves went back to Upton Park. It had not been a week of standard preparation for a big game, but next day we got a worthy 2-2 draw against Arsenal at Highbury, my old workshop, with Ron Tindall scoring with one of the best headers I have ever seen. It was a happy postscript to a stimulating week.

I felt we were heading in the right direction and, in fact, we finished eighth in my first full season, 1961–62. Spurs, a side of maturity, high quality and balance, were setting the standards but I felt our way was going to pay a dividend in the not too distant future. We felt it was the right way and certainly the best way for us; and I say 'we' because my players shared my beliefs. We aimed to play constructive, intelligent football at all times, even if this meant occasionally being turned over by a team that was direct and muscular in the traditional British way. We seemed most at risk when the opposition played as if it was their last day on earth. Cup ties, particularly, are like this and in that first full season of mine we were soundly beaten at Plymouth in the third round. That hurt!

We never thought of compromising, however, because we felt so strongly about our method and our attitude. We knew our road was uphill – but it was the only road we wanted to take. It may have been a gamble but we thought it worth the risk.

It was obviously essential I had the right kind of player and there was one man I wanted above all: Johnny Byrne. He was with Crystal Palace, who had just won promotion from the Fourth Division, and I set my heart on him the night he helped destroy West Germany in an Under-23 international at Tottenham. We won 4-1 before a crowd of nearly sixteen thousand and everything went like a dream. Bobby Moore was excellent,

Freddie Hill of Bolton looked full of promise and chaps like Terry Paine of Southampton and John Barnwell were clearly going to make their mark. But most of all there was Johnny Byrne. His performance was almost unbelievable.

At that time I was Arsenal's assistant manager and coach, but that night I promised myself that if ever I became a manager I would try to sign Byrne. The chance came in March, 1962, just a year after the Under-23 international and towards the end of my first full season with West Ham. Arthur Rowe, Crystal Palace's manager, let me know Byrne was available – at a price. It was simply a question of finding the money. I told Mr Pratt I wanted Byrne and how important he could be to the future of our side, and his response was everything I hoped for. He backed me to the hilt. I asked him if, as chairman, he would handle the financial side of the deal because I was in my early days as a manager and this was going to be very big business.

We were told Palace's negotiations were to be handled by one of their directors, Victor Ercolani of the Ercol furniture company. As he lived at nearby Woodford it was decided we should meet at his home. I accompanied Mr Pratt and we found Mr Ercolani had Arthur Rowe with him. I did not know quite what to expect but it all turned out to be very civilized. Mr Pratt handled things with tact and firmness and it was agreed we should pay Palace £62,500 plus Ronnie Brett, a skilful forward who had started his career at Selhurst before joining us. The package was worth £65,000 – a British record fee. It was also agreed we could put down part of the fee and pay the rest at the rate of £1,000 a week. That was the last time West Ham bought a player on hire purchase. From that day on they have always bought outright, cash down, the full sum. Palace were sorry to see Johnny go but were delighted with the deal, and so were we. Johnny himself was no problem. His wage: £40 a week. Sadly, Ronnie Brett was soon to be killed in a car accident. A tragedy and a waste.

We paid a record fee for Byrne . . . so what did we get in return? Byrne was a forward who, in my opinion, simply had everything. I used to call him 'the Di Stefano of British football' and I could pitch no praise higher than that.

Johnny was smallish, not quite five feet eight inches tall, but solidly built. He had a boyish face and a tongue that worked overtime – hence his nickname, 'Budgie'. He was born in the Surrey green belt but he bubbled and chirped like a real East Londoner. Life was never dull when he was around and the other players liked him immediately.

Byrne's talent was enormous. He was beautifully balanced, a short-strider and a master of the ball. He seemed to need no space in which to turn and no time to wind up. He could change his mind or his direction in a blink and was almost impossible to anticipate. He would stop the ball with his chest and, before it hit the ground, volley it out to a winger. The bigger the centre-half against him the better he seemed to play. He loved pitting himself against defenders the size of Maurice Norman of Spurs. Budgie would just back into him and then spin away like a top. But although he was an individualist he led his line well and was always looking to bring his team-mates into the game. He made us tick, and when Budgie played well we played well.

There was one little problem, alas, when he joined us. Nothing seemed to work out for him. He had a disastrous first eight months or so in which he could not put a foot right. This was partly due to bad luck, partly to attitude of mind and partly to the usual difficulties of settling down with new team-mates. He was trying too hard to justify his fee and, when the crowd inevitably became impatient, he started worrying. Sometimes it seemed he wanted to take the lace out of the ball before putting it into the net.

People started looking at me as if I was mad and I could sense them wondering why I had spent a fortune on a player from the wrong end of the League. I felt pressure myself because I knew my judgement was being questioned. But I had such absolute faith in Johnny that I was able to ride all criticism. Eventually I said to him: 'Just go back to the basics. Do the simple things and once that starts going right your game will come together.' I had no doubts about him and in time, of course, he fulfilled every expectation. He became a central figure in West Ham's success.

We rounded off that season with a tour of Nyasaland, Southern Rhodesia and Ghana, an African adventure which taught us more about ourselves than football. We scored twenty goals and conceded only two in our six games: that side of the tour presented no problem. It was only after we had left Nyasaland and Southern Rhodesia, two good stops, and arrived in Ghana that things started to go wrong. The army had taken over and we found the place in chaos.

Nobody met us at the airport at Accra – the excuse given later was that they thought we were on another plane. By this time, though, we knew there was only one flight a day from Johannesburg to Accra. We then found ourselves being shown into a hotel that was nothing more than a doss-house. The blankets almost crawled. Nobody slept, nobody even got between those awful blankets . . . except Johnny Dick, who could sleep anywhere.

I created a fuss and eventually, halfway through the night, a fellow from the Ghana FA turned up. Another hotel was found for us and we made the switch very early the next morning. It was a new hotel, they said, but it was damp and cold and nothing had been made up. Malcolm Musgrove, wearing a nice pair of suede shoes, found himself walking through what looked like red mud in the semi-darkness.

One of the Ghanaian officials was a prominent FIFA man, a six-foot six-inch mountain wrapped in colourful robes. I looked up at him and said with all the authority I could muster: 'If this goes on I shall report you to FIFA.' I was only too aware that he could have squashed me flat with one hand. I even threatened to pull out of the tour, but the Assistant High Commissioner then appeared. 'Please don't . . . it would cause an international incident' he said. I told the players about this and Bill Lansdowne – a responsible, level-headed man, who was then nearing the end of his playing days and was later to become a West Ham coach – said: 'I agree. We've got to stay. But please, Ron, don't ever take me on a tour again!'

Everything was eventually sorted out, after a fashion, and we got on with the football. We won our games convincingly and were then tipped off that we had stepped out of line: apparently visiting sides were supposed to settle for honourable draws!

The tour had a hidden bonus for us, however. Through all its adversity our team spirit grew even stronger. The problems we shared welded us together. It also taught me a lot about the character of my players. I noted those who had a good sense of humour, those I could count on, those who looked for problems and those who were idle. And on my first tour as a manager I discovered much about myself. I discovered I could be very impatient, even when the only real answer was diplomacy and courtesy. I discovered the need to be adaptable when abroad, and the value of laughter. Yet firmness is always an asset – it does produce results. Just before we left our hotel in Accra the assistant manager told me: 'I'm glad you stood up to them because every team that comes here gets this sort of treatment. Nobody has stood up to them before.'

I now felt I was on top of my job and involved myself in every aspect of the club – with transfers, finance, players' personal problems, the day-to-day routine, and, of course, training, tactics and selection. Foreign visitors to Upton Park would ask: 'How many jobs do you do?' I would reply: 'About a dozen – but I only get one wage.' It was no hardship, though. Total job satisfaction is a priceless thing which has nothing to do with pressure or the number of hours worked. I thought life was wonderful.

There was a wealth of young players coming through, most of them products of our own area, most of them unearthed by Wally St Pier whose contacts were second to none. He knew every corner of our parish and had connections in every school; but his net was spread from Scotland to the south coast. Wally had an old pro's eye for quality, that feeling for talent and character which are special. West Ham will always be in his debt.

Wally did most of the spadework in acquiring a player. I was usually only called in at the kill. A typical example was Johnny Sissons, whose lovely talents were all too obvious right from the start. This young Middlesex lad would hear thousands of youngsters shouting 'Sissons . . . Sissons' when he played in schoolboy internationals at Wembley. A lot of clubs were very keen on him but Charlie Faulkner, one of our scouts, lived nearby in Middlesex. We persevered, we said the right things and we won the battle for him. Our reputation for being a family club and bringing on young players did us no harm and, indeed, when young Johnny came to us we hid him away for a year and a half. I remember him saying to me at one point in his professional apprenticeship: 'This is a different game to the one I used to play. I don't know anything about it.'

We won the FA Youth Cup in 1963 and I find it impossible to describe how much pleasure this gave me. We had some tremendous youngsters in the side, Sissons, Trevor Dawkins, Bill Kitchener, Martin Britt, Dennis Burnett, John Charles, Peter Bennett, Bobby Howe, Colin Mackleworth, Harry Redknapp and John Dryden, all from London or just outside, and we had few doubts that they would go all the way. With two replays it took us nine games to win the tournament; and in every one of our five matches at Upton Park we scored four goals or more, including five in the home leg of the final against Liverpool.

Jimmy Barrett, a former West Ham player like his father before him, was our youth coach and I spent so much time working with him that Bobby Moore said to me jokingly: 'You're more interested in the youngsters than you are in the first team.' Ours was one of the most exciting youth teams I have ever seen, a side of talent, good habits and style. They were West Ham's future.

In the League we were inconsistent, full of sparkle one week, blue the next, often matching the best but disappointing against more ordinary teams. Our form was mid-table; and so was our final position. We had a run in the FA Cup once the terrible snow and ice of early 1963 had disappeared. We beat Everton, who were to win the championship, with a penalty by Johnny Byrne in the fifth round, but Liverpool narrowly edged us out in the quarter-finals at Anfield. A niggling feeling began to grow that perhaps we were better suited to Cup football than League, that we were sprinters rather than marathon men. A year before the opposite had seemed true: now I was not so sure. The blame was partly mine, of course. I began to wonder – not for the last time – if I had put enough concrete into the mixture. Was the team hard enough? Was I being too idealistic? Questions like this are easier to ask than answer but one thing never wavered: my faith in good, intelligent football.

Peter Brabrook had joined us in October 1962 from Chelsea after long negotiations. He was an East Londoner we had missed in the mid-fifties – an expensive slip! He cost us £35,000, a lot of money, but with several England caps and more than two hundred and fifty League games for Chelsea behind him I felt he would give us new pace and drive as well as experience on the right-wing. He had been inconsistent at Chelsea and he took time to settle with us; but once we had persuaded him to think more about his game he became a mature, much more effective player.

We also had a new goalkeeper, Jim Standen, following a wretched run of injuries to Lawrie Leslie – one of them sustained when he went in head first to salvage a bad back-pass. I knew Jim from my days at Arsenal where he was the stand-in for Jack Kelsey. He had then moved to Luton and, at the very time I was looking for a new 'keeper, I read that he was about to join a non-League club. I moved in quickly, got Jim for around £7,000, and what an asset he proved. He was an outstanding athlete with safe hands, good reflexes and a canny understanding of pace and line – some of the reasons why he was also a first-class cricketer with Worcestershire.

I now had all the players who were going to win the FA Cup in 1964, and their development into a team took a big step forward in the summer before that season. We took part in an American international tournament which involved outstanding clubs from all over the world, including Brazil, Mexico, Germany, France, Scotland, Italy and Poland. The experience gained was priceless: we couldn't have got it anywhere else at the time.

The clubs were split into two groups, with the winners of each meeting in the final. We were in the first section. Before we left home I told my players: 'This is not going to be a picnic. Burnley were in it last year and although they did very well they had a lot of problems. I know from my own experience that it's going to be hot and difficult, we'll be facing unusual styles and coming up against different attitudes and values. Let's see what you're made of.'

We played six games in our group, lost only one, to Mantova of Italy, and went into our last match against Recife of Brazil needing just a point to finish on top. The heat that evening in New York was around ninety degrees, it was humid, the Randall's Island pitch was a cow and the

Brazilians had some brilliant players. It was impossible to play in the usual English way, so we slowed things down and let the ball do the work. We drew 1-1, enough to win the group, and the reaction of the Brazilian coach said everything. Before the game I gave him a handful of badges: at the end he threw them all straight back at me!

We had to go home for a month while the second group was being played and then return to New York to play the winners in the final. The players asked me if they could take their wives and girlfriends out for the second phase and the directors, as good as gold, immediately agreed. They knew it would be a costly business, because our expenses covered only the players, but they did not hesitate. Their gesture did wonders for club spirit.

The second group was won by Gornik of Poland, a hard, intelligent side which had a seventeen-year-old prodigy in it called Lubanski, an inside-forward whom everyone was talking about and who became one of the most celebrated Polish players of all time. The final was a two-legged affair and we drew the first game 1-1. Everything now rested on one game, with the winners staying on to play Dukla of Prague, the previous year's winners, for a special Challenge Cup.

Victory meant an extra week in America so I said to all the wives and girlfriends: 'If you want to stay on you'd better gee up these men of yours. Make sure they win!' I fancy they did their best, but Gornik were still on top in the early stages. One incident then changed everything. The Canadian referee made a decision the Polish immigrants in the crowd did not care for so they poured onto the pitch and beat the poor fellow up. We had to leave the field and I said to the officials: 'If anything else like this happens it's all finished. We won't go on again.' Gornik seemed deflated by the incident, we raised our game and won with a goal by Geoff Hurst.

The first of our two games against Dukla for the Challenge Cup was to be played in Chicago, so I had to tell the ladies that we could not afford to take them with us. They would have to stay in New York until we returned for the second leg. Our departure was quite a scene. The players on the coach cheering because their girls were being left behind . . . while the girls on the pavement were delighted at being left on their own!

Dukla proved to be the best side we faced that summer; they had tremendous skill and strength, and about five men had played for Czechoslovakia in the World Cup final the year before, among them Masopust and Pluskal. Dukla beat us by a goal to nil and, although we had the better of things in the second leg back in New York, they held us to a draw to win 2-1 on aggregate. Masopust, a player of real distinction, came up to me afterwards and said: 'Mr Greenwood, you have a wonderful young side. They have a great future.' That comment pleased me no end, coming from a man of his ability and experience.

It could have taken two or three years at home to gain the experience we achieved on our American adventure. We faced the skill of Brazilians, the quick minds of Italians, the controlled strength of Germans and Poles and the all-round quality of Czechs. Every one of our ten games was a lesson in itself and our reward came in the form of increased confidence, understanding and team-spirit. I was convinced even bigger things lay just ahead of us.

13

Hurst, Moore and Peters...Part one

Geoff Hurst, Bobby Moore and Martin Peters (no order of merit that – just alphabetical) played more than fifteen hundred games between them for West Ham and won two hundred and twenty-four caps for England. They were products of West Ham's own allotment and they conquered the world.

All three were waiting for me when I joined West Ham, young chaps ready to be taken in hand. In football terms it was like hitting the jackpot on the pools three weeks in a row. I watched them develop from inexperienced youngsters full of doubts into central figures in the history of our national game. They gave me success, joy, deep, enduring professional satisfaction – and a few headaches. I was lucky to be part of their story.

The three might have been specially created to win the World Cup for England . . . the key figures in a plan ordained above. Moore, the captain, was voted the outstanding player of the 1966 tournament; Hurst was the first man to score a hat-trick in a World Cup final; and Peters scored England's other goal on that famous day at Wembley. George Brown, who supported West Ham and the Labour Party with just about equal intensity, sang *I'm forever blowing bubbles* at the victory banquet afterwards. West Ham, not England, he insisted, had beaten West Germany. Our cup, the World Cup, was full.

I cannot say I anticipated such success when I inherited the trio. Peters was the gifted one, his talent stood out like a chapel hat-peg, but he was still in the youth team. Moore was a first-class technician and a quick learner but he was heavy-legged, not a good runner and a poor header. His promise seemed limited. Hurst was just a big, strong, ordinary wing-half, happy when going forward but a terrible defender. The raw material was all there but the shaping and maturing of it took time.

There was even doubt about their best positions. Moore's climb to distinction began after I switched him from wing-half to central defence. Hurst only became a player when I moved him into attack. Peters was so versatile he wore every shirt from one to eleven and had to ask me: 'What is my best position?' At that moment I did not know but my answer in the end was to rid him of all shackles and give him a free role.

Moore had won his spurs as West Ham's left-half by the time I joined them at the end of the 1960–61 season although, curiously, he had just been dropped a couple of times by Mr Pratt, the chairman, and Phil Woosnam, who ran the side between Ted Fenton's departure and my arrival. Hurst had got their nod instead and Moore, mortally hurt as only youngsters can be, soon came to see me. I understood his attitude: pride is part of a good player's make-up. He said he was worried about his future, but I told him his future was West Ham's future. 'I've known you some time, in the England Youth and Under-23 teams, and I feel we can build this club around you' I told him. I was not flattering him. I meant it.

There was always something about Moore. He looked good, of course: nice height and strong build, blond hair, determined chin and cool, knowing eyes. He did not win any major acclaim as a schoolboy and, in fact, showed more promise as a cricketer, but once he started to move there was no stopping him. I first spotted him playing centre-half in a schoolboys' match at Stamford Bridge. I was impressed by his presence and solidness on the ball and, although West Ham saw him as a wing-half I used him in central defence as soon as we got together with England's Youth team. He began playing centre-half for West Ham's reserves though not with much success. A lot of goals went past him because he wasn't sure of himself in the air. I was manager at Eastbourne at the time but Geoff Hurst remembers how other players at Upton Park used to gripe about their number five. They all said much the same thing – 'Get Moore out of that position.' They got their way and Moore switched back to left-half, but this did not worry me because my Youth team played a lot of continental sides who tended to keep the ball on the ground. Moore coped splendidly with them.

There was no sign yet, however, that Moore was going to become a player of world stature. He looked as if he might be very good but there were a lot of better equipped youngsters about. He did not have much pace, or even variety in the pace he had, and there were people around who would say he couldn't cope with 'a chasing'.

Moore's critics could see he had weaknesses, and certainly he did not have the natural talent of Martin Peters. But what few people knew about was his fanatical dedication. Moore made himself into a great player.

I rarely had a conversation with young Moore. He simply asked questions. He wanted to know everything. He would quiz me for hours, just picking my brain, and I was delighted to oblige. He would slip into the seat next to me, on plane or coach, and in a professional sense we became very close. We talked for hours and, during practice and in games, I could see it was time well spent. I studied Real Madrid in one match and told Moore how their full-backs played early balls down the line with the outside of the front foot which meant their intentions were disguised. He mastered the technique – front foot, outside contact, early ball to target already in mind – and used it throughout his career. His front foot was always his right.

There were times when I was deliberately unkind to Moore. I even told him he would never win a place in Hartlepool's side because he couldn't head the ball. But he got round that problem, too. He would use his mind and feet to get into exactly the right position, so that he could let the ball drop and take it with chest or foot. He was difficult to fault. He was a perfectionist.

Moore's switch from left-half to central defence came in my first full season. We were playing Leicester, an intelligent, well coordinated side, and to counter one or two things I knew they would try I suggested a new role to Bobby. 'Drop back . . . play deeper and play loose' I told him. He slotted into the role beautifully, working alongside and to the left of Ken Brown at centre-half. That gave our full-backs a chance to go in and get closer to their opponents, and the balance of the side improved immediately. Moore had found his niche.

His international chance came suddenly in 1962. England reached the finals of the World Cup in Chile and Walter Winterbottom, his selection rubber-stamped by the International Committee, named his squad early. Not so long before departure, though, he told me he thought he had a wing-half problem and my reply was immediate. 'Why not take Bobby Moore? He won't let you down.' We had often talked about Moore and such a strong recommendation didn't surprise Winterbottom: he probably half expected it. Moore was on the plane. He was thus unable to join us on our club tour of Nyasaland, Southern Rhodesia and Ghana. When I called him into my office to break the news I said with contrived severity: 'You won't be coming with us on tour.' Then, as his face fell, I added with a smile '. . . because you're going to Chile with England.' Moore's face was now a mixture of surprise and pleasure, and even perhaps a flush of anger at my 'bad news, good news' way of letting him know. One thing is certain: my pleasure at Moore's selection was at least as great as his own.

Moore's selection was kept quiet for a day or two, to keep the pressure off him before they left, but Winterbottom then decided to take a chance and played him at right-half in the warm-up game against Peru. That one unexpected invitation was all Moore needed and he played in all the World

Cup games in Chile. He had come to stay. A hundred or so more caps were on the way.

Jimmy Adamson, Burnley's captain, much respected and highly experienced, was Walter's right-hand man on the trip and when he got back he told me he'd noticed one or two little faults in Moore's game. 'Bobby's a bad passer' was one comment. He meant Moore's passing was erratic under pressure. 'Well, I wouldn't worry about that. He'll cope because once he knows about a fault he irons it out', I replied. I knew there were still a few good habits to be ingrained into Moore, but this was just a matter of time.

Moore's timing was impeccable in everything – even the start of his professional career coincided with the removal of the maximum wage, and this led to an early difference of opinion. I offered £28 and Moore wanted £30. This sounds ridiculous now, but in those days a couple of pounds mattered – a point emphasized by the fact that we both felt it was worth arguing about. I was brought up never to spend what I hadn't got; and as West Ham were not a rich club my attitude to their money was exactly the same. The players used to think I was a Scrooge. I didn't like disagreements over money because they pinpointed one of every manager's main difficulties. One moment, in his office, he is expected to argue about money. The next moment, on the pitch, he is expected to ask for blood. But, in office or on pitch, it was my job to do right by the club. And, yes, Moore and the rest of the players eventually got their £30.

The only player with whom I'd compare Moore is Franz Beckenbauer of West Germany. Beckenbauer had a bit more pace but the quickness of Moore's mind compensated for that. He read the game uncannily well, his anticipation always seemed to give him a head start, he was icily cold at moments of high stress and his positional sense was impeccable. He was at his best when his best was most needed and his concentration never let up. He made football look a simple and lovely art.

Geoff Hurst was barely holding his own as a First Division footballer when I joined West Ham. He had played eight League games in two seasons and, at best, he was promising to become a strong, honest wing-half with no claim on history. He was handsomely built, always willing and loved to go forward, a simple, uncomplicated sort of player, but his game lacked foundation. He was useless at accepting responsibility. I told him early on: 'You're a horrible defender. When the ball's behind you, you don't even know where it is.'

I still felt Hurst had qualities we could work on, however, and I politely said 'No' when Arthur Rowe, Crystal Palace's manager, suggested him in part-exchange for Johnny Byrne in March, 1962. Arthur knew

Geoff's father, Charlie, from his playing days. Charlie, a useful player with Oldham and one or two other clubs, had moved south to link up with Arthur in his Southern League days at Chelmsford. This was how Geoff, who was born in Ashton-under-Lyne, came to live in East London. And Charlie, I think, would have liked Geoff to play for his old boss at Selhurst. They felt Geoff wasn't making enough headway with West Ham.

I had attempted to open up a place at right-half for Hurst by letting Andy Malcolm, a hard and reliable club man, go to Chelsea in exchange for Ron Tindall, but Geoff did nothing to change my opinion that this wasn't his best position. A brief memory, though, kept coming back to me. In my Arsenal days we had played West Ham in a friendly, after we'd both been knocked out of the FA Cup, and I could recall being impressed by a young chap who played up front. His name was Hurst.

That memory led to an idea; and soon after the start of the 1962–63 season I asked Hurst to have a go in attack. He put up a half-argument, but I made it clear to him that if he was going to have a future in the game it wouldn't be at wing-half. I told him: 'I want someone who is strong and aggressive and not afraid of work in attack and I think you're the man. It's my judgement that's at risk and I won't hold it against you if it doesn't work. All I want you to do is play your natural game. Do the things you want to do and like doing. That will do for now and in time we'll add all the rest. Have a go . . .' He did, too, and we beat Liverpool at Upton Park by a goal to nil. Geoff Hurst was on the right road.

Hurst had a lot to learn but he was a coach's dream. Nobody could have worked harder. He listened and practised, and kept on practising, and the improvement in his game was remarkable. He learnt to take the ball coming from behind instead of towards him, he worked on his heading and shooting from all distances and angles, his control improved a hundred per cent, his mobility acquired a new edge and he quickly grasped the basic principles of making and using space. 'You can make the stupidest runs in the First Division but defenders still won't dare let you go' I told him at the start. 'Look at it like that and you'll drag your opponents all over the place – even when you're going nowhere or heading in the wrong direction. You will always make space for others.' He then began to realize that once he had made room for others, that room was there for him as well. He would drag his opponents out and then come back in himself. His strength was his legs; his endless running and direction-changing were phenomenal. He was also as brave as they come.

Hurst was our leading goal-scorer that season but it was in America, during the international tournament the following summer, that he proved to everyone – including himself – that he had completed the transition

from midfield to attack. He scored nine goals in ten games, a very sub-
stantial contribution to our success there.

A partnership that was very special developed between Hurst and
Byrne. To begin with, Hurst just took the weight off Byrne. Their worth
to each other was a bit hit-and-miss. Byrne was the star, once he found
his real form, and Hurst the straight man. But, gradually, a real relationship grew. They were opposites in appearance and style: Hurst was the
strong type, Budgie the dapper twinkler. But it was this contrast that
made them so effective. Between them they had everything to undermine
other's defences. Hurst, with his late, angled runs, his controlled power
and aggression, his persistence and selflessness, posed one sort of problem,
while Byrne, with his deft touches, instant control, ability to beat his
man, quickness over the first vital yards and cheekiness, presented another.
Both, too, knew exactly where the net was. They got more than forty
goals between them in each of their first two full seasons together. Byrne
helped make Hurst, but in the end they were as equal and complementary
as bacon and eggs.

Jimmy Hill once put together a fifteen-minute montage for television
of Hurst running off the ball, and I think this should have been shown to
every club in the country. His movement was fantastic. Sometimes he
was just a decoy, sometimes he would just knock the ball off, one touch
and away, sometimes he was giving width to an attack and sometimes
making himself a new target. His skill was remarkable – though I wonder
if the fans on the terraces at these games always realized what he was doing.

A Bolton director once said to me after West Ham had knocked seven
past them in a League Cup tie: 'Your Hurst reminds me of Nat Lofthouse.'

'Afraid not' I replied. 'Nat did his work at the far post. This fellow
Hurst gets to the ball anywhere. Far post, yes, but also near the ground
and at the near post. It's a different game.'

Hurst's ability at the near post was something which developed over
a period. Not only for Hurst either: it was something which involved
everybody. The vulnerability of defences to a strike or knock-on in this
area came home to me again during the 1966 World Cup itself. I was a
member of FIFA's technical study group and, during the game between
Hungary and Brazil at Goodison Park (Brazil losing their first World Cup
game for twelve years), Ferenc Bene scored a near-post goal from an
early cross by Florian Albert. It only happened once in this game but it
struck me that in English football such a goal was scored by accident
rather than design. Here was a chance for profit.

Back at West Ham we put down a couple of cones, one on each side of the field. Each player had to take the ball up to one of the cones, screw the ball round it, as if it was a man, and then cross to the near-post area – between the post and the edge of the six-yard area. Johnny Sissons and Harry Redknapp got it to perfection. At the near post we had Geoff Hurst, Martin Peters and other front men hitting the ball as it came, high, low, fast, spun or angled. They knew roughly where the ball was going to drop; the rest was up to them. This practice tested technique: it improved technique: and it paid off handsomely.

The near-post threat proved difficult to counter even when it was expected. We played Manchester City, for example, and Malcolm Allison spelt out all the dangers to his defence which included a new full-back he had just signed from Hearts, Arthur Mann. But Hurst and Peters each scored a goal at Mann's near post and Malcolm said to me afterwards: 'It's no good talking to 'em, is it? Not with your two!'

A lot of sides attack at the near-post now. Some get it right, some never will. But back in the 1960s it was new. The near post was the soft underbelly of many defences and many people in the game did not understand what was happening. Peters would ghost up from midfield, timing his run to perfection, while Hurst would confuse the defence by going to the far post and then switching suddenly at the last moment to the near. Newcastle's John McNamee was once taken to the far post by Hurst, and was still there as Hurst knocked the ball in at the near post! People used to say we were lucky. Week after week.

Martin Peters was the most gifted of them all. He had so much natural talent that it would be ridiculous to claim that anybody 'discovered' him. He was an outstanding player as a boy; he was always at the front of the shop window as a youth; he was public knowledge. Every club with half an eye open wanted him, including Chelsea, Arsenal, Spurs and Fulham, but he was a cockney, a real East Londoner, and Wally St Pier talked the same language. There was never much doubt that Peters would join West Ham.

Peters was a natural games-player and he looked the part: he was tall, lithe and well balanced, and he had a nice, easy relationship with the ball which made him look as if he was never in a hurry. He did everything so perfectly he made it look too easy. But even with all these advantages he had his early problems: his very versatility told against him.

I gave Peters his first League game at Easter, 1962. The side had been playing reasonably well but that is rarely good enough and I felt the time was ripe for a gee-up. It was also the right time of the season for an experiment or two. So I dropped five players, including Phil Woosnam and Geoff Hurst, and Peters took Hurst's place at right-half. We beat Cardiff at Upton Park and I decided to play the same team against Arsenal, also at home, the following day.

Early in the second half Lawrie Leslie broke a finger diving at the feet of an Arsenal forward, so John Lyall went into goal and Peters was switched to left-back. We drew 3-3 after being 3-1 down. As Peters had done well at left-back, I kept him there for the return with Cardiff at Ninian Park on the Easter Monday. More drama was to come! Brian Rhodes, Leslie's deputy, dislocated his collar-bone after about an hour and Peters went into goal. He had proved himself a useful 'keeper in practice and in one reserve game he actually started in goal. He was a player who could turn his hand to anything and, as I have said, was eventually to wear every shirt from one to eleven for us. But, the question remained, what was his best position?

Peters played regularly the following season, mostly at wing-half but always ready to fill in where required. He was the answer to a manager's prayer although the fans did not always appreciate him. He brought refinement to whatever job he did and I think some people mistook that for softness. He was not a typical English player and the terraces didn't relate to him. In a way his ability went above their heads.

I had no reservations about him, however, and in that same 1962-63 season I happily recommended Peters to Walter Winterbottom for an England Under-23 cap. Walter rang me to say one or two players had pulled out of his side to play Belgium at Plymouth. He wanted Bobby Moore to play at left-half. 'You don't want Bobby. He's a full international now' I said. 'Have the other one, Martin Peters. He's ready.' So Peters played, scored twice in a 6-1 win and was England's best player.

The first hiccup in Peters's career came halfway through our FA Cup season in 1963-64. It followed an 8-2 thumping by Blackburn at Upton Park on Boxing Day. It was a terrible game technically but Blackburn capitalized on our mistakes, getting the ball inside our full-backs and into space which Fred Pickering and John Byrom made good use of. We had our chances – the score should have been about 8-6 – but we didn't take them.

I deliberately did not go into the dressing-room afterwards. I went upstairs to my office, just in case I was going to have a heart attack! I wanted to avoid saying anything I might regret, and also to have a few moments' thought in peace. The return game at Blackburn was only forty-eight hours later, so time was precious.

After a while I wrote down a team for Ewood Park. There were nine changes. Then I wrote another, and this time there were eight changes. Then another . . . seven changes. And another . . . six. The process continued until I felt I'd got the team exactly right: and now there was just one change! Eddie Bovington for Martin Peters at right-half.

Peters was going through a lean patch by his own standards and a knee injury was also bothering him. His style meant that if his movement or confidence was affected his whole game suffered: he could not compensate by pure physical effort. It was not in his nature. Bovington, on the other hand, was a gritty, efficient player who would give us firm control in midfield and who was itching for a chance to prove himself. The change paid off handsomely. We were able to pull in our full-backs and force the ball wide. Bryan Douglas, Blackburn's England winger who was a real trick-man with the ball and who'd never been pinned down at Upton Park, was no longer a threat. We won 3-1 and that same side went right on, unchanged, to win the FA Cup.

Thus Peters came in for only the odd game, to fill a gap created by injury, and like any player with pride he was far from happy. He eventually came to see me just before the Cup Final, obviously nervous and worried, and told me I had cost him his life's ambition – to play at Wembley. 'I'm afraid that's the way it is' I said. 'The side is settled and playing well. But I'll bet you one thing – you'll play more times at Wembley than I eat in the restaurant there.' I went on: 'Everything's gone right for you in your career so far. There have been no problems. But for the first time you've got a set-back. You've a dodgy knee and things aren't going well. This is a test of character for you. This is where you stand up or fall down. You've got to fight your way in again.' I knew his time would come but it wasn't then, not as part of our Cup team.

Martin then said he was fed up with being 'a general dogsbody'. 'What is my best position?' he asked. 'It's all right being a utility player but I never know where I'm going to play. You're making use of me.' That was a question I couldn't answer immediately. I promised him we would work something out and the solution, which came the following season, was simply to give him a free hand. Broadly, he filled in the gap behind our strikers, playing wide when he chose to, pushing forward when he wanted to, a role without restriction.

It was a job only a player of Peters's quality could have done. He really was the complete all-rounder. He had a steely temperament, intelligence, ideas, subtlety and vision. His long legs covered the ground surprisingly quickly, he volleyed beautifully, he was an artist in the air, he tackled surprisingly strongly and he moved the ball to order. He always seemed to have a pay-off pass ready, often knocking it away first time where others would have needed a second touch, and all through his game ran an uncanny sense of timing. He knew when to move and where to move and, importantly, he never gave up. Sometimes he would make a twenty-yard run and there would be nothing at the end of it. But he would go again and again and again – and that is hard work. His understanding of space and his timing were delightful. Peters was a connoisseur's dream. He would have been a sensation on the continent.

14

Cup Time

The League championship was a star beyond West Ham's reach but the 'other' game, Cup football, filled the seasons with hope and success. We were capable of winning any tournament we entered but equally capable of losing to any side that argued with muscle.

We won the European Cup Winners' Cup, the FA Cup twice, the FA Youth Cup and the American international tournament. We finished runners-up in the Cup-Winners' Cup and League Cup on other occasions and reached four assorted semi-finals. We were also upended, embarrassingly, by Plymouth, Swindon, Mansfield, Huddersfield and Hull.

At our best, engine ticking over smoothly, minds properly focused, we were a match for anyone. We used our wits, adapted our tactics to order and made our skill count. We were even better in Europe than we were at home: we were perfectly suited to the game on the other side of the channel. Nothing gave me greater pleasure than our first European season which culminated in victory over Munich 1860 in the Cup Winners' Cup at Wembley. The game was seen by tens of millions on television all over the continent and proved we could beat them at their own game. It was a wonderful night of fulfilment for me.

First, however, we had to win the FA Cup: this was to be our key to Europe. Right at the start I used the sudden end to John Lyall's playing days as a way of motivating everyone. 'This is tragic news', I told the players. 'Wouldn't it be great if we could win the Cup and tie it up with a big testimonial for him. Remember, this could have happened to anyone.' That is exactly what we did – with Lyall, still officially a member of the squad, in charge of the players' pool.

We scored three goals against every club we faced, Charlton, Leyton Orient (after a draw at Brisbane Road), Swindon and Burnley. Geoff Hurst scored in every round except the sixth, we had a little luck when it was needed and our form never wavered. We did a good, honest job and there was steel in our game.

Two First Division clubs and two from the Second reached the semi-finals and at this point our luck seemed to run out. The two outsiders, Preston and Swansea, were drawn together, leaving us to face Manchester

United. They beat us at Upton Park in the League a week before the semi-final and, as they fielded a side containing seven youngsters, the omens for us were clearly not too good. George Best played in that game and Matt Busby said to me afterwards: 'I think in Best I've got the best young winger I've ever seen.' I replied: 'No you haven't. I have. John Sissons.' It was a reasonable argument. Their talent was prodigious.

West Ham's chances for our semi-final at Hillsborough were completely written off by the press. We had been beaten over two very good legs in the semi-finals of the League Cup by Leicester, a sound, intelligent side built around the likes of Frank McLintock, David Gibson and Colin Appleton, and apparently this was to be the limit of our run in the FA Cup. There were columns on the game in the Northern papers but we were only mentioned in passing, down page, as a sort of afterthought. All Manchester United's major stars, the Laws, Charltons and Crerands, were coming back for the semi-final and we were seen as mere doormats.

Before the game at Hillsborough, however, I wandered out onto the pitch and there, a homely touch for us, were the Dagenham Girl Pipers. Also there, shorts already on and looking superbly relaxed, were half the United team, having a laugh and a joke with the girls. I went back to our dressing-room, where my players were looking grim and keyed-up, and told them: 'Hey, United think this is going to be easy. We've got a chance here!'

Jim Standen, as always on a big occasion, had a sore throat. It never failed. The more important the match, the worse his throat. Bill Jenkins even told me the night before he didn't think Jim would be fit – our goalkeeper not only had a nasty throat but a high temperature too, and he looked terrible. Bill said he'd give him an injection; and he did, with the biggest syringe I have ever seen. I have no idea what Bill pumped into him but Jim's scream must have been heard back at Upton Park. It worked, though. Standen played a blinder – and so did just about everyone else. We kept things tight, cut off the supply to their match-winners at source, didn't waste possession and got the ball forward quickly to Hurst and Byrne who played off each other. We did things our way despite the mud. We buzzed. Our pride had been hurt and it showed. Bond, Burkett, Bovington and Brown were rocks while Moore, I need hardly say, was immaculate.

Boyce got two of our three goals, one whacked up and over from almost the halfway line – brilliant, and typical of the man. He kept his goals for the important games. Hurst got our third and decisive goal, and it was another gem. Moore set it up from his corner of the pitch with good control in a tight situation, playing a perfect ball forward. Hurst was in space, as always, and he took the ball on to score from the edge of the penalty area. Moore and Hurst: no one else was needed.

I said on the radio afterwards that I was glad we'd won because it would have made people in the north realize we were playing as well as Manchester United. After the interview I discovered the team coach had left without me, and I had to get a lift to catch our train. I understood their excitement. Our performance had been superb and Matt Busby told me in later years it was one of the biggest surprises and disappointments of his career.

West Ham were thus in an FA Cup Final for the first time since the famous 'White Horse' opener at Wembley in 1923. I felt so emotional as I was being driven to Sheffield station that I did not have a worthwhile thought in my head. There are times when feelings take over. But I knew the journey back to London was going to be special. We had reserved a diner-carriage and it was going to be party time all the way home. A private affair for the players, the officials, the directors and all their wives: just for us.

That, at least, was the idea, but what we found was chaos. There were so many people on the platform, getting in and out of our carriage, that half our party had difficulty in boarding. But worse still, daft British Railways had put our carriage last but one instead of last. The folk in the end carriage obviously couldn't be shut off so there was a right of way past us. Everybody on the train seemed to be in our compartment. Our bar was open but nobody could get near it for the crush. It was like the January sales, Wembley Way and the London rush-hour all rolled into one. To say I was upset is a mild understatement. I'd wanted the journey home to be memorable, and instead it was a disgrace. I wondered 'Is this success?'

Eventually one big chap found a solution. 'Don't you worry', he said, 'I'll sort this lot out'. He stood at the door to the main part of the train and nobody got through who didn't belong to the last two carriages. He was an unofficial, unpaid bouncer – and he was big enough and bright enough to do a very good job. I'll never forget him.

The period between semi-final and final is exciting but difficult. The letters pile up, the 'phone never stops, those with propositions form an orderly queue. But life beyond Wembley goes on: there are still League matches to be played and important points to be won. Standards have to be maintained because losing, like winning, can become a habit. It is particularly hard when for all concerned the final ahead is a first. Wembley is never out of one's mind. I was watching a junior game a week or so after the semi-final when a fellow came up and said: 'D'you know, I wake up in the middle of the night and I still can't believe it. West Ham at Wembley! I have to pinch myself.' That sort of comment, multiplied a few hundred times, helped me realize how important our achievement was to East London.

At the end of my first full season with West Ham I went to watch Spurs play Burnley in the 1962 final. I arrived late and stood just behind the player's tunnel, and as Bill Nicholson and Harry Potts led their sides out I felt tears in my eyes. I knew them personally, I identified with them, I shared their pride. I also wondered what I would feel if the chance came my way. In fact, when I led West Ham out in 1964, I felt no emotion at all: I was doing my job. Only once have I shown real excitement at a match: that was when we scored our winner against Liverpool in the final of the FA Youth Cup at Upton Park. I jumped to my feet. I was, you might say, over the moon. Mr Pratt turned to me and asked: 'What's the matter with you?' But, normally, I have my feet squarely on the ground. It is not my job, nor is it in my character, to start punching the air.

Before and after the FA Cup Final was when I showed pride. Wembley was where I had worked as a lad and where my father had been maintenance engineer. The old place was so familiar I felt I knew every brick and blade of grass personally. It was like coming home, and when I left the gloom of the tunnel a few minutes before the match and walked out into the sunlight I knew exactly where my father was. He had retired by then and gone back to Burnley to live, but nothing would have kept him from that final. He refused to sit in the main stand and stood with his old work-mates on a little platform directly above the entrance to the tunnel.

We had done our homework on Preston. Right through our Cup run, any player who was injured was sent to watch our next opponents, and for the final I even managed to get the whole team to a Preston game. Our team coach got a battering from their fans but, most important, what we saw confirmed that they were a very useful side. Alex Dawson was their main threat – an enormously strong, traditional British centre-forward who was lethal in the air.

Preston were a Second Division side but that meant nothing. They had played with a great deal of drive and resilience on the way to Wembley. My team picked itself but other decisions had to be made, and I decided Moore would play as a sweeper, covering the threat in the air and the inevitable knock-downs, and that Bovington would pull back as an extra marker. This apart we intended to play our normal game. A system good enough to get a team to Wembley should also be good enough to win at Wembley.

Alas for mortal plans. We were a goal down in ten minutes: Doug Holden, who had twice been to Wembley with Bolton in the 1950s, was the scorer, from a toe-in after a shot by Dawson had been half stopped. We equalized quickly, Moore and Byrne setting up Sissons, but Dawson, timing his run and header well, put Preston ahead once more just before half-time.

It is at moments like this that managers earn their keep. I felt we were giving Preston too much time and room in midfield and that our set-up wasn't right for the dual threat of Dawson and Alec Ashworth. They were making good use of the big pitch and Moore was being bypassed. He was doing nothing. My answer was to play squarer at the back than I'd have liked, with Moore shifting up alongside Brown to mark Preston's two strikers, and to push Bovington forward to make earlier impact. In short, we reversed our tactics, and it worked. We got to grips with things at the back and began to stamp on them in midfield. Our service forward got going and with Hurst getting an early equalizer, the reward for sustained pressure after a corner, the game turned our way. Even so, dramatically, Boyce didn't get our winner until a couple of minutes from the end. The Preston defence just watched a ball from Brabrook and little Ronnie was in for one of his specials.

There have been better finals but there have certainly been much worse. The game was competitive, always close and in the end very thrilling. I know we could have played better but we had won, the Cup was ours for twelve months, and now we could relax. We had a 'do' at the Hilton and later I slept with the Cup under my bed, the same Cup I had first seen as a boy all those years before in Cornholme. Then came the journey back to Upton Park, a trip which started quietly and ended with a real old knees-up.

We travelled in an open-top bus and central London was its usual Sunday-morning self when we started. Budgie Byrne said he didn't think there would be anyone about to welcome us, and for a while I thought he was going to be right. The roads were clear all the way to Aldgate and Petticoat Lane but then, suddenly, the whole of East London seemed to be there – thousands and more thousands. Six miles of smiling faces, deafening cheers and waving banners. The lads and the Cup were on top. I sat inside relishing every second. All these lovely people were proof that our achievement mattered.

Now we were into Europe and this, for me, was the real prize, the test for which I had worked and waited. The prospect excited me but it did not frighten me, because I had never felt surer of anything than the ability of my players to cope with the continent. I did not care whom we played. I was convinced that at our best we would be more than a match for their best. I wanted to do something for English football.

Clearly our preparations had to be first-class. I remembered the Spanish dossier I had found in a hotel drawer in Porthcawl in my early days as West Ham's manager, and I decided to give my players a similar service, with an original extra. I watched each opposing club as soon as I could after every draw, so that I could give each player of mine a vivid word-picture of his likely immediate opponent. To do this I related every opposition player to a British player my men would know. If a man ran like a Bobby Charlton or tackled like a Mackay or dummied and tricked like a Greaves I would say so, though the comparison was not often at this level. Even the continent is not over-stocked with such men. My aim was to paint a realistic and useful verbal portrait of each opponent.

We did not play particularly well in the first round against La Gantoise of Belgium. We made our first trip into Europe by coach, train, boat and coach again, via Ostend and then on to Ghent. The Belgians proved a rigid side and we took the tie in reverse order – winning away and drawing at home. In the second round, against Spartak Sokolovo of Prague, we were much better. Sokolovo were a good side, hard, disciplined, without much conscience, and were comfortable leaders of their League. Although we scored twice against them at Upton Park I was far from sure that this would be enough in Prague. Moore was unfit, an added complication, and my solution after a lot of thought was to play Boyce as a sweeper. He was a revelation, quick, adaptable and able to cover the whole of the back area, while Byrne and Sissons were lone heroes in front, picking up our service, linking up with each other and holding possession until support arrived. We were up against experienced opponents, a large, hostile crowd and a Bulgarian referee who did not give us much protection. But we survived with single-minded efficiency. Though we lost the game 2-1, we took the tie 3-2 and their officials paid us the compliment afterwards of asking me where they had gone wrong.

Next it was Lausanne whose manager was Karl Rappan, the father figure of Swiss football, a great character and a kind, caring man. His experience was enormous, going back forty years as manager, coach and player, and I found him excellent company. He believed in flexibility and skill in front and clever strategy in defence. He was a man to learn from – and I did, from our first skirmish. We had a battle of wits over who should play at home first. He won, eventually, but our answer was to beat his team 2-1 on their own ground. The tempo of the game was slower, patience was a virtue and possession was everything. We outwitted Lausanne at their own game, but at Upton Park they produced one or two new tricks and we were hard pushed to win an erratic but enjoyable match by 4-3. They were friendly people and first-class opponents.

We were now in the semi-finals and, not surprisingly, we faced our toughest hurdle so far – Real Zaragoza of Spain, who had a celebrated line of forwards known as the 'Magnificent Five'. We did well enough to beat them at home but our advantage, a modest 2-1, meant we were on thin ice for the return. I decided nothing was going to be left to chance: hotels, transport, food and practice facilities were checked and double-checked. I was determined no one was going to pull a fast one on us.

Our lead was so slender that I said to Sissons before the game: 'If we get just half a chance we've got to put it away.' We played without an orthodox centre-forward with Sissons to the left, Hurst and Dear holding back and Sealey playing wide on the right; and this format obviously confused their centre-half, Santamaria. He was left on his own, poor chap, and he spent most of the game waiting for employment. It wasn't until the closing stages that he cottoned on and started to use the acres of space in front of him. He could have forced us to change our whole plan, but by the time the penny dropped it was too late.

Zaragoza scored first but eventually Sissons got his half-chance and, to the letter of his instructions, he took it well. We then marked them down, despite frantic efforts by the Magnificent Five, and we were through to the final. It was a splendid, fascinating game played in a big-time atmosphere. Brian Moore was doing the commentary in an open position for BBC Radio and he told me later he could hardly make himself heard. The din, he said, was deafening, even when he listened to a recording of the broadcast.

The decision to play the final at Wembley was taken long before we made our mark, of course, but obviously it gave us a big advantage. Our players also saw Munich 1860 play twice that season – once by sheer chance, once as a routine part of our careful preparation. The first time was in the middle of our pre-season tour. We played in Vienna and Graz and, on the way to Nuremberg for our last match, we passed through Munich and discovered that 1860 were playing Tommy Docherty's Chelsea. We knew 1860 were in the Cup Winners' Cup so, just in case, we stayed over to watch them. What a piece of luck!

I then sent the whole team to watch 1860 play Torino in a semi-final play-off in Zurich. It was a chance that was too good to miss, and the only man who missed the trip was me. I have always kept quiet about the reason for my absence but, in fact, I was being confirmed at Loughton. The date of my late confirmation had been settled a long time before and it was of very great importance to me. The players returned to say I knew

a thing or two. They had had to watch the game in open seats in a tremendous thunderstorm, but all agreed it was a priceless trip. We felt we
knew as much about 1860 as we did about most English clubs.

Byrne, sadly, was a non-starter for the final. He damaged a knee while
playing for England against Scotland at Wembley, and a cartilage operation was necessary which meant he also missed our second leg in Zaragoza.
His absence was an almighty blow but Brian Dear had done well in
Budgie's place in Spain and I had no qualms about picking him for the
final. Dear, who had grown up at West Ham, was a powerful, headstrong
chap who was endlessly willing and packed a wicked shot. Hurst played
deep again, his all-round strength a significant factor, while the main
raiding was left to Sissons and Sealey. Alan Sealey was a straight running
winger-cum-centre-forward, more direct than Brabrook and a fair runner
off the ball. Alan was also a very newly-married man. We all went to his
wedding about a week before the final, with German television recording
every second. The cameramen couldn't understand him getting wed just
a few days before the big match: they were to discover it did him no harm.

The team, then, was significantly different from the one which won
the FA Cup a year before. The whole right-flank had changed. Its legs
were younger. Kirkup had taken over from Bond at right-back, Peters
had replaced Bovington at right-half and Sealey, not Brabrook, was on
the right-wing. The stealth and intelligence of Peters gave us a new
dimension and he made excellent use of the space created by Sealey's
diversions. I could not resist saying to Martin before the game: 'I thought
you said I'd cost you your lifetime's ambition to play at Wembley.'

The match exceeded my wildest hopes. We won with two second-half
goals by Sealey, the first a thumping drive, the second from a free kick,
but it was the manner of the victory that counted most of all. I said to my
players before the start: 'Here's our chance to show the world what we
can do.' And that is precisely what they did. Three years of hard work and
faith went into our win. Our principles were justified: we proved that
football at its best is a game of beauty and intelligence. Players and ball
were in happy harmony, while skill and method flourished together. Ideas
and passes flowed, For me it was fulfilment.

It was pleasing to see Sealey emerge as the match-winner. Before the
game he would not have been rated by many as the man likely to turn the
match, but this is the way football works. He needed help, of course. His
second goal, for example, was the product of a free kick often tried in
training. Trevor Dawkins, one of our youngsters, even told me this
particular variation would never work, a solicited opinion because we
tried to get everyone involved and to have a say. It was not a complicated

kick. Hurst ran over the ball and then Moore floated it over for Peters coming in on a late run. Martin timed his movement and contact perfectly but the ball came back off Radenkovic, 1860's excellent goalkeeper, and Sealey was there to find the net. But Dear also played his part. A late run of his had almost got him behind the 1860 defence and forced a desperate defender to concede the free kick. Sealey will be remembered as the scorer but four other players were also involved. Football is a team game above all.

Our defence, too, was excellent because it takes two sides to make a great match and 1860 were full of flair and determination. They kept at us. Moore gloried in the occasion but Burkett, one of the more unsung members of the side, did a first-class job at left-back, fitting in efficiently just behind his captain. Moore, magnificently, and Burkett, quietly, played their parts in their different ways. Standen also had a super match in goal, although something I said to him before the start proved useful. 'If you go down don't forget you've a pair of legs' I told him. Brunnenmeier, the 1860 captain, broke through at a crucial point in the match and seemed to be past Standen who'd gone for the ball and missed. A goal seemed inevitable, but then a pair of legs suddenly swung round, contact was made and the ball spun to safety. 'Good job you mentioned that' said Jim afterwards.

More people, a hundred thousand of them, paid more money than ever before to watch a floodlit match in England and they were all fans who cared about the game. It was a warm evening, an unforgettable match and that song of ours about bubbles seemed to fill the stadium. But I could have done without the postscript. Wembley laid on a meal in the restaurant afterwards but it was just for players, officials and directors. No provision was made for all the wives and girlfriends, who understandably were not very happy. I ran all over the place fixing them up with drinks and saying the right things. Who'd be a manager?

Now was the time I should have begun to make changes because little cracks were appearing in the fabric of the side, but one of my reasons for keeping the team together was more success in the Cup Winners' Cup in 1965–66. We began our defence of the trophy by beating Olympiakos of Greece 4–0 at Upton Park and then drawing 2–2 in a stadium full of fanatics in Piraeus. Then we overcame Magdeburg of East Germany with a narrow win at home and a grim draw in Magdeburg – a city I remember all too well. I went there on a lone scouting mission before we met them, a journey which involved a flight to Berlin and then a train ride to the west. It was the middle of the night, pitch black, snow was falling, shadowy figures kept flitting past my compartment and the whole world was silent and cold. I felt like someone in a movie about espionage. I'd have believed anything. As I said before: who'd be a football manager?

The four teams who reached the semi-finals were Liverpool, Celtic, Borussia Dortmund, all leaders of their national leagues, and ourselves. The chances of an all-British final at Hampden Park looked bright, and I was happy enough when we were paired with the West Germans.

Peters put us ahead just after half-time in the first leg at Upton Park, watched by Alf Ramsey with the World Cup less than three months away, and we might well have scored at least a couple more. Jimmy Bloomfield had by now joined us from Brentford, an old friend I'd bought to give us a bit of short-term stability and composure, and he did us proud. But we overstretched ourselves going for another goal, a familiar story, and we were cruelly punished in the last five minutes when Lothar Emmerich, West Germany's leading scorer, turned in two goals. Emmerich was a dark, broody sort of chap without much general ability but he had a lethal finish. We simply did not have the defensive pace to counter him.

It was a magnificent match but, realistically, we were now in trouble. Borussia were unbeaten at home that season and on all the evidence they were one of the best sides in Europe. A little voice inside me kept insisting we had no chance in the second leg but what manager ever admits private thoughts like that? I talked about courage and composure and looked confident. I did feel we might stand a chance if we could hold steady for half an hour and perhaps steal a goal ourselves. So much for hope. Borussia scored with their first movement of the game. Sigi Held centred, Emmerich headed the ball against the cross-bar and then pushed home the rebound. Held and Emmerich, of course, were to be in the West German side that faced Moore, Hurst, Peters and company in the World Cup final a few weeks later. We played well enough for the next eighty-nine minutes, and Byrne even managed a goal, but there was no real way back for us. Borussia won 3-1, and then went on to beat Liverpool in the final. We had gone down to a better side, so there were no complaints.

The next trophy we had a tilt at was the League Cup: we reached the final in 1965–66 and the semi-finals the following season. Each time, too, it was West Bromwich Albion who bettered us. We beat Albion 2-1 in the first leg of the final, with Johnny Byrne stealing a goal twenty seconds from the end, but up at the Hawthorns they got their rhythm going and scored four in the first half: we were not a pretty sight. But our defeat by Albion at the semi-final stage twelve months later hurt even more. Again we let in four at the Hawthorns, Jeff Astle murdering Ken Brown in the air, which ended there and then our chances of appearing in the first

League Cup final to be played at Wembley. It would have meant a fourth successive appearance at Wembley for Bobby Moore and Geoff Hurst – FA Cup, Cup Winners' Cup, World Cup and League Cup.

What made that defeat even harder to take was the memory of our form in earlier rounds. We beat Tottenham, Arsenal, Leeds and Blackpool – and against Leeds we looked like world-beaters. We annihilated them by seven goals to nil, with Sissons and Hurst each getting a hat-trick, on one of those nights when everything went right. I think we'd have kept finding the net even if the floodlights had gone out. Poor old Leeds had their full side out, too: Johnny Giles, Jack Charlton, Norman Hunter, Billy Bremner and company were all present. Back at their hotel they stayed up all night asking themselves where they had gone wrong.

It was a victory we paid for. Leeds were as cold as ice, a team and a club without heart or mercy, when we played them over the next few years. They always saved up something special for us and even carried the 'cold war' into their boardroom. I would go in after a game and immediately their directors would start chipping away. 'Thought you played reasonably well', they would say with little smiles, 'but, y'know, perhaps you're not quite . . .'. They would leave me to complete the thought. I hated it.

We did not beat Leeds again until 1972 when a far-post header by Clyde Best in extra time put them out of the League Cup. It was at Elland Road, too, and in the boardroom afterwards I wasn't very charitable myself. 'This time' I said 'it's somebody else's – – – – – – turn to be polite'.

The real sequel to that famous win over Leeds came after Don Revie's appointment as England manager. He called the country's top players together – we were the best represented club with about eight of the sixty – and then he toured the clubs to have a chat with the managers.

My turn came and Revie opened the conversation by saying: 'We've never really talked, have we?'

'I don't know why not' I replied.

'I'll tell you' said Don. 'Remember when you beat us 7-0, well we were demoralized but I still went into your dressing-room afterwards to congratulate you. You were over by the radiator and I came over and said "Marvellous. Miraculous. What a game you played." And you looked at me and all you said was "Thank you very much". I felt snubbed and I went back to our dressing-room and told my players "We'll never lose to that bloody man's team ever again".'

I think Revie felt I should have done a handstand when he congratulated me . . . but I also know the expression I must have had on my face. It is what my wife Lucy calls my 'llama-look'.

We reached the semi-finals of the League Cup after that extra-time win at Elland Road in 1972. Next we beat Liverpool efficiently by 2-1 and Sheffield United easily by 5-0, both at Upton Park, but then we found ourselves locked in a marathon semi-final with Stoke. We won the first leg at the Victoria Ground by 2-1 and Tony Waddington, their manager, a lovely chap, was despondent when he came round to our hotel for a drink afterwards. We tried to cheer him up – it's not difficult to be big in victory – and kept reminding him there was still the second leg to come. We felt good and he felt terrible because we all believed West Ham were at Wembley. We had done it!

Then, alas, we had a stinker at Upton Park. Stoke scored through big John Ritchie, which made the aggregate score level, and the game went into extra time. A replay looked inevitable but with only three minutes left Gordon Banks fouled Harry Redknapp and we were given a penalty. We only had to put it in and we were at Wembley. Geoff Hurst was our man for the job, he had the shot, experience and temperament to make sure of it and, once again, we were there. A draw would be enough. We couldn't fail.

Hurst hit the ball with everything. It exploded towards the left corner of the net but, somehow, Banks of England got to it. His leap was prodigious. I don't know to this day how he reached the ball and never will. It was a save only Banks could have made. On reflection, I blamed myself. I reasoned that Hurst should not have taken the penalty because Banks, his World Cup pal, knew him so well. Hindsight? It is not worth a bean.

I lost the toss over the replay and so the match went north to Hillsborough. 'You're bloody useless' the players told me. But that spin of the coin led to the funniest, maddest, most bizarre and in a way most dangerous coach-ride any of us had experienced.

We stayed at Buxton before the replay and arranged with a Manchester firm we always used to provide us with transport. But the coach arrived late, very late, and by the time we reached the outskirts of Sheffield the situation was desperate. Cars were solidly locked nose-to-tail, every road was choked with traffic. Spotting a policeman at some crossroads, I leaned out and shouted:

'Which is the quickest way to Hillsborough?'

'You'll never get there in time for the kick-off' he called back.

'In that case it's a waste of time all these other people going there because we're West Ham' I replied.

His mouth just opened. No words. No advice.

By this time our driver knew he was in dead trouble but all the players were thoroughly enjoying it. The coach was full of wisecracks and laughter. 'Go up the other side of the road' one of them shouted. Very little was coming the other way: the traffic jam was pointing towards Hillsborough. Our driver snatched gratefully at the straw. Suddenly our coach turned onto the other side of the road, the wrong side, and started accelerating. The cars that were coming in the opposite direction scattered in all directions. Some were actually hit glancing blows as white-faced drivers wrenched at their steering-wheels. Onlookers just gawped. Our driver was now going faster and faster and from the back came shouts of 'Go on, my son'. The players were hooting and cheering and loving every second of it. Some of the cars we hit even turned round and started chasing us: it was part-farce, part-lunacy. I can describe the incident but not, of course, condone it – though we did get to the ground on time. Then we discovered that Stoke had also been late. Traffic problems, they said!

The result, after all this, was a goalless draw after extra time. I thought the second replay would automatically go to a ground near London but we had to spin a coin again, I lost again and Old Trafford was nominated. The postscript to the night was still to come, though. 'Mr Greenwood' said our old friend the coach-driver. 'What now?' I asked. 'I'm sorry', he went on, 'but somebody's put a load of sand in my petrol.' We had to get another coach to take us back to our hotel.

We lost 3-2 at Old Trafford but it was an eventful night to say the least. Bobby Ferguson was concussed in an early collision and, while Bobby Moore took over in goal, a brave and responsible act, we tried everything we knew to bring Ferguson round in the dressing-room. He kept insisting he was all right so we started throwing balls at him to test his reactions, but I'm not sure he even knew where he was. To begin with he just flapped at the ball but gradually a light came back into his eyes and after about quarter of an hour he went back out.

By this time Moore had faced a penalty. He stopped Mike Bernard's kick, which was a bit straight, but couldn't hold the ball and the Stoke man knocked in the rebound: Stoke 1, West Ham 0. But then, still with ten men, we equalized through Billy Bonds and – with Ferguson back in goal and Moore stabilizing things again – we took the lead through Trevor Brooking. Ferguson was still desperately wobbly, however, and though we tried to protect him Stoke went for the throat. It may have been wretched sportsmanship but their tactics paid off. Peter Dobing and Terry Conroy got their winners and Stoke were on their way to Wembley and a major trophy for the first time in their history.

It was a semi-final we should have won. I looked back at our win at Stoke, at Tony Waddington's despondency, at that crucial penalty confrontation between Hurst and Banks in the last seconds at Upton Park and at Ferguson's injury in that tremendous second replay and was left with one, simple conclusion: Stoke, all along, had been meant to win. It was their year.

Our failure was a watershed for West Ham. By the time we won the FA Cup in 1975 and reached the final of the Cup Winners' Cup again the following season there was a different team – and it was John Lyall's team. I was sitting on the bench as John led his men out at Wembley and I can only say I was as pleased as Punch. Fulham, one of my old clubs, were led by Alec Stock, a rare and warm man, and just behind him was Bobby Moore. It seemed totally unreal to see him in opposition colours.

We knew exactly how Moore would play, of course, which meant we would not get away with much at the near post. He would always be there, so we decided to play the ball away from him all the time, and it worked very nicely. Alan Taylor got our two winners.

The following year, via Finland, Southern Russia, Holland and West Germany, we reached the final of the Cup Winners' Cup. Again we observed, prepared and motivated ourselves thoroughly and, by any standards, ours was a notable achievement. We met Anderlecht in the final in Brussels and knowing their coach, a Dutchman who was not a brilliant tactician, I said that whatever they tried would be the result of individual effort rather than collective efficiency. That is exactly what happened. An injury upset our defensive balance and Francois Van der Elst destroyed us down the right. Anderlecht 4, West Ham 2. A few years later, Van der Elst was wearing the claret and blue of West Ham.

There were other Cup days, though, that had nothing to do with finals and exciting trips into Europe. There were defeats by small clubs that made me wish the ground would open up and swallow me. Teams that we should have spanked and sent to bed would rise six feet above themselves. Players past their best would suddenly peel off the years, just for ninety minutes. They would say 'Hey, let's show you what we can do' and they would run and kick like young bucks again.

The football wasn't always very pretty. Peter Brabrook once turned the ball into the net in a League Cup tie at Walsall and, turning round with arm raised, saw all five of the players who had been involved in the build-up lying flat on their backs. But Walsall's muscle did not work that night. We won 5-1. Before another tie, against Port Vale, I told the team: 'Let's keep it moving. Let's play one-touch football.' It proved to be a 'physical' game – and afterwards Bobby Moore said that 'one touch was one touch too many'.

There is no secret to Cup football, but there is one golden rule. Never take anything for granted.

15

Hurst, Moore and Peters...Part two

England's triumph in the 1966 World Cup lifted the nation, gave a hefty boost to the game and transformed the lives of the young men who beat West Germany on that famous day at Wembley. They started the World Cup as footballers but finished it as household heroes. They were lionised honoured, wined and dined, flattered, pointed at and whispered about; and, as the club manager of Bobby Moore, England's captain and perhaps the outstanding player of the whole tournament, and of Geoff Hurst and Martin Peters, who scored all four of England's goals in the final, I saw at first hand the effect it had on them. Success always has a price.

All three changed as men. They became more assured and more ambitious and all of them, at different times and in their own way, asked to leave West Ham. They felt the grass – almost any grass – would be greener on the other side. Each got his way eventually but in West Ham's time. Peters went to Tottenham four years after the World Cup in England, Hurst to Stoke after six years and Moore to Fulham after eight. But before then I could have sold them many times. They were among the hottest properties in football.

The three players gave West Ham the best years of their careers and they gave me great pride and professional satisfaction but they were also the cause of some thumping headaches. I even wanted to sack Moore at one point and our relationship became unhappy and strained. There was an icy corridor between us. I upset Matt Busby when he made an offer for Hurst, although Hurst would have loved to join Manchester United. I let Peters go to Tottenham, in exchange for Jimmy Greaves, because he felt he was 'the third man'. He believed the other two were getting all the credit and limelight.

Moore, in fact, refused to sign a contract in the months before the World Cup. He wanted richer pastures and I know Spurs would have liked him. But Bill Nicholson, a straight and genuine man, never approached me and, in any case, we had no intention of letting Moore go, either before or after the World Cup. It was deadlock: problems loomed. FA officials were concerned that unless Moore signed and became a properly registered player he would not even be allowed to play in the

World Cup. Just imagine the rumpus that would have caused. Alf Ramsey was keen that he should sign because he did not want a captain with other things on his mind. He wanted players with only one objective: winning the gold Jules Rimet trophy.

Eventually I was called to the England headquarters, the Hendon Hall Hotel in north London, and this time there were no hiccups. I had a chat with Alf, who as a former club manager himself understood the problem, and then with Bobby. The signature was a formality.

By this time I had taken the club captaincy away from Moore. His attitude clearly meant he was less than a hundred per cent for the club and I gave the job to Johnny Byrne who bubbled with enthusiasm. It was not a difficult decision because it made the important point that no player is bigger than his club. Moore did not show a flicker of emotion when I told him: I am not sure he ever did show any. Only once in all my years with him did he congratulate a player for scoring a goal. That was when Ted MacDougall scored his first goal for West Ham after joining us from Manchester United – and Moore ran the whole length of the field to him. Normally he regarded such a gesture as a waste of energy.

Phil Woosnam, my first captain, was always popping into the office, full of chat and ideas, but Moore never followed this line. He took responsibility but led by example more than anything else. He did not use his voice a lot but when he did he made it count. He would take command, his arms would start going and an order would be barked out, but he was not a noisy captain. Moore had presence and style and, above all, he had standards. That was his real strength. He always put in a good performance on the field no matter what battles he was fighting off it. In action he was always a first-class professional. He had pride.

It has been said of Moore that he was a big occasion player who did not put himself out in lesser combat. Not so. He *was* a big occasion player – but only in the sense that he somehow scaled new heights when it mattered most. He loved the big stage and the big challenge but never, whatever the game, did he drop below those standards of his.

Moore also had nerves of steel, as he showed during the Bogota incident before the 1970 World Cup when he was ludicrously accused of stealing a bracelet. I was in Mexico at the time, as an official technical observer, and my hair stood on end when Helmut Kaser, FIFA's secretary, broke the news to me. 'Your Bobby Moore's in trouble' he said. 'He's been arrested in Bogota.' My imagination worked overtime but as soon as the details filtered through I calmed down. I stopped worrying because I knew he was in good hands and that everything would be sorted out, although no one could have guessed just how long the wretched business would drag on. I cannot imagine many players of this or any other generation who would sail through that kind of experience and then become one of the outstanding players of a World Cup tournament. Nobody could have handled it better: and great credit to him.

Off the field, however, we had a problem. I felt he became very aloof, locked in a world of his own, and although his cold detachment was a strength on the field, and even a shield in situations like the one in Bogota, it was an attitude which made things very difficult in the small, everyday world of a football club. Moore even started to give the impression that he was ignoring me at team-talks. He would glance around with a blasé look on his face, eyes glazed, in a way that suggested he had nothing to learn. 'Who needs a manager?' he seemed to be saying. The danger was that other, less experienced players would believe what they saw.

I called him into my office and told him: 'Don't give the impression that you're not listening. You may be kidding some of the players but it doesn't wash with me. Whenever I ask for something to be done on the field you're the first to do it. I know you're listening to every word. So why the act?' He did not argue.

It was impossible to get close to Moore. There was a big corner of himself that he would not or could not give. To begin with I think it was a sort of protective act, but eventually the act became reality. He seemed to step inside an image from which he couldn't escape. It worried me, because I knew what a nice person he was at heart. I remembered him as a lad, full of enthusiasm and determination, and the way we had shared our passion for the game. I had given him his first chance with the England Youth and Under-23 teams and recommended him for his first full cap. I had shaped his understanding of the game and his attitude to it, and moved him into the specialized defensive position he made his own. I had tremendous faith in Moore and would never listen to criticism of him. Lucy says that even at home I would never hear a word against him. It hurt that he could be so cold to someone who cared about him and who had helped him so much.

I suppose it was basically a case of different personalities not gelling; and this was my fault as much as his. We were two proud and reserved men – with the one difference that my first concern was always West Ham in particular, but football in general. I tried to bridge the gap between us once or twice but it never worked.

There were incidents which did nothing to improve our relationship. One, oddly, took place in the bar of a jumbo jet over the Atlantic in 1970. We had just been walloped by Newcastle and were on our way to a profitable 'friendly' in New York against the Brazilian club Santos, Pelé and all. Bobby Moore, Jimmy Greaves and a friend of theirs, Freddie Harrison, went to the bar soon after take-off. I had plenty on my mind because the side as a whole was not firing well but after a while I went up for a glass of coolness. I ordered a Coke but while we were chatting I could see Moore and company were quietly lacing my drink with something stronger. I knew exactly what was happening but I didn't mind and I didn't spoil their little prank. It was the end of a terrible day, we had a long journey ahead of us and the talk was bouncy. There's a wrong time to drink – and a right one!

The session led to two admissions. Greavsie suddenly said: 'D'you know what? For the first time in my life I froze in front of goal.' I remembered the missed chance he was talking about in the game against Newcastle but it was still quite a statement coming from someone who had always made scoring look a supremely easy art. I decided to cap his confession. 'I'll tell you something now' I said. 'For the first time in my life I felt like resigning.' I wasn't joking. I was so down after our defeat by Newcastle that I genuinely felt like calling it a day. But by the time I admitted it, with New York ahead, the temptation to quit had long since passed. It just proved that managers have feelings too.

The lowest point of all was the Blackpool affair in January 1971. I trusted my players. I treated them as I would like to have been treated as a player – but four of them and one of the staff let the club and me down badly. It led to my asking the West Ham directors to sack Moore, Greaves, Brian Dear, Clyde Best and our physiotherapist, Rob Jenkins.

They chose to step right out of line on the night before an FA Cup third round match at Blackpool. We had gone north early because I wanted the team to have a pleasant, relaxed meal at our hotel on the Friday evening. They were then free to do whatever they wanted: cinema, cards, even the dogs if they wanted to. There were no restrictions because I had faith in them.

The weather was atrocious, the pitch was ice-bound and there were even doubts whether the match would be played. But it did take place and Blackpool, who were heading for relegation, beat us 4-0. I had no idea anything was wrong at this point, except that we'd played horribly, and back in London on the Sunday morning the reports in the papers made dire reading. It wasn't the best weekend of my life.

I was in my office on the Monday morning when our chairman, Reg Pratt, looked in. 'I've just come through the front door', he said, 'and there's a lot of supporters down there all moaning about what happened on Friday night'.

'What happened on Friday night?' I asked.

'They say all the players were out drinking' he replied.

'You're joking!' was my instant reaction. All managers get silly rumours fed back to them, usually after a defeat, and I always dismissed them out of hand.

'Well, that's what they're saying and they're up in arms about it' Mr Pratt added.

I said I'd make enquiries but still did not believe the story. I preferred to believe in my players. But next morning all the papers were full of the story. They didn't know the whole truth but they had enough to justify big headlines. Some of the fans at the door had been on the 'phone to Fleet Street.

I now made a couple of telephone calls myself – and the real facts emerged. Five men were involved, Moore, Greaves, Dear, Best and Jenkins. They had all been out to a club together, getting back to the Imperial Hotel some time after one o'clock on the Saturday morning of our cup-tie. I was furious. I felt so let down. I had the five in and, one by one, they apologized but insisted they had done nothing wrong. They had 'just gone for a drink'. Nothing more, nothing less.

Moore even said he thought I'd let him down by not denying the story to the press. 'Let *you* down' I said. 'It was you who went to that club before a big match. Not me. Not the fans who came banging at the front door. And you tell me I've let you down!'

Greaves came in and cried his eyes out. One of the papers had claimed there were some women involved at the club in Blackpool, and Jimmy had had a row with his wife, Irene.

After a lot of thought, I felt there was only one thing to do. I went to the directors and asked for all five to be sacked. Moore, Greaves, every one of them, but above all Rob Jenkins, who had succeeded his father as our physio and who, as a member of the staff, should have known better than anyone else.

Now it was the turn of the directors to do some hard thinking. Their answer, when it came, was firm. They said 'No' to the sacking of Moore, Greaves, Best and Jenkins, because they felt it too big a decision to make, but 'Yes' in Dear's case. Dear had left us a few years earlier but after playing a few games for Brighton, Fulham and Millwall he had gone on the dole. I had taken him back – 'I'll give you a second chance' I had told him – and the board felt he had let us down in more than one way.

I said it would not be right to sack only Dear. They had all been in it together and all should go. But the directors would not change their minds. They said they couldn't do it. Instead there were moderate fines and suspensions.

Greaves retired at the end of the season, a decision undoubtedly precipitated by the Blackpool affair. Although I had wanted to sack him I still feel he packed in too early – there were still goals in the man. Best had just gone for the ride in Blackpool, a youngster who didn't have the character or experience to refuse, but the one I really had a go at was Jenkins. He should have set an example.

Moore and the other four let everyone down. I felt this, so did the fans and so, in a way, did the newspapers. If there was no harm in a spot of night-life before a big match they would not have given the story the treatment they did. But the issue went deeper than this. There was a heavy social scene available to many of the players. We had been successful, one or two players uniquely so, and inevitably there were queues of people wanting to latch on. Invitations rolled in.

Moore's world was particularly big. He would travel with us on an away-trip in casual clothes but before we got back to London he would disappear into the toilet for a while and then emerge all dressed up in immaculate fashion. His wife, Tina, would be waiting for him and, at ten o'clock on a Saturday night, off they would go into town. There was nothing wrong with this. I had no objection to any of the players enjoying themselves. A good social life is one of the rewards of success. But there are built-in dangers, and self-discipline is required. Collective responsibility does matter because a player never lets just himself down. He lets his whole team down. I trusted my players and they owed me that. I believed in their ability to make the right decision off the field as well as on it.

Those who lack personal discipline always have an excuse for their weakness. They will claim they 'do the business' despite a lager or a Bacardi or two. They will say it relaxes them and removes tension and that without a bit of fun poor old Jack is sure to become a dull boy. The gap, in any case, between what is acceptable and what a player *thinks* is acceptable is always growing. A player may perform well after a few drinks; but might he not have played even better without them? I repeat: there is a right time for a drink – and a wrong time. A night-club in Blackpool a few hours before an important cup-tie is the wrong time.

Moore the player would have improved any team in the world. Brian Clough even decided he would be an asset to his championship side at Derby, and made an attempt to buy him that was almost unbelievable. Around the start of the 1973–74 season he suddenly walked into my office with one of his directors. 'I just want a chat with you' he said. 'Have you got any whisky?' I obliged. 'Any water?' he asked. 'Sure, the kitchen is just round the corner' I told him. He went out – and didn't come back for twenty minutes. 'I've been looking round the place' he said. 'Isn't it lovely? All nice and spruce.' 'That's because we're a well-run club' I replied. (I learnt later that Clough had approached our receptionist and persuaded her to open up the directors' box where he asked her all sorts of questions about the club.)

The conversation in my office got under way. 'I want to sign Bobby Moore and Trevor Brooking' said Clough.

'You can't be serious' I replied.

'Every man's got a price' he insisted. I told him there was no point in going on because neither were for sale.

'Well, if I can't have Moore can I have Brooking? And if I can't have Brooking can I have Moore?' Clough continued.

'They're not available, Brian' I said. 'But I'll pass your offer on to my board.'

Clough carried on talking about money as if he hadn't heard me. The figures were rising by the minute. So eventually I said:

'I'll tell you what. We've got a board meeting next Monday. You ring me at half past six and I'll tell you their decision. I'll pass on your offer and recommend we refuse but it's then up to them.'

'They might say okay . . . you're not in charge' said Clough.

'Fair enough' I replied, 'but I'm still going to make my recommendation'.

The board would have liked the money but they had no hesitation in backing me. Moore and Brooking were not for sale. I excused myself from the meeting to take Clough's call. I waited. And waited. But no call came. I never heard another whisper from him.

Clough let the story out, though, and the papers ran a story, part-fact, part-fiction, that Derby had offered more than £400,000 for the two players. Moore got uptight and accused me of standing in his way. What I did not know at the time was that Clough had been in touch with Moore privately, but the word always gets back sooner or later. Football is like a village community. Nothing is secret for very long.

A week or so after that extraordinary conversation in my office Clough got the sack.

In all his years with us – until then – a side without Moore seemed inconceivable. Even in his last year with us I would get threats of bomb damage to my house if I dared let him go. I received them by 'phone and letter and, far from worrying me, I used to think 'Good, it shows people care.' Moore *was* West Ham. But not even a man like him lasts forever and eventually Mick McGiven, whom we'd brought from Newcastle, started to do a good job at the back whenever Bobby was injured or out of touch.

I felt the time had come when we could let him go. We had talked of a free transfer but in the end I worked things out differently. We sold him to Fulham for £50,000, £25,000 for West Ham and £25,000 for Moore. Not a bad handshake.

Geoff Hurst was a man I would have been happy to have at West Ham forever. I was delighted later on to have the chance to make him an England coach.

His three goals at Wembley in 1966 did more than win the World Cup for England. They reshaped his whole career and personality. He had always been a nice chap with a bit of style, but after that historic hat-trick he grew in stature both as a player and a person. He became much more assured and confident off the field while on it he really started to express himself. But he never became selfish. He was always willing to help others. Clyde Best scored twenty goals in his first season basically because of the assistance he got from Hurst.

Hurst would have liked a chance to play for one of the country's biggest clubs but he never made a major issue of it. Matt Busby wanted him to join Manchester United, an interest sparked off by a mistake of mine. I sent a routine circular around the clubs which said simply that we had 'First Division players available for transfer'. Matt Busby rang me to ask if those players included Hurst. I said: 'Sure, if you throw in Bobby Charlton, George Best and your grandstand.' Nothing more happened for a week or two but then there was a story in the northern papers that Manchester United wanted Hurst. Matt had let it 'slip' that he had made an inquiry for Hurst. A sum of £200,000 was mentioned and Geoff, reasonably enough, pricked up his ears.

Manchester United were in the European Cup that season, 1967–68, and just before they left to play Gornik Zabrze in Poland there was another call to Upton Park from Matt Busby. I was not in, so Eddie Chapman, our secretary, took the call – and when I got back he told me Matt had definitely offered £200,000 for Geoff and that he wanted me to contact him in Poland.

I sent off a telegram which read: 'Busby, Manchester United, Gornik. No. Greenwood.' It was curt and rude and I was told later the telegram upset Matt. I later regretted that, but at the moment I banged off that terse little refusal it reflected exactly how I felt. I should not have given Matt a loophole but, equally, Matt should not have used the newspapers to help push the deal. Hurst was very interested because he seemed to have achieved almost everything he could with us and the call of Old Trafford was a powerful one. It offered him a new challenge and a new world and, in fact, Manchester United rounded off that season by winning the European Cup. But Geoff took my refusal well: he always did.

Later on, however, I promised Hurst that if a good offer came along, which would give him a chance to make some money, I would not stand in his way. Stoke eventually said all the right things in 1972 and, although Geoff was still playing well and the fee was modest, I thought the timing was correct. Geoff did well out of the move and that was the main thing.

Hurst was irreplaceable. The game is not exactly full of players capable of scoring a hat-trick in a World Cup Final. But I cherish our association. Geoff Hurst was a loyal club man, a brilliant team man and an outstanding player himself. Can any manager ask for more?

Who was it who said, 'Martin Peters is a player ten years ahead of his time'? And who was it who said, 'This boy Peters cannot play'? The answer to both questions is Sir Alf Ramsey. Sir Alf's comment about Peters' 'futuristic' style is well known, of course, and was made after England's triumph in the World Cup. It was a compliment to Peters's tremendous all-round ability, perception, understanding of space, perfect timing and stealthy running. His qualities were not of the obvious kind. He was often unappreciated and sometimes cruelly misunderstood but he was a true artist in a game which has too many labourers.

The other comment was made just after Ramsey had taken over as England's manager and three years before Peters was to play his major role in winning the World Cup. Peters played in an Under-23 international and Alf rang me afterwards. 'This boy Peters *cannot* play' he said in that clipped, emphatic way of his. 'I shouldn't worry about it, Alf . . . he *can* play' I replied. What Alf didn't know was that Peters had a niggling knee injury which was affecting his movement and confidence. Peters obliged Ramsey to change his mind before very long because he had gifts that were very rare, but the story proves that early impressions of a player are not always right.

I do not want to sound boastful but I think Peters is a player that perhaps only West Ham could have produced. I believe he would have done well with half a dozen other clubs, but it was our style and philosophy which enabled him to flower properly. He did not need to adjust with us because he found the understanding he needed at Upton Park. He had players around him who were on the same wave-length. We were right for him. He was right for us. The result was a player who did full justice to all his talents.

It was a personal opinion which finally ended Peters's career with West Ham. He became convinced that the other two, Moore and Hurst, were getting most of the credit and rewards after 1966. He saw himself as a sort of quiz question – 'Who scored England's other goal in the World

Cup final?' – with most people getting the answer wrong. Martin was a very likeable person but he became fed up and eventually sure in his own mind that things would be different elsewhere. He began to ask for a move regularly but I did not agree immediately because once again I felt it important that he should go to the right kind of club. He needed a manager who understood what his game was all about.

Tottenham, I felt, would be best of all, so I rang Bill Nicholson and said I wanted a chat with him. We agreed to meet outside Chingford Greyhound Stadium, a convenient halfway point, and we arrived there almost together. I got into Bill's car and at this point he still didn't know why I wanted to see him.

'Martin wants away. What do you think?' I said. Bill's face lit up. We talked about values but I had a deal already in mind. 'What about a straight swop for Greavsie?' I asked him. Agreement was immediate. Bill was getting rather the better of the bargain because Jimmy wasn't doing much at Tottenham at the time, but I knew a change could sometimes work wonders. I fancied a go.

The two players were happy and Jimmy even said to me: 'Just give me a blank contract and I'll sign it.' I felt Jim would give us a new kind of target to play up to and that he would score those extra few goals which can make such a difference over a season. Everybody at Upton Park was delighted, directors, players (especially his old pal, Bobby Moore), and fans. He was a Dagenham boy who'd watched his first football on the terraces at Upton Park and now he was coming home.

Jimmy introduced himself to West Ham in the best possible way. He had scored in all his first games for other teams, England and England Under-23, Chelsea, Milan and Tottenham, and in his first outing for us he scored twice against Manchester City. He was so pleased he asked me if he could wear his number ten shirt home.

I think everyone believed he would go on scoring like that, and for a while he was certainly good news at the box-office, but he enjoyed a drink or three, this chap, and his interest in football was cooling fast. He retired at the end of the following season, 1970–71, and threw away one or two useful years of his career. He was at the crossroads when he joined West Ham. It was a worthwhile gamble but it didn't quite pay off.

16

West Ham...Part two

Three members of the England team that beat the world in 1966 were West Ham men, and there was nearly a fourth. Bobby Moore, Martin Peters and Geoff Hurst could have been joined by Gordon Banks. Just think: the best goalkeeper in the world backing up the massive authority of Moore, the elegance and stealth of Peters and the goals of Hurst.

I doubt that many managers even dare dream about having such a powerful backbone to their sides. But I had the chance to sign Banks, he wanted to join us and I refused. Hindsight tells me that was one of the biggest mistakes of my life – but the reason for my decision was at least honourable. To sign Banks I would have had to break my word to an old friend and I could not do that.

I inquired about Banks before the 1966 World Cup but Matt Gillies, his manager at Leicester, said he wasn't available. England's ultimate success changed things for a lot of people, though, and Banks decided soon afterwards that he wanted a move. He got his way and Matt Gillies, remembering my inquiry, rang me out of the blue to say, yes, Banks was now for sale. We could certainly have afforded him, and I was told that Banks was keen on joining us. The idea of linking up with Moore, Peters and Hurst must have been irresistible to him. It rather appealed to me as well!

Alas, there was a mountain of an obstacle: my conscience. I had just made a huge and firm offer for Bobby Ferguson of Kilmarnock. The fee was £65,000, a record for a British goalkeeper, and I even agreed to hang on until the Scottish club was knocked out of the European Fairs Cup before completing the deal. I was prepared to wait to get my man. Kilmarnock's manager was Malcolm McDonald, a good pal from my playing days at Brentford, and we had shaken hands on the sale.

Then Gillies made his telephone call. I had the chance to sign the best goalkeeper in the game, a man with every physical and mental quality a 'keeper needs. Defenders in front of him would always say: 'We're okay . . . even if they get past us they've still got Banksie to beat.' And he was a long-term buy as well: he had years left in him. But I had given my word to Kilmarnock. I told West Ham's directors about my dilemma, admitting that I would prefer Banks, but I insisted that we went through with the Ferguson deal.

The story that Banks was for sale and that we were interested came out in the papers, and Malcolm McDonald 'phoned me to ask if I still intended to stick to our agreement. 'I've given my word: the deal is still on', I told him.

Roland Brandon, one of our directors, told me that it was one of the biggest mistakes West Ham ever made. He said we should have pulled out of our deal with Kilmarnock and gone for the best man. I know he was right in one sense. Professional football is a hard little world. Promises are broken daily. Expediency rules. Nice guys are supposed to finish last. But I did what I thought was right, and honesty *should* matter. Only if that is wrong was I wrong.

I can only wonder about what we might have achieved if Banks had joined us. Banks, Moore, Hurst and Peters were still the backbone of the England side in the World Cup finals in Mexico nearly four years later. Together, in the claret and blue of West Ham, I fancy they would have been a match for most.

We had to wait for Ferguson because Kilmarnock reached the semi-finals of the Fairs Cup, and when he did arrive he was not a great success. He took a long time to settle down and even then he couldn't prove consistently that he was the man for the job. His signing (and one other at the same time: the early summer of 1967) emphasized a defensive problem that was one of the major reasons for our modest record in the League during my years at West Ham.

Our basic trouble was in two positions: centre-half and goalkeeper. Ken Brown and Jim Standen did a fine job early on and we won the FA Cup and the European Cup Winners' Cup. But from then on we always seemed to be a little short in one or other of these key positions. We were not the bosses of our own penalty area in the way we should have been. We had good goalkeepers and good centre-halves, but not at the same time.

I was set on signing a new centre-half at the same time as I bought Ferguson. I had hung on to my old guard because they'd served the club well but – later than I should have done – I then went for a double buy. Bobby Moore wanted me to sign Maurice Setters from Stoke, an aggressive and durable player I knew from my days with the England Under-23 side. I felt Maurice was rather short for a centre-half, however, and I went instead for John Cushley of Celtic.

Cushley was not much taller than Setters but he was a defender who was positive and strong, he had done well in Europe, Jock Stein spoke highly of him and he was a man of character – something he proved when he trained hard for nearly a year to get and keep himself fit after a nasty Achilles tendon injury. He had a degree in both English and History and after joining us he taught at a grammar school in East Ham. I thought he would make it but time proved he was below par technically. He had his moments but he sometimes struggled in the air. Perhaps Setters would have been a better bet after all.

In short, Ferguson and Cushley were not my most successful signings. I made the changes too late, and the replacements were not as sound as they should have been. There were, though, other reasons why we never made a serious challenge for the League championship but why we sometimes had to play like champions at the end of a season to avoid relegation. One reason was the style of football we believed in and another was the character of myself and some of my players.

Our aim was always to create rather than to destroy. That was my philosophy and I brought up my players to believe in it. We tended to open up the game while the majority of clubs tried to close it down. Opponents would often say they enjoyed playing against us but I do not think they always knew why. We were constantly trying to make space by drawing the defenders, by making dummy runs, high mobility, late involvement, dropping back off the ball and changing angles and direction. But if we gave possession away we also gave that space away. It was there for our opponents to use. When we were playing well we made and employed space brilliantly, but when we were out of touch our ambitious methods cost us dearly.

Opponents enjoyed a freedom against us which they did not have in other matches – and often they would put this down to their own craftsmanship. This was the strength and weakness of our game. Sometimes our own weapon turned on us.

I have no regrets on this score. Entertaining football is a thing of chance, and I never saw the game as anything else. Our football was good to watch. It amused and fascinated people. We made friends because we were different. Sometimes we were made to feel we were the last of a dying breed. We did not win the championship but, oh yes, there were compensations.

But this is not the same as saying that I saw West Ham as football's court jesters, providing a bit of light relief in an otherwise very serious world. Such a notion is a million light years from the truth. I desperately wanted to help West Ham win the title and it is a matter of deep regret to me that the best we ever managed was sixth. It is no consolation to me that many other clubs have never been champions although I do take pride from the fact that in all my years with West Ham we were never relegated. I think we lent an important extra dimension to the First Division but I have to say we were never good enough to win it. We could be brilliant – and in cup tournaments we frequently were. We were at our best in the sprints. But we lacked staying power over the full marathon course of a winter.

I accept much of the blame for this myself. Perhaps I was too idealistic. Certainly I was not ruthless enough. My conscience sometimes got in the way and loyalty was occasionally a handicap. But I was not a dreamer. I believed in our style and was always convinced it was the best and right way to play. I honestly thought it could win the championship for us. At the same time I also recognized it would be necessary for us to sweat and battle and this, over the years, was what let us down.

A player's attitude of mind is largely his manager's responsibility, of course, and motivation is an art. Sometimes I did it with reason, sometimes with passion. There are times, too, when a hefty kick up the backside is essential. I even remember telling my team once, after a galling defeat, to 'grow up and be men'. But real determination, the blunt, uncompromising refusal to accept defeat, is something that comes from within a man. I could give my players knowledge and polish their techniques until they shone but I could not turn them all into warriors. We had plenty of artists but not enough willing artisans. We were short of good jobmen, men who once we lost the ball would win it back, men who could turn the tide. The fault was one of balance.

I bought men I believed would fit the bill – centre-halves, for example, such as Alan Stephenson from Crystal Palace and Tommy Taylor from Orient. I honestly thought they were right, and they didn't do a bad job; but once again, technically, they weren't quite up to the mark, although I think Taylor might still have been England's centre-half if he'd had a little more personal self-discipline.

Billy Bonds proved a magnificent buy, a perfect example of a good, hard professional. I first saw him playing for Charlton in a five-a-side at Wembley in 1967. He looked so capable and strong that I made an immediate inquiry. Bob Stokoe, his manager, was not very encouraging but soon after he came back on the 'phone to ask simply: 'D'you want to sign Billy?' I said I did. Very much. 'There's something going on here' he went on. 'My chairman has been in touch with the Sunderland chairman and I think they're doing a deal behind my back. I don't think Billy will want to go to Sunderland – so if you want him I reckon you've a chance. What will you pay for him?'

I offered £47,500. Bob asked for £50,000. I agreed – £47,500 down and another £2,500 if Billy got an England cap. He was ours.

To begin with I think Bonds was a little overawed at Upton Park. He had noticed the likes and dislikes of our crowd and wondered how they would react to him. He is a sensitive sort of chap, even a little introverted, but he had no reason to worry. What a marvellous buy he was. He started off at right-back but later proved to be equally at home at wing-half or in central defence in a career that was to take him right through the seventies and well into the eighties. Billy was a resolute, tireless winner and, if every buy had proved as good, life would have been very sweet.

But men like him come along only once in a while, especially in the south, and I began to feel that what we needed was a player or two from the north. I am not saying the south does not produce men of character because we had a few ourselves, among them Moore, Peters and Boyce, men who knew how to fight. Yet there is something in the northern temperament that is particularly suited to rough times and survival. It is something to do with grimy brickwork, smoking chimneys, indifferent weather and the dole queue. Environment, after all, is a character-shaper and life in the north can be a battle. Success is not offered on a plate. Northerners may take exception to some of this but I make the point as a northerner myself. There is a narrow but important band of truth in the argument.

For years West Ham were essentially a southern side in their make-up and attitude. Nearly all the men who made any sort of impact with us were born south of Watford; and even Hurst, who was born at Ashton-under-Lyne, was brought up in Essex. Frank Lampard, John McDowell, Pat Holland, John Charles, Kevin Lock . . . there were so many who did us proud.

Bryan 'Pop' Robson was one northerner who sparkled brightly in the early 1970s. He was born in Sunderland and scored a stack of goals for Newcastle before we bought him for £120,000 – a deal made possible because he was given a lot of stick for missing a penalty in a European Fairs match. Robson asked for a move and, with Tottenham showing interest, we had to move quickly; but what a good signing he proved to be over the next three years. Our style fitted him like a glove. He was bright, full of courage and his timing was almost as good as that of Martin Peters. He was dangerous at the near post but he had the technique and goal-sense to threaten from anywhere. Robson scored twenty-eight League goals for us in 1972–73 of which only five were away from home, but that was a reflection on the side rather than him. He won one or two Under-23 caps at Newcastle but I am sure that if he had come to us earlier he would have won full caps for England. He then moved to Sunderland for family reasons but later returned to West Ham for another three years. He was a marvellous little player.

But no manager can ever be a hundred per cent sure about a signing: his fingers are always crossed. I thought Ted MacDougall would score a lot of goals for us when we bought him from Manchester United in 1973. He had made his mark at a lower level, at Bournemouth under John Bond, and although he didn't click with Manchester United he took a drop in salary to come to us and I believed we could get something out of him. He was a moody person, however, and we didn't keep him long. John Bond had by now become manager of Norwich and he took MacDougall on again; there he did much better. Peter Eustace was another who couldn't settle in our parish. We bought him from Sheffield Wednesday for £90,000 because I thought he would fill the hole left by Martin Peters: his build was similar and he had a lot of style but his game lacked grit. Eustace had been something of a squire in his part of Yorkshire and East London wasn't to his taste. You never can tell.

On one thing I am very definite: I do not believe I failed at West Ham. The title eluded us and, as someone with a championship medal from my Chelsea days, I know what it would have meant to my players. But there was success and there were good times. There was great satisfaction in our Cup achievements, pride in our standards and pleasure for the people on the terraces. I loved the job and its day-to-day problems, the contact with people and sharing life with a first-class permanent staff who backed me all the way. We had respect and that is one of the greatest prizes of all. For years, too, we produced a steady stream of accomplished young players who were to make their living as professionals, some with West Ham, some with other clubs.

Reg Pratt and his directors were central to the club's buoyancy. They were intelligent, honest and caring men who did things for the right reasons. They were always with me and only twice in all my time at Upton Park did they say 'No' to me. They refused to sack Moore, Greaves and company after the Blackpool affair and the other occasion came in the first month of my sixteen years with them.

When I joined West Ham the man in charge of our youth players was a part-timer, Tom Russell, who was headmaster of the school Bobby Moore went to, the Tom Hood School at Leyton. He was doing a useful job and knew the area well but I felt only a full-time coach would get the best out of our youngsters.

The man I wanted was Malcolm Allison. He was then playing non-League football for Romford after recovering from tuberculosis but I was well aware of his ability as a coach. He was one of several men who, in a sense, prepared the way for me before I took over at Upton Park. There was also Noel Cantwell, Frank O'Farrell, Dave Sexton, Jimmy Andrews,

Phil Woosnam and Malcolm Musgrove – and their lively and endless debates in a little café around the corner, Cassettari's, is a colourful part of the West Ham story. I inherited fertile ground and Allison was one of the men responsible. He is a natural coach, a man with real insight into the game, and he proved his ability with youngsters right from his early days with West Ham.

I thought he would be ideal but when I put the proposal to the board their reaction surprised me. They listened attentively, but then said, firmly, that they did not think Allison should come back to the club. They told me one or two things had happened which would not make it a good idea and they were clearly not going to change their minds. I had to accept their decision. I had not mentioned anything to Malcolm so it was just a bright idea which never got off the ground.

It would have been his first full coaching post and it is of course impossible to say how things would have worked out. I still believe he would have been perfect for the job for a while. Sooner or later he would have been on his way. It is impossible to keep outstanding lieutenants.

The real joy of a manager's job is in working with players, watching them grow up, understanding them as men, shaping them as performers, sharing their laughter and taking pride in their success. There will always be peaks and lows because they are highly-strung thoroughbreds but the relationship with them is endlessly rewarding.

Johnny Byrne, for example, was a delightful character as well as an immensely gifted player. He was all chat and humour. I visited him in hospital once, a Catholic hospital down Lambeth way, and he had the nuns there running in circles for him – even putting his bets on. And in New York, when we popped into a television centre, Budgie introduced himself to every doorman, secretary and potted plant in the place in about five minutes flat. Bobby Moore was to appear on *What's My Line?*, good publicity for the tournament in which we were playing, and one of the American producers came up to me and – nodding towards Budgie – whispered: 'What a pity Bobby hasn't got the personality of that little guy.'

Budgie was everybody's friend yet, in a way, he was his own worst enemy. I told him early on that he should play for England until he was past thirty, but he was not a moderate man and by the time he was twenty-eight his lifestyle was telling. He couldn't say 'No'. He lived life to the rim but while he was young he recovered quickly and never gave a thought to the eventual cost. Nobody can have it both ways, and there is always a bill.

It was a cartilage injury, however, which effectively ended his career at the top. While he was playing for England against Scotland at Wembley, Byrne was switched to left-back in an emergency and came up against that tricky chap, Willie Henderson. The Scottish winger played a quick one-two and if Byrne had been an ordinary forward he would have followed the ball when it went inside him. But at West Ham we taught all our players something about every job on the field and Budgie, instead of ball-watching, did what a good defender should do – he turned with his opponent. His studs caught in the Wembley turf and his knee went. Yet if he had not been a West Ham player he might have thought like a forward instead of a defender and remained uninjured. The accident kept him out of the European Cup Winners' Cup final in 1965.

Byrne also ran into trouble of his own making in New York that same summer. His wife, Margaret, asked if he could come on tour with us. 'Don't for God's sake leave him behind. He'll be terrible' she said. We decided to take him because we could work on his knee while we were away.

Munich 1860, the team we beat at Wembley, were also in the New York tournament and by this time we had got to know them quite well. Byrne and some of their players went to a big World Fair that was going on there and, fooling around, he jumped or fell off a big coach. I am not sure whether it was a stagecoach or a brewer's dray. Bill Jenkins was so angry he nearly throttled Byrne and told him he'd let everybody down, especially me. Bill worked hard on Byrne's knee, though, and even got him fit for the last match of the tour. What happened then? Budgie broke a bone in his foot!

The time came soon afterwards when I had to accept that Byrne was past his best, and as Crystal Palace were keen to have him back we decided not to stand in his way. Really I was just keeping a promise. He did not make any money on the side when he joined us, because that wasn't the way we did things, but I told him that when the right time came for him to leave us we would make sure he did well. His return to Crystal Palace was a good move for him.

Byrne was one of five players who formed the axle of our successful Cup side in the mid-sixties. The others were Moore, Peters, Hurst – and Ronnie Boyce. Boyce's inclusion here will be the unexpected name for many, but he was vital to us.

Arsenal had been keen on him when I was at Highbury. I even interviewed him there and can only thank my lucky stars that I didn't persuade him to stay. Boyce took over in midfield when Phil Woosnam moved to Aston Villa, and he really was exceptional. He was a first-class technician, a wily architect and a tireless worker – hence his nickname 'Ticker'. He did everything simply but all the other players knew how valuable he was. He even shaped the way Peters, Moore and Hurst played. They depended on him more than most people realized. We could play Peters loose because we had Boyce as our springboard. Peters and Hurst could make their runs knowing that Boyce would always find them, usually with an early ball. And Moore knew that whatever the pressure Boyce would be available in front of him.

Boyce read a game expertly and this was always apparent in five-a-sides. Another player would make a perfectly good pass, with exactly the right weight and direction, but Ronnie would somehow intercept because he had read the passer's mind. You could sense everyone wondering: 'How did he spot that?' Ronnie Boyce was another player, however, who didn't catch the eye in an obvious way and perhaps that is why he only won caps at Under-23 level.

Trevor Brooking's career was under way by this time – and we stayed nicely in step. I watched him play for Ilford Schoolboys at Leytonstone and, as England's manager nearly twenty years later, I saw him score twice against Hungary in an overwhelmingly important World Cup match in Budapest.

Brooking was a tall, angular centre-forward when he first started to make an impression. He was very promising and I felt he had the talent for a worthwhile career; but he was inconsistent and, as Arthur Rowe used to say, he 'needed a squib up his backside'. He was elegant, even in those days, but he was too casual and sometimes even lethargic. That was his style and I knew I would have to take him as he was.

There was certainly a doubt or two about him. He came to see me in his early days in the squad and complained that he was always the one who was left out. 'Unless you pull your finger out you always will be' I told him. We even put him on the transfer list one summer with an asking fee of £67,000. The only inquiry, though, came from Ted Bates of Southampton and even he couldn't make up his mind. Ted asked everybody about Brooking but still hadn't come to a decision by the start of the season. Then, after an indifferent start, I gave Trevor his chance and he took it well. 'D'you still want to go?' I asked him. 'No' he replied. 'You've changed . . . for the better' I said. He had got married by then, which is often a very good thing for a young player. He was a more responsible person and it showed in his game.

Brooking went on improving with age. He grew in stature, his personality rounded off and he thought more about the game. He developed, in short, into a midfield player of the very highest quality. But his floppy ankles remained. His ankles were loose – floppy! – and they posed a problem when it came to shooting. Unless he locked his ankle, and hit right through, the ball was liable to go anywhere. I used to say to him: 'Have you got your handbag with you?' It was part code, part private joke, a reminder to keep his ankle locked. I even used the phrase during England practices and the other players would wonder what I was on about. But those floppy ankles had their uses. Their flexibility meant he could screw round the ball and get some wonderful angles.

Brooking had many qualities, including, importantly, a strong personality and natural authority. He could see a game as a whole, a complete picture, and was always quick to spot an opposition weakness. He was the best runner with the ball since Bobby Charlton – almost a lost art these days, but one that is vital in a midfield player. It is all about confidence and knowing when to carry the ball and when to let go. Brooking would also involve himself in a movement at just the right moment, and once in possession he was difficult to know off the ball. He was an expert screener. He could play one-touch football with the best and his angles were usually just right. He knew when to let the ball run, often beating a man without making contact, and sometimes, just sometimes, he even headed the ball.

Trevor also happens to be a wonderfully amiable chap, bright, courteous and willing. He has a wife, Hilkka, who helps keep him up to the mark, successful business interests and an enviable lifestyle. He was good for the game and the game did right by him.

There are no rules or guarantees, however, and no one can be sure that any player will do himself full justice or make it all the way. Johnny Sissons had rare gifts, including a left foot that was a miracle, and medals to prove he helped win the FA Youth Cup, FA Cup and European Cup Winners' Cup while he was still just a kid. But he had personal, family problems that were beyond our solving. Those problems knocked the legs from under his career and eventually we let him go to Sheffield Wednesday just so that he could get out of our district. He was desperately unlucky.

I was widely and correctly reported as saying I thought Mervyn Day would be West Ham's goalkeeper for 'the next ten years'. That was in 1973 and, in fact, he did the job for the next five years. But he didn't fulfil his promise, and that was largely his own fault.

Day was a schoolboy when he joined us, a big, soft hap'orth of a lad. Then his father died and I told him: 'You're the man of the family now'. Although we didn't normally sign players as full professionals until they were eighteen, we promoted him early so that he would have a decent wage to support his family and mother. Day matured quickly and took

over from Bobby Ferguson, and to begin with he seemed a brilliant prospect. But then he stopped making progress. He became involved with
one or two people who gave him grand ideas. He became a bit spoilt,
didn't work as hard as he should have done and went back to being a big,
soft hap'orth. He was a nice lad but lacked the drive and self-discipline
that men like Peter Shilton and Ray Clemence had.

One or two players just slipped through the net, among them Mordechai Spiegler, captain of Israel and an inside-forward of intelligence,
great ability and boundless enthusiasm. I saw him first during the 1970
World Cup in Mexico when Israel drew with both Italy and Sweden.
Spiegler was leanly built, rather like Martin Peters, and I was enormously
impressed by his technique. He was an amateur but he was highly professional in everything he did. And when I got to know him I discovered
he was a football 'nut'. He knew everything about the game. He read and
talked about it endlessly and when I first suggested that he should come to
Upton Park I thought he was going to burst with pleasure and pride. He
came over before the start of the next season and everyone at Upton Park
was highly impressed.

Then, alas, the League baldly refused to register Spiegler. I explained
to Alan Hardaker, the League secretary, that he was coming to England
to study the game because he wanted to be a coach, but Hardaker said if
that was the case he could study while he was in the reserves. I had
thought we could overcome the residential qualification because Spiegler
was an amateur but the League stuck to its ruling. Spiegler was terribly
disappointed and so was I, because I was convinced he would have been
successful in the First Division. He then went to Paris St Germain, where
he made a lot of money, and eventually joined New York Cosmos. We
put him on the market but we would have liked him ourselves. He would
have given West Ham a new dimension. I am not sure I have ever met
a keener chap. He overflowed with football, which Jimmy Greaves will
confirm.

Spiegler sat himself next to Greaves on the team coach for a trip
to Epping Forest where we did our pre-season cross-country running.
Mordechai obviously felt that sitting next to the great Jimmy was one of
the highspots of his life. I was sitting just in front of them, and for the
whole of the half-hour journey Mordechai gave poor old Jim one of the
biggest ear-bashings ever. He talked about English football, its history
and style, players and prospects – the words just gushed out, endlessly.
He was unstoppable. Jimmy sat there numbly just saying 'Yeah . . .
yeah.' We got off the coach and Jimmy sidled up to me. 'Please Ron' he
said. 'Don't let him sit next to me again. I don't know what the . . . . . . hell

he was talking about.' That was Jimmy then. The game started and finished on the park for him.

Jimmy was not the only celebrated ex-Spur we had at Upton Park. Bill Nicholson himself was with us for a year. I felt really upset when Bill dropped out of football after leaving Spurs and I got my board to put him on our pay-roll. Bill's experience was an enormous help in all kinds of ways, and I liked having him around. When Wally St Pier left I offered him the job of chief scout. But Bill said he didn't think he could do it, and I said I didn't think I could either. Chief scout is a specialist job. It means a lot of cloak-and-dagger work, endless frustration, dogged persistence and watching all kinds of football in all kinds of weather. It is hardly a job for a manager who has won everything worth winning. Bill asked for a week to think about it; but in that very week he was asked by Keith Burkinshaw, who had now taken over at Tottenham, to go back to White Hart Lane. 'Get back there quickly because you shouldn't have left in the first place' I told Bill. I was delighted for him.

This brings me to the strange story of how that recall by Spurs of an ex-Spur led to us taking on another ex-Spur who persuaded us to give a job to another former Spurs employee – all of which led to West Ham signing Alan Devonshire for £5,000.

I still needed a chief scout after Bill Nicholson's departure and the man I chose was Eddie Baily who had played for Spurs in their great push-and-run days under Arthur Rowe and then become Nicholson's assistant manager. He had been out of football for a couple of years and was a sportsmaster at a local school. His headmaster said I was stealing the best sportsmaster he'd ever had; but Eddie was delighted to get back into the game and his wife told me that when I offered him the job he really smiled for the first time in two years. We were very lucky to get a man of his quality to replace Wally St Pier. Eddie is an exceptional person, a typical cockney who mixes easily and has a lovely, impish sense of humour. He fitted in as if he'd been a West Ham man all his life.

Eddie quickly suggested we brought back Charlie Faulkner as one of our scouts. Charlie had left us to join Spurs but he was out of work at the time, and I felt it was Eddie's right to pick his own team. So Charlie came back and he started by telling us about a lad called Alan Devonshire. His was a name I knew. Alan Devonshire had been released by Crystal Palace about a year before and his father, Les, who had been at Brentford during my time there, had asked me if I would like to take him on. That wasn't possible because we had our full quota of apprentices, and Alan started playing non-League football for Southall and working as a fork-lift driver at a local factory.

Charlie Faulkner said Reading were offering £3,500 for Alan and, entirely on Charlie's recommendation, I got in touch with Southall. I said we would send Eddie Baily to look at the player and if he came up to scratch we would give £5,000 for him. Eddie said it took him about five minutes to make up his mind and the deal went through.

Devonshire, it must be said, did not look like a future international. He was frail and nervous and he was sick after his first morning's training. The second day he did not even turn up. He rang to say he'd been sick again on his way to the ground and had gone back home. I was given some odd looks, looks which said there are better ways to get rid of £5,000.

The boy had talent, though, and it started to come through when he switched positions. He was an outside-right to begin with but he said he didn't like playing there so we moved him to the left side of midfield. He tended to move inside all the time, using his right foot to cut across his opponents and this meant he had almost the full width of the pitch to work in. A lot of teams found his diagonal runs very disconcerting; and he kept on running until he found himself in the England team. It was my pleasure to give him his first cap.

Alvin Martin was another lucky signing who went on to play for England. He is a Liverpool lad who was first recommended to me by a schoolmaster friend, and I invited Alvin and his father to have a chat with me at the Adelphi Hotel on the morning of a Saturday game at Everton. They were nice people and I had their interests in mind rather than West Ham's when I gave them some advice. 'Alvin is coming up to fourteen and still at school', I said, 'and if he signs as an associated school-boy with us we're only going to see him in the holidays. You say Everton have offered to take him. Well, if he was my son that would be the offer I would accept. They are your local club and he'll be able to train twice a week there and become properly involved. He's well recommended and he's obviously got promise but this is still my advice. I am just being honest. It's up to you.'

They took my advice and I forgot about it. Two years later, however, I got a letter from Mr Martin saying Everton had released Alvin because they'd got Mark Higgins who was the current England Schoolboys centre-half. Mr Martin said he'd always remembered my concern for Alvin's future and wondered whether we'd like to have a look at him. Alvin came down, we were impressed, and he joined us as an apprentice. The rest, as they say, is history. Alvin played alongside lads such as Paul Brush, Alan Curbishley and Geoff Pike in the side beaten by Ipswich in the final of the FA Youth Cup in 1975; and he went on to develop into a strong, influential defender and again I was delighted to be able to pick him for England.

Alvin took great pleasure in proving Everton wrong, and it pleased me to have such wonderful proof that honesty can pay.

The business and art of man-management is a complex one which changes day by day and player by player. It is all about ambition and frustration, dealing with personal problems as well as professional ones and big issues as well as small; and if a manager is going to cope he must know when the moment is right for tea and sympathy and when it's right for tough, practical judgement. Every manager has his own methods and all I can say is I did things my own way.

I was always 'Ron' to my players, rather than 'Boss', because that was the kind of relationship I wanted. I did not want to force anything on them. Respect is not something a manager can demand or expect simply because he has a desk and a chair. A manager should be respected for his knowledge and for his ability to improve his players and help them win matches.

My man-management was based entirely on mutual respect. I believe in people and, although I was let down once or twice, I don't think I met some of the problems encountered by managers who rule with an iron fist. I did not consider it necessary to shout. Bob Paisley has said, rightly, that nobody listens to a ranting voice. Speak quietly and everybody will listen to make sure they miss nothing. Sometimes I was angry, of course, and for this reason I never had a pop at players immediately after a match. I always left it until Monday when things had cooled down, I'd had time to think and everything was in perspective.

I encouraged youngsters to open bank accounts, to visit local schools, to attend courses and to wear suits and ties when travelling or staying away – in short, to have pride in their profession, their club and their district. But at the same time I did not believe it was necessary to impose curfews, to clock-watch or to use a whip. I never had lunch because I always made myself available in the office in case anybody wanted to see me. A player's problem was also my problem. Nobody had to worry on his own. West Ham is a family club.

Criticism was something I reacted to in different ways at different times. I could take criticism of our form, because this was often justified, and I could accept a dig at the way we played if the comment was interesting or perceptive or fairly intended. But I would become very prickly when there was criticism of the club as a whole. This was because it was often about good people who weren't in a position to defend themselves such as the directors or permanent staff. I saw this as a very definite part of my job.

Talking to the press is an integral part of a manager's job. He is the voice of the club and a major part of its image whether he likes it or not.

Reporters and commentators are all individuals with different backgrounds, different IQs, different attitudes to the game and different demands from their employers. Some understand the game and some do not. Some are honest and some are not. Some I liked and some I didn't.

I used to invited the press into my office after every game. Our conversation was off the record after ten minutes and, over a drink, there was a chance to relax and chat and listen. It cemented relationships and even friendships and became quite a ritual. I learnt from them: perhaps they learnt from me. We used to have some very enjoyable natters. Football is not famous for its communication and I felt anything which helped that had to be good.

But nothing lasts for ever in football: a point I have made before. A manager can stay in a job too long. He can begin to take things for granted. He can stop being hungry and start being cosy. Things had not reached that point when I decided John Lyall should take over in 1974. I simply felt that it was better early than late, and the decision was made easier by the fact that in John the club had the perfect man to take over from me. I was also becoming increasingly angry at the way the game was developing: a point, of course, which I made right at the start of this book.

John Lyall's playing career had been abruptly ended by a knee injury in his early twenties. He became a wages clerk but then Jimmy Barrett, our youth coach, left and when I suggested to John that he took over he reacted like a man who has just been told he's won the pools. We sent him on courses and, as a man with the right qualifications and attitude, he began to grow with the job. By 1971 his youngsters were coming through into the first team and to provide continuity I decided to make him my assistant manager. Ernie Gregory was a bit disappointed, and I could understand why, but I felt we needed a younger man.

Our relationship was a very good one. John is a strong character with a Scottish background, stable, straight and single-minded. He has a nice, easy manner and I discovered very quickly that he was a person after my own heart. He wanted to know everything about the job but, more than that, he cared passionately about the club and the game. He was also a family man and he cared about people for their own sake.

The time came when I knew he was ready to take over. 'You be team manager and concentrate on that', I told him, 'and I'll become general manager, and deal with financial matters, look at opponents, size up players we might want to buy and handle everything else'. I told John that tactics and selection were now his job and that I wouldn't even go near the training ground. 'That's stupid' he said. 'Look, if both of us are at the training ground', I replied, 'we'll have two voices hammering away and two opinions. I remember what happened to me at Arsenal – and I don't want that to happen here.' Inside it hurt me. I hated the idea of divorcing myself from the players but I felt I had to be absolutely fair to John.

I had, alas, forgotten one thing. I'd told John about the changes without first telling the directors. I overlooked this important formality because I'd become so used to running things. It was wrong of me. A day or so later I mentioned the switch in roles to Michael Hart of the London *Evening Standard* who was helping me with a regular column in his paper. My comment was off the record and I did not give it another thought.

The following weekend I was in Newcastle watching Keith Robson playing for their reserves against Liverpool. Afterwards, on the station, I picked up an early edition of the *Standard* – and there was the full story. Michael had let the news slip out in the office and his sports editor had told him, in no uncertain terms, to write the story. That is the business of newspapers, but I was very put out that a confidence had been broken and more conscious than ever that my directors were the last to know.

There was a board meeting on the Monday, the first since I had made my decision, and I steeled myself for some rough treatment. In fact, the directors were marvellous. I told them exactly what had happened and how the story had leaked out. They said they could see the wisdom of the move and the continuity we would get but then, inevitably, Mr Pratt had to ask me: 'Why didn't you tell us about it in the first place?' I explained, apologized and asked them to forgive me. 'Well, we think you were wrong and we're not very happy about it', said Mr Pratt, 'but we back your decision and approve the appointments'.

We signed Keith Robson from Newcastle, Billy Jennings from Third Division Watford and Alan Taylor from Rochdale in the Fourth Division – and at the end of the season we won the Cup. Robson couldn't play because he was injured but the other two did their bit at Wembley with Taylor scoring our two winning goals.

When I left West Ham to take the England job I knew I was leaving the old club in very good hands. John Lyall is a harder man than me and I know that over the years he not only noted the things I did which worked but also benefited from my mistakes. And with a harder manager West Ham are now a harder side – though the important traditions remain.

West Ham are still one of the most watchable and most admired sides in English football and I take great pride in that. Old habits die hard.

17

Yours Sincerely

Retirement came at me like a crafty opponent on the blind side. It had come and gone before I realized it.

The game goes on, though, and I am still part of it; but I know now what the real prizes in life are. Cups and medals are important but football offers nothing more precious than true friends. A warm handshake and a shared memory, such simple things, mean more than a line in the record books. It is a lesson only time teaches.

A glance around our home in Brighton tells my story well. On one wall there is a Wedgwood plate, hammers in light blue on a claret background, which West Ham presented to me. The club has a few specially made and Bobby Moore, Geoff Hurst, Wally St Pier and Ernie Gregory are among those who also have one. I have a picture of Gigg Lane at Bury, a memory of early days in the north which was painted by Howard Riley, the Manchester artist, and commissioned by my friends on the English coaching staff. And beside the fireplace there is a Lladra replica of the new World Cup: we didn't quite manage the real one.

There is a handsome collection of glass which was presented to me by the England players before our famous victory over Hungary in Budapest in 1981. But they didn't know they were going to win when they gave it to me and they didn't know I intended to retire immediately after the match. It was a gift from their hearts. They made me another presentation before we left for Spain. This time it was a video, camera and stereo set – 'Now you can film all your grandchildren', said Kevin Keegan.

Even time itself has a special significance for me. On the back of my wristwatch there is a simple inscription: 'To Ron with thanks and best wishes from your fellow travellers. May 1982.' It was presented to me by the football writers who were such excellent company on many of my scouting trips around Europe I value it highly.

I was also touched beyond words by a special dinner organized by the Football Writers' Association at the Savoy Hotel in London. The front of the menu described it as a 'Tribute to Ron Greenwood CBE'. Jeff Powell, the chairman of the FWA, and his committee went to remarkable lengths to make it a lovely and memorable night. It wasn't a stag do, either: Lucy and all the ladies were there to share the fun.

A lifetime of friends came, there was film of moments past and I was presented with a marvellous old statuette of a footballer. But there was more: the FWA arranged for Enzo Bearzot to travel from Milan just to make the presentation. He was delayed by fog but finally made it to Heathrow via Brussels. How good it was to see him on such a night.

Enzo said some very kind things in his speech and I was especially pleased that he remembered how we had been introduced by Gigi Peronace and how he and Gigi used to come to Upton Park in the early days to watch West Ham play and train. 'Ron and I became opponents and friends, always loyal and respectful of the rules and professional etiquette', Enzo said. 'Our job has been one of joy and trouble, of experience and friendships – and friendships like ours I will treasure forever.'

When my turn came to speak I felt very emotional. I said the whole evening was 'tremendous and unbelievable', and I meant it. I paid tribute to Gigi and said how he would have loved to have been present, expressed the hope that Bobby Robson and Bryan Robson would lead England to another 1966, and thanked Enzo and everybody from the bottom of my heart.

I remembered, quietly, Gigi's funeral in Rome. His death was sudden and I was the only Englishman able to travel over for the service; but all the young professionals from AC Roma and Lazio were there to pay their tributes to a lovable little man. It was a Christian occasion and it mattered to me.

The memories and friendships endure; and so will football. It is a game; but it can be more than a game. It is what we choose to make it.

INDEX

237